Reviewing the Forties

Introduction by Paul Fussell

Diana Trilling

Reviewing
the Forties

Harcourt Brace Jovanovich, New York and London

Requests for permission to make copies
of any part of the work should be mailed to:
Permissions, Harcourt Brace Jovanovich, Inc.
757 Third Avenue, New York, N.Y. 10017

Printed in the United States of America

Library of Congress Cataloging in Publication Data
Trilling, Diana.
Reviewing the forties.
Includes index.
1. Fiction—20th century—Book reviews.
I. Title.
PN3503.T7   809.3′044   78–5182
ISBN 0–15–177084–0

First edition

B C D E

Introduction

The context of this book is the culture of the nineteen-forties, and not just "culture" in the high-minded sense. In *Notes Towards the Definition of Culture* (1949), itself a book notably of the forties in its serious deployment of reason as traditionally conceived, T. S. Eliot understands "how much is . . . embraced by the term culture," which includes, he says, "all the characteristic activities and interests of a people: Derby Day, Henley Regatta, . . . the dog races, . . . the dart board, . . . boiled cabbage cut into sections, . . . nineteenth-century Gothic churches and the music of Elgar. The reader can make his own list."

Let's try. The home-front American culture of the forties would embrace the Chief and the Super Chief (which for all their class seemed to smell just perceptibly of urine) plying between Chicago and Los Angeles in less than three days; and it would embrace the snood and "The Hut Sut Song." It would include *The Road to Morocco* and service flags with blue or gold stars hung in windows and the Andrews Sisters and military supply shops in deplorable towns near camps and bases. Add to these the signs WHITE and COLORED—BLACK would have been an insult—over the public toilets in the South and well-shined reddish-brown loafers with a penny in the instep. Throw in "Elmer's Tune" and "I Left My Heart at the Stage Door Canteen" and *Oklahoma* and the black-and-white A-stickers on auto windshields. TWA stood not for Trans World Airlines but for Transcontinental and Western Air. You had to turn in an old toothpaste tube to buy a new one. Trains—there were more of them than planes—had upper and lower berths screened at night by heavy green curtains ("Silence is Requested for the Benefit of Those Who Have Retired"), and the adman told us that "The

Kid in Upper 4" on his way to training camp needed the berth more than we did: "Wide awake . . . listening . . . staring into blackness . . . thinking of . . . the taste of hamburgers and pop . . . the feel of driving a roadster over a six-lane highway . . . a dog named Shucks or Spot, or Barnacle Bill . . . There's a lump in his throat and maybe a tear fills his eye. It doesn't matter, Kid. Nobody will see . . . it's too dark." In those days there was virtually no suggestion that cigarettes and sweets were not actively good for you, and all classes were supposed to assemble at the soda fountain and manipulate the pinball machine while remembering Pearl Harbor, listening to Glenn Miller's "American Patrol" on the jukebox, and resolving to buy more war bonds and stamps.

The popular culture of the forties was rigorously cheerful and trivial and optimistic ("We'll Have a Barrel of Fun") because the events it was trying to "take your mind off" were not just so distressing but so resistant to satisfying interpretation. Earlier wars, like the First World War and the Spanish Civil War, had begun in illusion; the disillusion came only at their end. The Second World War, as Robert Sherwood says, was "the first war in American history in which the general disillusionment preceded the firing of the first shot." Although the Jews knew better, to most people the United States seemed to be merely defending itself against something that had happened at Pearl Harbor, and one man recalls, "All of a sudden, for the first time in our generation, we were underdogs." What were we fighting for? "The Four Freedoms" was one official answer, but even warmly depicted on the Norman Rockwell poster "Ours to Fight For" they failed to grab the heart, let alone the mind. As the war went on there grew a sense that sheer unverbalized action on behalf of the common cause would somehow replace the need for formulations of purpose or meaning. Thus a double-spread Goodyear ad in 1943, in which one full page shows a mother at her doorstep looking up from a telegram; the facing page reads: "What can you say to those whose hearts bear the aching burden of this conflict? That their sons have died in a noble cause? . . . That these men shall be avenged, that we shall see to it that they shall not have died in vain?" And then the crucial *No,* which in an earlier World War would have been thought cynical and even brutal: "No, you can't say these things and have them really mean anything. You can't say anything—you can only do.

You can only bend a bit more grimly to whatever task is yours in these stern times." Until 1945, when empirical evidence of the Final Solution fully disclosed itself, the troops shared the muddle over what the war was about. "The Marines didn't know what to believe in," Robert Sherrod reported from Tarawa, "except the Marine Corps." The President had implied what we were in for on December 8, 1941, when, referring to the destruction of the Pacific fleet the day before, he said: "I regret to tell you that very many American lives have been lost." There was no blinking his *very many,* nor failing to understand that the task facing Americans sent abroad would be unspeakable. Hence the labored levity of the popular culture that ministered to the morale of those at home, who learned to sing, "Mairzy doats and doazy doats and liddle lamzy divey."

"It is an odd fact," notes the social historian Alan Jenkins, "that in war, when people are so busy prosecuting hostilities that they should theoretically have no time to read, they somehow find time to read more than they ever read in peace." One effect of gasoline rationing—four gallons a week was the standard allowance—was to confine people at home, where they listened to the radio, played parlor games like "Chinese" checkers, and read books and magazines in unprecedented numbers. Television had not yet appropriated the popular imagery business, and in the forties all the old American magazines, *Life, Look, Saturday Evening Post, Collier's, Liberty,* were busy promulgating the local values of cheerful efficiency and success. And although paper rationing made books smaller and less imposing, with poor paper, thin margins, and tiny type, they were frantically in demand. At Christmas, 1944, someone at Scribner's New York bookshop was heard to say, "At nine o'clock we just open the doors and jump out of the way."

As always, nonfiction books were the most popular, beginning with *The Red Cross First Aid Manual,* a best seller throughout the forties. People liked to read about the services and the war in books like Marion Hargrove's *See Here, Private Hargrove,* William L. White's *They Were Expendable,* Richard Tregaskis's *Guadalcanal Diary,* and Ernie Pyle's sympathetic, sentimental accounts of infantry fighting, *Here Is Your War* and *Brave Men.* In 1942 most books were hardbound, but there were paperbacks (or "Pocket

Books") which sold for a quarter and offered material thought racy, like Erskine Caldwell's *God's Little Acre,* a favorite with sex-starved servicemen in those days before unlimited pornography. (It is in his tattered copy that Ensign Pulver, in Thomas Heggen's *Mister Roberts,* scrawls "well written" next to one particularly salacious passage.)

Except that there was no *New York Review of Books,* the book-reviewing scene was remarkably like what it is now. There were the five main weeklies: the "sophisticated" *New Yorker,* the middlebrow *Saturday Review* and *New York Times Book Review,* and the intellectual liberal-to-radical *New Republic* and *Nation.* Books were also reviewed in the two main monthlies, the conservative *Atlantic Monthly,* the unflappable voice of New England, and the liberal *Harper's.* If *Harper's* didn't lean far enough left for you, there was the monthly *Partisan Review.*

Among the weeklies the liveliest was the *Nation.* It had a reputation for initiative, vigor, and clarity. The average number consisted of thirty pages of paper-towel stock, by now browning badly and flaking at the edges. It cost fifteen cents a copy, and five dollars (three if you were in the service) got you a year's subscription. In the rural reaches it was thought wickedly radical, or, to put it another way, offensively "New York"; and I remember finding no copy on any newsstand in the whole of Georgia, Texas, and Arkansas during 1943 and 1944. The first two-thirds of each issue offered political essays and comment. There, liberals, socialists, and fellow-travelers like Harold J. Laski, I. F. Stone, Dorothy Thompson, Michael Foot, and the *Nation's* editor, Freda Kirchwey, lambasted "reaction," excess wartime profits, and racism, while the British cartoonist David Low sent up Blimps and other Tories. The last third of each issue, the back-of-the-book section titled "Books and the Arts," constituted virtually a separate cultural weekly anomalously disjoined from—and sometimes openly hostile to—the ideologies dominating the front. Here one found essays and reviews by a rare gathering of regular critics permitted a remarkable freedom of speech by Freda Kirchwey. Every week James Agee reviewed films, B. H. Haggin music, Clement Greenberg art, and Margaret Marshall (who edited the back pages) theater. F. W. Dupee and Delmore Schwartz covered poetry, and nonfiction was handled by David Riesman, Eric Bentley, C. Wright Mills, Reinhold Niebuhr, and other such reviewers. When poems appeared they were likely to be by Marianne Moore or Randall Jarrell.

Diana Trilling's work for the *Nation* began with short unsigned notes on new novels. She proceeded after a few months to signed fiction reviews, and within the year she achieved her own weekly or bi-weekly column, "Fiction in Review." As it turned out, she had undertaken to read a new novel virtually every day for the next six and a half years, of which at least a few remain vital thirty years later, novels that included James T. Farrell's *My Days of Anger,* Lawrence's *The First Lady Chatterley,* Isherwood's *Prater Violet,* Waugh's *Brideshead Revisited,* Warren's *All the King's Men,* Sartre's *The Age of Reason,* Bellow's *Dangling Man* and *The Victim,* and Orwell's *1984.*

But these are special, half of them imports. Most of the novels that passed through her hands were in no way special. Their concerns and devices were thus invaluable for Diana Trilling the cultural registrar, who from these novels was able to infer a profile of assumption and conviction, a body of implicit doctrine constituting, as Eliot puts it, a people's *"lived* religion."

On the evidence of these novels, what did people want to believe in the forties? What struck them as important? For one thing, they wanted to assure themselves that the choice of a career had intense moral as well as monetary meaning. Novel after novel—books like Frederic Wakeman's *The Hucksters,* Helen Haberman's *How About Tomorrow Morning?,* and Herman Wouk's *Aurora Dawn*—explores the degree of dishonor attaching to "the parasitical professions": advertising, the vending of cosmetics, commercial radio, low journalism, making a living by working for Henry Luce, even selling. (*Death of a Salesman* was the Broadway hit of 1949.) The world of big advertising and flagrant merchandising was still new enough to occasion moral doubts in the innocent. If the seventies are obsessed with the power of corporate commerce to screw the consumer, the forties were concerned with its newly revealed power to pervert the seller.

Set against the big businessman and his toads was "the artist"— or, in Ayn Rand, the architect—conceived as something very special, struggling against Philistines and heroically resisting invitations to insincerity. Because of their remove from commerce, women and children were thought to be attended by sincerity too, a signal of their natural virtue. And a similar absence of evil, Diana Trilling tells us, characterized "the little guy" or "the ordinary Joe," an iconographical legacy of the New Deal to the forties, with its swarms of all-but-anonymous G.I.'s. The Kid in Upper 4 is one such, and so will be the hero of Norman Corwin's Victory program for CBS Radio, *On a Note of Triumph:* "They're finally done in, and the rat is dead in an alley back of the Wilhelmstrasse./ Take a bow, G.I.,/ Take a bow, little guy." As Philip Roth's Alexander Portnoy remembers, "Just the rhythm alone can cause my flesh to ripple." If little guys were more interesting and virtuous than big, so were little countries: Diana Trilling registers dismay over all "the novels which weave a rainbow of poetry about the resistance to German domination of a small country or 'small' people." Like the Dutch, poeticized in the weepy popular song "My Sister and I," one of the hits of 1941.

Another idea attractive to the forties was that being "pixilated"— the term is from *Mr. Deeds Goes to Town* (1936)—was not only charming and beneficial but was even a secret source of wisdom. Thus the popularity of Saroyan and Joyce Cary and similar celebrators of adolescent anarchy, as well as of plays like *Arsenic and Old Lace* and *The Madwoman of Chaillot.* In a similar way, the vogue of Thurber's reminiscences of family eccentrics, the play *Life with Father,* and Osbert Sitwell's memories of his madly willful parent suggests a need to reanimate some powerful images of individualism and outré personality as an antidote to the stultifying uniformity of life in wartime.

A further article in the forties' popular credo, as Diana Trilling observes, is that the South is very different from everywhere else, a theater of steamy passion, often homosexual, as in the writings of Hubert Creekmore and Truman Capote, a venue at once of sadism and exquisite sensibility. In these reviews, once Mrs. Trilling has reported of a novel that its setting is "a small Southern town," we are already prepared for the fictional clichés that are going to pass in review. The forties shared with the seventies the assumption that a solution to human unhappiness is a course of sexual adjustments and repairs, although before the Kinsey Report in 1948 these tended to be short on adventurousness. Another forties belief still lingering is that a person psychically sick or unsatisfactory, or even boring, can cure himself by dedication to a progressive cause. "One recalls," says Diana Trilling, "the novel of a few years ago in which a young woman was cured of neurosis by giving visas to refugees, or a more recent fictional instance where the heroine was saved from nervous collapse by joining the movement for cooperatives." Indeed, she says, "If I were asked to name, on the evidence of contemporary fiction, the chief trend in our progressive literary culture I would no doubt point to this mechanical notion that the individual finds himself by losing himself in some larger social manifestation." A further mechanical notion apparently irresistible in the forties is that human motives are to be comprehended as validations of Freudian theory simply understood. But alas, as Mrs. Trilling concludes about the fiction of Anaïs Nin, "we have only to compare the novelist's insight into human motivation before Freud and after him to see how steady has been the deterioration in psychological understanding as the post-Freudian novelists have tried to incorporate the findings of psychiatry into their art."

One of the pleasures of immersing oneself in these reviews is watching the force, control, and precision—"Let me make myself unmistakably clear"—with which their author demonstrates the hazard these and similar undiscriminating orthodoxies pose to a literature for grownups. Her theme is the threat of monomanias and systems and theories and sentimentalities to fiction, or, as she puts it, to "the world of useful imagination." As she says when finding John Hersey's *A Bell for Adano* primitive, what's wanted is "a valid and useful complication," and as she observes of Sinclair Lewis's *Gideon Planish,* "even weakness or error or villainy must be shown in its full humanity." Hence her weariness with novels depicting Germans as inherently brutish or liberal reformers as inherently attractive. Indeed, one thing she is proposing is a generic reform of the American radical novel, urging its authors to make it less like a strip cartoon, and a self-righteous one at that. "I like books," she says, "in which men learn to be heroes. The quest for greatness is an eminently proper subject for fiction. But the novelist who now attempts it must beware a peculiar pitfall prepared for him by our culture, the sentimental danger of supposing that someone can come to moral stature merely by identifying himself with the righteous cause of an oppressed people."

Impatient with the simplicities of radical fiction, as with any novels of the *a priori,* she is best described as a democratic humanist. In her notices of Waugh's *Brideshead Revisited* and J. P. Marquand's *B. F.'s Daughter* she proves staunchly immune to the reactionary sentimentality of both. And we note her coolness towards John Dos Passos's *The Grand Design*, held by its admirers to be "conservative" but actually describable as simply ungenerous. She has no patience with refractions of life uninformed by a deep democratic sensibility betokening an understanding of the human situation as imperfect, problematic, and profoundly difficult. The authoritarianisms of both left and right express an immature "impulse to perfection." Dos Passos is a case in point: "In all his novels we recognize [his] profound impatience with people because they are less than ideal. [In his latest novel] it is politics itself which falls so lamentably short of the ideal because it is the creation of fallible people." (Perhaps we now understand that it was just this American idealism in its most absolutist and self-righteous form that by devising the formula of Unconditional Surrender prolonged the war and extended the Holocaust.)

If the simplifications of politics are one menace to the mature practice of the novel in this country, another is the self-love of artistic people, doubtless occasioned by the American writer's exaggerated consciousness of being uniquely called to Higher Things in the midst of a grossly pragmatic and value-careless business environment. Whatever the cause, a fact Diana Trilling cannot help noticing is the self-congratulatory subjectivity and the self-conscious overwriting of much current fiction. There, she says, "the imagination is like nothing so much as a series of dye-pots in which the author successively dips his or her own image, each time bringing it up with fresh surprise at how pretty it looks in its new tint."

But we should not conclude that she is essentially a negative appraiser. From the outset she avoids that folly of the beginning reviewer, the dazzling condemnatory notice which shifts attention from the object under scrutiny to the reviewer, and which thus provides nothing useful to either novelist or novel reader. As a reviewer Diana Trilling behaves as she urges her women novelists to behave, as if she not only fully understood but also had actually herself conceived Count Caloveglia's exhortation in Norman Douglas's *South Wind:* "Delve deeply; [but] not too deeply . . . into yourself. . . . Delve into the living world and strive to bind yourself to its movement by a chain of your own welding. . . . Externalize yourself!" Diana Trilling is generous in recognizing real merit, as in Isherwood's *Prater Violet*. And despite her suspicion of the generic female novel of the forties, palpitating with delicate sensibility and ready to burst any moment into cascades of self-applause, she notices immediately that the novels of Jean Stafford and especially Isabel Bolton (Mary Britton Miller) are fully humane exceptions and hastens to accord them high honors.

"I have several times commented," she writes, "on the refusal of American fiction to discuss any of the political, social, or psychological realities of this war. Ideologically, the war plays about the same role in our current novels that a storm plays in murder mysteries: it is something noisy going on outside the house to add to our indoor tensions." Those words, which appeared in the *Nation* on June 10, 1944, she probably wrote on the day of the Allied invasion of France, or the day after, and I'm sure with an anxious heart. If the novelists can ignore the war, she cannot, and her awareness of the insensate power raging outside the house sustains her insistence on reason and intelligence and complex human sympathy at least indoors. She is aware as well of the flight from paradox, wit, and subtlety in public wartime rhetoric, and she seeks to protect the humane tradition of the novel from that kind of coarsening too. To see her in September 1947 reminding readers that "non-rationality . . . normally is and should be under the dominion of reason" is to sense the impact of the war on all her writing since, as well as to perceive that she is going to grow into a formidable adversary of such later chic and cruel notions as the idea that ignorance and lunacy and suicide and violence are equal in value to wisdom and clarity and life and poise, or that trances are a source of information about human life. Her reprehension of even Orwell's "fierceness of intention" in *1984*, her recoil from something strident and intemperate in that book, seems to reflect her civilized suspicion of the crude antitheses the war and its politics had enjoined. It is like her civilized distress that so many people of trained mind have not noticed that the promise of the Russian revolution has decayed into the monstrosities of Stalinism.

The words *conscience* and *responsibility* occur often in these reviews, reminding us of the moral sense that most people in the forties, swept up in a war, exercised instinctively. People seemed more willing than they are now, compromised as they suppose by Hiroshima and Vietnam and content to embrace the prevailing value of institutional success, to take moral predicaments seriously and to worry honestly about them. In contrast, the culture of the seventies increasingly tends to invoke "style" as its main criterion of the interesting. In the forties Diana Trilling could write words that in their sharp moral focus may remind us of some Victorian prophet: "Ours being in all spheres such a 'know-how' culture, a civilization so brilliantly skilled in turning out anything it sets its hand to and yet so appallingly ignorant of what is worth making or to what use the things it makes should be put, we cannot be surprised that our literature, too, shows a marked ascendancy of craft over conscience. Probably there has never been a time when so many people wrote so 'well' as now but to such meager purpose; when, indeed, the emptier a novel's content, the surer its technical proficiency." If the reader thinks that sounds more like a critic than a book reviewer, he is right. And as a critic, Diana Trilling has range; she is not satisfied to leave literature sitting there uninterpreted in its fullest psychological, social, and political meaning, for she perceives that "literature is no mere decoration of life but an index of the health or sickness of society." It follows that "just as dictatorship, war, and all the other hideous phenomena of our political day undoubtedly answer a profound need in the modern mass-personality, so the debasement of our literary standards reflects a loss of standard throughout our lives." To read these reviews is to see what such a standard might look like, both for literature and for life.

—PAUL FUSSELL

Reviewing the Forties

There is no biographical or historical apparatus in this collection of eighteen Latin American stories and novelettes, *Fiesta in November* (Houghton Mifflin, $3.00). Except for some bits of information given us by Katherine Anne Porter, who provides an introduction, we are not told whether the writers are young or old, professional literary men, workers or diplomats, successful or still unknown. But whatever the background of their authors, only two of the stories are about people of education and social privilege. "Fiesta in November," the title piece by the Argentinian Eduardo Mallea, is an impressionistic study of a decaying upper-class family, symbolically interwoven with the account of an incident of fascist violence; it has considerable emotional power but it is turgid and forced, sentimental in its detail. "Brother Ass," by Eduardo Barrios of Chile, is a subtle, clever, almost brilliant story of the making of a latter-day saint, told through the mind of a sophisticated fellow-Franciscan. For the rest, these are stories of simple people: Negroes, Indians, halfbreeds, fishermen, woodcutters, peons.

These people live either in the country or on or near the sea. They are hot-blooded and reckless, generous and superstitious. Miss Porter points out the absence from their lives of all the familiar paraphernalia of civilization: there are no electric lights, radios, automobiles, or airplanes. But in our own fiction, too, it is current fashion to write about the periods of our history and the sections of our country in which life is still un-

3

mechanized. There is this difference: these Latin American stories have none of the self-conscious virtue and false innocence of our "primitive" writing. They deal with a primitive society but their level of worldliness is very high. When we in the United States write about simple people we implicitly pay homage to modern industrial urban life by reducing man's stature in proportion as we strip him of machinery; these Latin American writers know that man is no less complicated and dignified for living in a simpler culture. This is a true worldliness and the sense in which I can agree with Miss Porter when she says that artists lie less than other people. *Good* artists lie less than other people—bad artists probably lie rather more than less—and these are good artists.

And what is striking, although it might have been expected, is that all the stories, not excepting the two sophisticated novelettes I have already mentioned, have as their theme the struggle between the individual and a hostile environment. Miss Porter speaks of the amount of weather in these stories, and certainly storms and cold and drought rage through their pages. But by the opposition between man and his world I do not mean merely this reiteration of "man pitted against the elements." Weather is only one of the hard conditions which these people must conquer, a reality of course but also the symbol in nature of the fierce, almost unbroken circle of enslavement in which they live. When the fleeing peon in "The Fugitives" meets his death in a torrential downpour, nature is only paying off with the last blow, and his companion who survives is inevitably returned to serfdom; the monk in "Brother Ass" is the prisoner of his vows; the wealthy Ragues of "Fiesta in November" are enslaved by their class; and in "Country Girl" the bondage of Vicenta to her family tradition is represented by the little hoard of gold and jewels stored in her father's cupboard, just as in "Rain" the bondage of the old couple to their dry soil is dramatized by the freedom of a child to wander at will into and out of their poor lives.

But it is the economic bondage which is the master-bondage

of them all, and how could it be otherwise in a land with such a history of economic exploitation and oppression? These are stories of economic prisoners and, read with conscience, they must make any white man feel the guilty burden of his race and any North American blush for our good neighborliness. "I have no master, nigger. Slavery came to an end long ago," says a character in "The Sloop Isabel Arrived This Evening," and she is answered, "But how about the belly? Live without eating and I'll call you Queen!" The quotation from one story might be the epigraph for the whole book. For it is the belly that chains these people to their fate and makes the weather so tragically important for them.

In her introduction Miss Porter says: "Of 'social consciousness,' which has been a fighting issue between writers all these years in the United States, there is almost none in the explicit sense. The wrongs committed by one class of society upon another are touched upon obliquely, by inference, in sorrowful little stories of evils endured in silence or rebelled against without hope." Clearly she does not mean that the disease has not been recognized because the writers don't give it a label or name its cure. These are stories about people and not about victims, and they are constructed not of attitudes but of understanding and insights; there are no slogans or parties, and certainly there is little hope. But they are as politically effective as any stories written by our own most socially conscious writers of fiction. They are just better stories.

September 19, 1942

Besides the accident of being published in the same month, the four novels brought together in this review have in common their intellectual decency and their effort to deal intelligently with modern life. While none of the four is wholly successful, all four are readable and each has merit. In better literary times books like these might not warrant special notice but in the current flood of Civil War novels and frontier novels, novels about a single river in Georgia or a single acre in Mississippi, they take on lifegiving disproportions simply because they try to cope with the world of their authors' and readers' experience. It may be significant that three of the four are first novels and their authors are young.

Arnold Manoff's *Telegram from Heaven* (Dial Press, $2.50) will remind you of Clifford Odets's *Awake and Sing*. Although it has not the ingenuity of detail of Mr. Odets's first and best play, it surveys the same territory, the Jewish Bronx, from much the same point of view, well left of center. It has the same awareness that the lives of its poor Jews are part of a larger political picture and the same essential vagueness about what is to be done about it. But a lot of water has flowed under the bridge since Odets made his first appearance: where the author of *Awake and Sing* hadn't the war to complicate his problem, the author of *Telegram from Heaven* uses the war both to complicate and solve his problem, too easily. Before Pearl Harbor, what Sylvia Singer, Manoff's heroine, was waiting for was the right feller with the right prospects and the right bank account. After Pearl Harbor her telegram from heaven is her boy friend's draft call to fight for democracy. One is tempted to ask Mr. Manoff, "And after the armistice, what then?" Even with all the political breaks on her side, and obviously Sylvia Singer deserves them, one suspects she will still (impossibly) want to be Hedy Lamarr.

Mr. Manoff's gifts are considerable. Like Odets, he not only has a feeling heart but a beautifully accurate ear for the harsh poetry of American Jewish speech. (Attention, Arthur Kober, on both counts!) There are scenes—the moment in which Sylvia's friend Francey breaks down and confesses her sexual fears; the interviews between Sylvia and her Riverside Drive employers—that have the sure ring of truth. And Mr. Manoff deals even more successfully with his secondary characters than with his hero and heroine, which is a sign of grace in any novelist but especially in a beginner.

Beatrice Borst won first prize in the Avery Hopwood competition with her novel called *Nearer the Earth* (Random House, $2.50). A far cry from the Bronx of *Telegram from Heaven, Nearer the Earth* is the biography of a nice spoiled child brought up in a comfortable home in a comfortable medium-sized city. Even the genteel poverty which confronts Karen Greenwald after her father's death is luxury compared to Sylvia Singer's one step from the relief rolls. Yet Karen's problem too is the problem of how to grow up and face reality; in her case maturity is made difficult by an oversheltered childhood. The "reality" her author concocts for her has one too many deaths to be convincing. For all her efforts at self-education, Karen Greenwald never develops into an interesting personality. But Miss Borst's story is written with great good taste in a style that neither inflates nor whines, it is poignant without being tremulous, and for a first novel in which author and heroine are closely related, it is remarkably objective—so objective, indeed, that one is uncertain whether it is Miss Borst or Miss Greenwald who peters out in the end.

Miss Borst needs to enlarge her range. It isn't so much that her world is too small as that she moves in it as if it were a cloister. I don't mean by this that, like so many women writers (for recent examples see Gladys Schmitt's *Gates of Aulis* or Ann Chidester's *Young Pandora*), Miss Borst thinks she is a priestess. Her lack of self-exaltation is one of her signal distinctions.

The most interesting if also the most uneven of these three first novels is Betty Baur's *The White Queen* (Viking, $2.50), which at moments is so skilful as to be astonishing, at moments so skilful as to look machine-made, and then again—as in the timing of the heroine's change of heart—not skilful at all. Much more ambitious than either Mr. Manoff or Miss Borst, Miss Baur divides her attention among several characters, interweaving their lives to the better understanding of each. The story is set in England in 1937 while Spain is fighting its war to determine all future wars. The heroine is an American girl married to a well-placed Englishman. In the course of discovering the connection between her own destiny and the destiny of the world, Deborah Abbott falls out of love with her husband and into love with an impecunious radical. Politics and social conflict boil down to one woman's choice between two men: a perfectly good way to write about world events in fiction. In fact, it is only when Miss Baur's social conscience gets the better of her and she leaves the sphere of private emotion to describe the practical workings of her Workers' Party or her Tenants' Association that she sounds naïve. Miss Baur's chief gift is her energy; she has genuine zest for what things look like and how people are, individually and in disharmony with each other. If there was ever a day when novels like *The White Queen,* about pleasant articulate young men and women trying to make the right kind of lives for themselves, was the expectable substance of first novels, Miss Baur's book makes one wistful for it.

And then there is Dawn Powell, who is of course no first novelist and should require no introduction to *Nation* readers. Miss Powell is one of the wittiest women around and our best answer to the familiar question, "Who really says the funny things for which Dorothy Parker gets credit?" The central figure of *A Time to Be Born* (Scribner's, $2.75)—certainly not to be called its heroine—is the fabulous Amanda Keeler Evans, blond, beautiful, author of a successful novel and wife of a publishing power. The world is her oyster; she knows exactly what she wants—everything—and she is in a fair way to getting it. The war, on which she is solemnly articulate, is the perfect break for Amanda's career. A ruthless debunking and the quintessence of unashamed cattiness, Miss Powell's novel is an instance of female venom made into a social force-for-good. She cries out to be quoted, and not just one or two sentences at a time—"A gypsy should be required to be wrong, or else she becomes an affront to science.". . . "She was thirty-two, but she looked like a woman of forty so well-preserved she could pass for thirty-two"—but paragraphs and pages. Her description of the women's magazine formula for how to cure a broken heart, her picture of women girding themselves for war or her analysis of contemporary literary trends are not only funny, they convince us of the educated no-nonsense intelligence that lies behind them. It all adds up to a first-rate satiric talent; one wonders what went wrong for *A Time to Be Born* to fall apart as it does in the middle. Perhaps it is because there is no longer a proper satiric tradition for Miss Powell to work in that she loses heart and dubs in the kind of love story—nice little small-town girl wins away the big tough newspaperman from the glamorous beauty—that she would herself be the first to ridicule. At any rate, the wee drop of cynicism she introduces into this love potion doesn't make it easier to swallow.

November 14, 1942

Stefan Heym's *Hostages* (Putnam's, $2.50), about the Nazis in Czechoslovakia, will set your hair on end. No doubt a faithful record of what it is like to live under the Nazi terror, it piles horror upon horror in nearly unbearable quantity and photographic detail—torture, rape, all the excruciating paraphernalia of Nazi sadism. You get the impression that Mr. Heym hates violence almost too much. But neither his passion against Nazism nor the emotions which his readers will bring to his subject can raise his book to the place claimed for it in the ranks of serious anti-fascist literature. It takes more than a serious audience to make a serious novel. For the most part *Hostages* is only a grand-scale thriller. This is not to ignore the difference between the fear we feel as we contemplate a whole nation of murderers and the fear we feel as we contemplate the individual acts of terror of an ordinary thriller. But it is also not to confuse the emotions an author plays on in his readers with the emotions he himself creates. When you have finished *Hostages,* with your equanimity restored, you have the cheated sense of having written the best part of the book yourself. What Mr. Heym has contributed is shabby, sterile, sentimental.

A group of people are in a Prague café on an afternoon when a Nazi officer disappears from the cellar. The Gestapo knows the officer is a suicide but prefers to act as if he were murdered; all the people in the café are held as hostages for the nonexistent murderer, among them a group of five men who are placed in one cell—an industrialist, an actor, a journalist, a psychoanalyst, and a janitor. It is with these five, their lives before their arrest and their conduct as they await death, that the novel chiefly deals; the janitor, a member of the underground, has comrades outside of jail who provide the free-moving action of the story. Here is material for any kind of novel: using the microcosmic device, Thomas Mann wrote *The Magic Mountain,* and Vicki Baum wrote *Grand Hotel.* Mr. Heym's novel, when it is not a thriller, is an anti-Nazi *Grand Hotel.* His psychoanalyst woos immortality by taking notes on the reactions of his cell-mates; the actor gives himself a big scene by trying to confess to the uncommitted murder; the pitiless industrialist is unpityingly shown up as a coward. Mr. Heym's characters are contrived of all the simulations of actual life that other novelists have taught us to look for.

It is a not uncommon fault of meretricious fiction that it likes to deal with the biggest subjects: *kitsch* walks in where better intelligences may fear to tread. Mr. Heym is much concerned with death and with the problem of how we must live in order to know how to die, and like so many modern novelists solves his problems politically. Only Janoshik, the philosophizing janitor, knows how to meet death courageously for of the five victims he alone has lived with a sense of his continuity in freedom. In so far as his companions are improved by their few days of association with him, they too come to face death bravely. Well, it is Mr. Heym's novel to do with as he likes. Still, we have at least the right to ask that he demonstrate his thesis instead of stacking the cards for it. It would seem, though, that like other subjects of size, death defies the novelist with a political ax to grind, whatever the cause in which he sharpens his weapons.

Angela Thirkell, prolific chronicler of life in Barsetshire, continues her literary love affair with the English upper classes. Like the other volumes in her Barsetshire cycle, *Marling Hall* (Knopf, $2.50) concentrates on a single household but once again we meet the Grahams, Leslies, and Crawleys of Mrs. Thirkell's previous novels; her cast of characters is as familiar as her plots or her anatomy of good family. Here again are those sterling middle-aged women of such gentility and wisdom, so devoted to their families and the local choral society, and her men so strong on duty and the decencies; there is even the usual younger daughter with a morbid interest in pregnant cows. *Marling Hall* is Mrs. Thirkell's third novel since the war. The Marlings are making genuine sacrifices for their country: one son is in service and a son-in-law has already been killed in action. But as might be expected, it is with the threats to security on the home front that Mrs. Thirkell is chiefly concerned.

For example, there are the secretaries and typists in one of the local government offices of whom Oliver Marling marvels, "as so many others have marveled, at the gulf which was set between himself and his friends and what were at the present moment the actual pillars, if not the saviors, of society." Mrs. Thirkell complains that "the rationing of petrol, more stringent and rightly so, cut people off from most of their friends, while the six hundred highly paid men and girls employed at the aeroplane reconditioning works . . . were driven in motor coaches to and from their work over distances varying from five hundred

11

yards to a mile and a half every day, besides being driven over to Barchester to the cinema every week at their employers' expense." There are the Marling servants who insist upon roast beef for Sunday dinner while the family is reduced to pigeon. There are the evacuated, the war's sternest duty, of whose children Mrs. Thirkell writes:

"And that," said David, "is the Brave New World."
Mrs. John Leslie said it was so nice to have those poor bombed children at the class and it was a good thing for their own children to mix with all kinds while they were too young to know the difference.
"No, Mary," said David. "You may have married my elder brother, but as he is not here I am going to say that you are talking nonsense. If your children don't know the difference between those two girls and Clarissa, it's time you took them to a mental specialist."

Advertised as a pleasant bundle of froth, Angela Thirkell is in fact quite a grim little person. For all her gentle voice, she is one of the great haters on the contemporary fictional scene. She hates sex, the movies, and the lower classes, except an occasional half-wit mechanic. The cousin of Rudyard Kipling, she hates "natives" and foreigners; she hates servants, except the governess who can frighten the grown son of a peer by asking him if his hands are clean. She hates writers, except the ubiquitous Mrs. Morland, created in her own image. Despite the fact that there runs through Mrs. Thirkell's books an amiable inanity —"daftness" is the word most recently used to describe it and it has become her trademark—she knows precisely where she is and what she is about. Daftness is a property of the upper classes and a *leitmotif* for virtue; it disguises but never hides Mrs. Thirkell's opinions and prejudices. It is a disarming device for persuading us that a powerful class of grown men and women— England's upper middle class, gentry, and minor aristocracy— are lovable children.

And on the level of feeling, especially of sexual feeling, Mrs. Thirkell's characters are, to be sure, childish enough. For instance, the husband of the older Marling girl has been killed before Dunkirk and she addresses her reflection in the mirror: "But there one is, alone, and it seems so silly to be a widow; the sort of thing other people are, not oneself. Oh, dear. Well, there it is," to which Mrs. Thirkell adds, approving such good sense, "with which philosophy she went down to breakfast." On the level both of conduct and opinion so much retarded growth sounds a note of the malign.

In each of her novels Mrs. Thirkell stalks the current threat to the tranquility of the people of whom she can approve. With a love story added, this usually constitutes her plot. Sometimes the menace appears in the form of Jews (the Warburys of *Cheerfulness Breaks In*), sometimes it is a pretty Irish girl (Miss Grey of *High Rising*), more often it is an intellectual, easily identified by his bad manners and his fondness for Russia. In *Marling Hall* Mrs. Thirkell hunts a young poet with long hair. At the end of the book the poet goes back where he came from, Bloomsbury, and civilization is once more safe in Barsetshire. Against the intellectual, whose books sell only in the hundreds, Mrs. Thirkell likes to set Mrs. Morland: her books sell in the thousands.

And Angela Thirkell's own books sell in the thousands; no one will ever accuse her of being an intellectual. But perhaps it is just because she is so popular a writer, with a wide English audience and a growing audience in America, that she warrants consideration beyond her literary merit.

January 23, 1943

To dispel some of the mystery that surrounds the life of Italians in America, two new books have appeared in these last weeks: *Maria* by Michael De Capite (John Day, $2.50), and *Mount Allegro* by Jerre Mangione (Houghton Mifflin, $2.50). With the exception of the Negroes, probably no large minority in the United States has received so little serious attention in fiction or been so stereotyped in popular art as the Italians. If this is a situation in which the Italian Americans themselves are not without responsibility—after all, despite their numbers they have produced very few writers and artists—here are two books which should help explain why they are such ready victims of ignorance and condescension.

Both books are first novels, both are written by young men born in this country of Italian parents, and both make it clear that the Italians, of all our foreign-language groups, are probably the most resistant to absorption into a new culture. Although the people in *Maria* and in *Mount Allegro* live in large American industrial cities, they are aware of the life around them only to fear it. They huddle together in their "little Italys," clinging to their native land by all means at their command: language, food, religion, social and family ties. The parents left Italy in most instances because of poverty but the slightly better livings they earn over here are small compensation for the fields and the olive trees and sunlight to which they dream of returning. Even their gregariousness doesn't tempt them beyond the family group. When Mr. De Capite reports that in 1914 his "little Italy" learned that war had broken out in the old country only when a fire attracted sightseers from "outside," we begin to grasp the problem of Italian-American assimilation.

But apart from their backgrounds Mr. De Capite's novel and Mr. Mangione's have few points of similarity. *Mount Allegro* is not even strictly a novel but a well-ordered series of recollections of Mr. Mangione's Sicilian childhood in Rochester— lively, witty, easy in the manner of the *New Yorker,* a kind of Italian *Life with Father.* Mr. Mangione has traveled a long distance in the course of his self-education; at moments he may appear uncertain whether he is any the better for having now reached the place where he can poke even such serious and tender fun at his past but this is a self-consciousness he shares with most of the first-person writers for the *New Yorker* and has little to do with the fact that he is an Italian. The reminiscence form, with its substitution of tolerance for passion, has a way of betraying both author and subject. Mr. De Capite's *Maria,* on the other hand, though full of expressed feeling is dull compared to *Mount Allegro*—passion without personality turns out to be less good reading than personality without passion. The heroine of his title is an American-born Italian girl who at sixteen marries the man her parents choose for her. Maria's detailed history through two marriages, motherhood, and up to the brink of old age is Mr. De Capite's indictment not only of the Old World culture that formed her but also of the New World culture in which Maria has such difficulty making her way.

The America of MacKinlay Kantor's novelette *Happy Land* (Coward, McCann, $1.25) bears little resemblance to the America of Mr. De Capite or Mr. Mangione. Rusty Marsh is a "typical" small-town boy who has been killed in the Pacific. To comfort the boy's father by showing him that where there is something to live for there is something to die for, Rusty's grandfather rises from his own veteran's grave to reconstruct Rusty's life. The biography has its charms but in the opinion of one reader it is too high-minded for credibility; the men fighting in the Pacific are heroic but they are also human—we at home should be able to draw fortitude from stronger stuff than this.

Of the latest, the fourth, volume of Upton Sinclair's fictionalized history of the modern world, *Wide Is the Gate* (Viking, $3.00), it is hereby noted that Mr. Sinclair has completed the period between 1934 and 1937 and that Lanny Budd, that wonder boy of ubiquity, is still as much at home with Hitler and Göring ("Ja, Lanny!" he is greeted by Göring) as he is with the depressed masses of Germany and Spain. If you are not too much mesmerized by the naïveté with which Mr. Sinclair describes the world of wealth and power—he has the innocent leer of a small-boy socialist watching a capitalist strip-tease—*Wide Is the Gate* is an easy way to refresh your knowledge of historical events not very distant in memory.

In the interest of good neighborliness it would be pleasant to concur in its publisher's opinion that Erico Verissimo, author of *Crossroads* (Macmillan, $2.75), is the Brazilian Dreiser, just as in the interest of quiet sincerity it would be pleasant to notice, for more than its effort, Jonreed Lauritzen's *Arrows into the Sun* (Knopf, $2.50). But in any language Mr. Verissimo is closer to the Elmer Rice of *Street Scene* than to the author of *An American Tragedy,* and as for Mr. Lauritzen's story of a half-breed Navajo, although it is decent and earnest, it is dull. Also dull and earnest, but not at all decent, is a novel called *Memo to a Firing Squad* by Frederick Hazlitt Brennan (Knopf, $2.50). A thriller with a message, it revolves around a sell-out peace conference in Lisbon; its action is an account of how the machinations of the appeasers are circumvented by the local underground. It is a muddled, pretentious, vulgar book, to be noticed, in fact, only for its indecency.

It appears that Mr. Brennan is one of those tough "wise" descendants of Hemingway who are no doubt an embarrassment to Hemingway himself. An ex-newspaperman turned political brooder, he is another of our popular authors (*Collier's,* the *Saturday Evening Post, Red Book, Cosmopolitan*) for whom even the writing of a thriller has its serious purpose: Mr. Brennan would warn us against a negotiated peace. He also has a serious hobby: the study of comparative methods of killing. This is a typical passage of dialogue:

"One should be judged on how he hates—on that alone," Dutch said.
"It is no time for watery guts."
"Or for laughter."
"Liberalism got us into this."
"They and the pacifists."

"A liberal is worse. I have heard such a one make excuses for Judas."

"They said 'Live and let live'—of Germans, they said it!"

"They talked—blah, blah, blah—while the Germans built tanks and bombers."

This is not an isolated passage in Mr. Brennan's book. The speakers are members of his underground: they are going to save us from the evils of Nazism. Each is fanatically devoted to murder and in Mr. Brennan's world murder becomes a fine art: whether you line yourself up with Spigo, Mr. Brennan's blood-drunk refugee from Franco, with Dutch, his blood-drunk refugee from Holland, with Jules, the French chef who is leader of the movement, or with Karen, the heroine and blood-drunk refugee from Poland, you can have your choice of dagger, pistol, strangling with the bare hands, or strangling with the garrote. Killing is not only the whole of Mr. Brennan's plot, it is the whole of his political philosophy.

One would like to dismiss such books by simply calling them "corny," corny being one of Mr. Brennan's own favorite words. Surely if there is anything cornier than a newspaperman being virtuous about love, it is a newspaperman being "realistic" about political morality. But sentiments like Mr. Brennan's now find too much support among supposedly thoughtful people to be dismissed this easily. For instance, reviewing *Memo to a Firing Squad* in the *New York Times* of Sunday, January 31, William du Bois says of Mr. Brennan's "colorful characters": "And yet they carry out all these tasks [their killings] with such nonchalance that one's heart warms to them. . . ."

Whose heart, and what's going on here? In war—and we are at war—you kill because you have to, because that is your job, but it has never been my impression that you kill with nonchalance. Or perhaps Mr. du Bois means not nonchalance so much as finesse: certainly Mr. Brennan has a Hemingway-like interest in the techniques of death. But at least in the way of literature, it is a far cry from *Death in the Afternoon* to the day when the author of every third-rate book for the rental libraries

17

has to boast a degree from the best-methods-of-finishing-them-up school.

Hemingway is a good writer. False notions can be introduced by good writers, then made into folk myths by bad writers. Hemingway gave us the false notion that it is in his more violent activities, such as killing bulls, that a man confirms his virility. Continuing this unhealthy confusion of manliness with brutality Mr. Brennan assures us that the sexual prowess of Jules, his leader of the underground, is all that might be expected of such a prodigious killer; in the words of Reba, his wife, Jules is "much man, much man." But if the first object of manliness is woman, women might be allowed to speak for themselves on the subject of their heroes instead of through the mouths of their male authors. I have yet to see the novel by a woman that affirms this foolish and dangerous test of masculinity.

One had thought that a reason we are at war is that the Nazis find slaughter so heart-warming. How ironic it is, then, that at the same time that we are fighting to outlaw the violence of Nazism, we are this busy creating a literature that glorifies it.

February 27, 1943

Most of the fiction of the last few weeks can pass in review only too quickly. Two women published novels which by staying closely within the limits of their authors' talents win at least minor laurels for good sense: Janet Lewis's *Against a Darkening Sky* (Doubleday, Doran, $2.50) is a nicely-felt biography of a middle-aged woman devoted to her home and family, and Grace Campbell's *Thorn-Apple Tree* (Duell, Sloan and Pearce, $2.50) is a small but very gracious restoration of Scottish-Canadian life a century ago. *Beneath Another Sun* by Ernst Lothar (Doubleday, Doran, $2.75) is the tragic account of what happened to a South Tyrolean family under Nazism; by no means a book of first rank, Mr. Lothar's story is conscientious and moving and has the distinction among anti-Nazi novels of avoiding the exploitation of horror. More pedagogy than fiction is Chard Powers Smith's *Turn of the Dial* (Scribner's, $2.00), in which the history of a small-city radio station provides the opportunity to repeat excerpts from several of Roosevelt's important speeches as well as for the author to argue his own logic of personal and international morality. Twenty-five of S. J. Perelman's funny pieces—why do they always start so much better than they end?—are collected in a volume called *The Dream Department* (Random House, $2.00) but like most occasional humor they are less amusing in mass than taken one at a time.

There are four thrillers to be reported on. Although none can be guaranteed to set your hair on end, surprisingly enough only one of the four rides its story as a political hobby-horse. The political equestrian is Mark Saxton, whose *The Year of August* (Farrar and Rinehart, $2.50) is a tedious tale of intrigue among the treasonable anti-Administration forces in this country; it would have been improved by more action and less ideology. The other three books deal with spies and therefore with international affairs but they are action stories whose authors announce their politics more indirectly. David Rame, author of *Tunnel from Calais* (Macmillan, $2.50), is an orthodox old-school Englishman; his characters go through their unconvincing adventures with more energy than thought but with excellent manners. David Keith, author of *A Matter of Accent* (Dodd, Mead, $2.00), is an orthodox American or what I like to think is an orthodox American; his paralyzed hero—he had his first appearance in Mr. Keith's prize-winning *A Matter of Iodine*—loves Free France and undergoes his discomforting adventures in order to preserve for freedom the short waves to that stricken country. J. B. Priestley, author of *Black-Out in Gretley* (Harper, $2.50), is what I very much hope is a type of new-school Englishman; his agent of the British Intelligence has the mind to pause in his not very exciting adventures to speak forcefully if briefly of the social changes that the war must bring.

Finally, there is a novel by Stephen Longstreet. Last fall, under the name of David Ormsbee, Mr. Longstreet published a novel called *The Sound of an American*. Now, under what I take to be his right name, he publishes a novel called *The Land I Live* (Random House, $2.50) in which David Ormsbee's brother, Driscoll Ormsbee, is nominated for President of the United States. If I fail to respond properly to the element of fancy in these splits in Mr. Longstreet's personality—and, oh yes, I forgot to mention that Gramp, maternal grandparent to the four Ormsbee brothers, in another phase of *his* life concocts recipes for the readers of *Gourmet* magazine—it is probably because I thought *The Sound of an American* one of the really unpleasant books of recent memory, so lush and self-indulgent that in comparison *The Land I Live* is almost a work of mature restraint. By any name, Stephen Longstreet is scarcely my favorite literary figure. The man I read is not the kind of man I like to think wandering with a typewriter through the land I live.

The Land I Live is dedicated to "all the little people"; so it is undoubtedly a patriotic effort. Although the narrator is an artist, the hero has no such weakness: Driscoll Ormsbee is a lawyer who comes to power with the aid of a corrupt political machine but in maturity breaks with the organization in favor of support from the masses and a life of idealism. But he, too, has his touch of schizophrenia; victim of a common form of political split personality, he is half savior of the little people and half a little person himself. Still, he is neither entirely distasteful nor wholly incredible as a potential President; it is Driscoll's youngest brother, David Ormsbee, creator of Presidents, who worries me no less for the future of American politics than American art. For example, Driscoll is himself still an adolescent when his author has him talk to his kid brother about "good rich mud"— this single phrase (but there are scores of others) is enough to persuade me that no member of the Ormsbee family will ever

20

grow up to be *my* hero. Or when David is inspired with a vision of Driscoll's future, his author writes on his behalf:

A star fell and hit me. This was the time for Dris! I had figured it all out suddenly. Logic—schoolroom logic. What was lacking in the world was faith. A faith like old-time religion. A faith honest, earnest, and true to all these things handed down from a mountain in Sinai . . . a return to a faith of the little people, a love of mankind, an understanding, a tolerance of the rights of people. Of the rights of lovers and children and fields and . . . Perhaps my head was a little hollow, my stomach empty of everything but whiskey and schoolroom logic.

Faith, stars, mankind, lovers, children, fields, and little people! Surely to put together this particular combination of words in such small space is to be drunk with platitudes, and the alcoholic excuse is the final platitude of them all. Do we not have all the proof we need these days that to be this soft with words is to be irresponsible with ideas and eventually dangerous? Here, then, is one reviewer who gives notice that should David Ormsbee's brother be nominated for the presidency of her country she will not vote for him. She doesn't like his author's style.

March 13, 1943

Except for members of the Communist Party, or a few sentimentalists who think that the fine victories of the Russian army justify the sins of Stalinism, and of course Martin Dies, it is hard to know who can take seriously Ruth McKenney's long and serious new novel, *Jake Home* (Harcourt, Brace, $3.00). As history—and it is in large part an account of the labor movement in America between the last war and 1932—it is written from the Communist Party-pris and therefore suitably tailored to fit the wavy line. As much by what it leaves unsaid as by what it says, it tries to create the impression that the history of labor in this period is identical with the history of the Communist Party, indeed that trade-unionism and communism are always one and the same thing. As frank fiction, on the other hand, Miss McKenney's story of the small mining-town boy who comes to the big city and makes good as a proletarian leader is basically such pure fourteen-carat goldwyn that you need only soft pedal the cops and occasionally turn the camera on a kindly capitalist to wind up with one of those movies in which idealism triumphs over low sexual-commercial temptation and Hollywood saves its soul.

A large section of the book is concerned with the Sacco-Vanzetti case. Jake Home, Miss McKenney's six ft. three in. of red-headed hero, organizes Sacco-Vanzetti workers' defense committees across the country. Happily in 1943 the air on the literary front has been at least temporarily cleared of the need to rehash the old left-political issues so, if you will, you can skip Miss McKenney's version of the factional divisions in the case and concentrate on the cultural implications of her narrative. Perhaps even before Jake goes on his tour you will have noticed the delicate distinction between the way he addresses his upper-class associates and his fellow-proletarians: Jake's self-taught English, which is so elegantly equal to the Boston lady who buys him his first lobster thermidor but which comes up with the good old proletarian "ain't" the moment he is back with the workers. Then the trip itself is fabulously successful, largely because of the Vanzetti letters which Jake carries with him. Of course by the time he has read these fine documents to half a dozen public meetings, using Vanzetti's words to play on the emotions of his audience like Aimee Semple MacPherson at a revival meeting, now murmuring them in a hoarse whisper, now blasting them to the heavens, holding up one finger for the accompanying orchestra to play "the dead march" soft and now two fingers for the orchestra to come up loud, the "Marseillaise" and the "International" and the "Battle Hymn of the Republic" finally mixing hysterically with the sobs

22

of the women and the shouts of the men—by that time, I submit, the serene soul of a martyred fish-peddler may be turning in its grave, but atta-boy, says Miss McKenney, the workers of the world are behind Jake Home.

It used to be said that revolutionary theory and revolutionary practice cannot be separated. Revolutionary culture and revolutionary politics are similarly inseparable in Miss McKenney's novel. Here is a random sampling of its cultural-political mode:

1. At the age of ten Jake Home knows *Hamlet* by heart; this is acceptable because "Shakespeare had to keep the boys in the pit in mind." At twenty-one he discovers Beethoven for the good, and Rachmaninoff and Debussy for the bad. At twenty-six he knows of James Joyce, "poet of imperialism," that "this guy is covering up a pretty cheesy mind with a lot of style."

2. Sex for a worker is home, wife, son, and curtains, preferably ruffled curtains sewn by the wife's own hands after a jolly day at the revolutionary stencil.

3. Nothing, in the last analysis, is as pernicious as an intellectual. For author McKenney, as for the author of *To Have and Have Not* (remember?), the final insult is to call someone a writer.

4. Scratch a writer and you'll find a Freudian. When Kate, the second of the two evil (female) geniuses in Jake's life, takes to drink instead of having either a baby or curtains, Jake is ashamed of her until one of the comrades gives him a good talking to. "You have a positively medieval mind on this subject, Jake," says the comrade. " 'Freud!' Jake snarled. 'A bunch of intellectuals picking over their elegant libidos!' " The comrade answers: "Do you know no one, no one at all, who uses the works of Karl Marx to confuse, or even to amuse? I am not saying that Freud himself did not evolve a completely bourgeois theory. Of course he did, but he also suggested lines of inquiry to others which have opened a new world."

In short, the proletarian novel which but a short decade ago was a promise of literary glory comes into this decade trailing clouds as musty and bedraggled as scenery at the opera.

March 27, 1943

Among contemporary novels Joseph Freeman's *Never Call Retreat* (Farrar and Rinehart, $3.00) must claim a special place for itself. It is serious, scholarly, ambitious. Its theme is one of the greatest available to the imaginative writer: the relation of the individual to the forces of history. If, then, it is twice as long as it should be and if, as fiction, it suffers severely from its heavy burden of erudition, these faults may be seen as an excess of good purpose and be forgiven. Less easy to forgive on this ground are the woodenness of his central character, Professor Schuman, and the naïveté of his women characters. For all Schuman's learning, this bloodless professor of history is scarcely the companion I would choose for a long journey through contemporary civilization, and for all their virtue—or because of it—the women in the professor's life are unbelievable. Yet what really troubles me about this novel is not its length, its frequent tedium, or the emotional non-dimensionality of its characters so much as its evasion of moral-intellectual responsibility.

As the book opens, Paul Schuman, the Viennese historian whose years correspond to the tragic years of this century, is a refugee in America. He suffers from recurrent visions and a failure of will, and has come to consult a psychoanalyst. The interview with the doctor occupies ten pages of Mr. Freeman's 750-page novel; the rest of the book is the record of Schuman's "thousand and one Freudian hours," although stripped of "everything that pertains to the somatic data and symptoms of the disorder" and keeping "only the human and social circumstances which explain how Schuman came to see what he saw." Yet what the patient is saying psychoanalytically is presented in conventional novel form: the narrative is divided into the usual sections and chapters, and there are even epigraphs at the beginning of each chapter. Schuman's recollections, far from being freely associated, are as ordered and polished as his author can make them, and except for the interjection of an occasional "I hesitate to describe it, Doctor," or "Are you still there, Doctor?" to remind us that the narrator is undergoing treatment, Mr. Freeman's patient might be at home writing his intellectual biography on his typewriter. Why, then, the psychoanalytical device?

Well, an obvious, artistically valid explanation would be that modern history can in no better way be summed up than in a man sick with visions and paralyzed in will. Just as Schuman struggles now for his personal sanity, he has been part of a world struggling for political and social sanity. Too, it adds a small but attractive fillip to Mr. Freeman's indictment of Nazism that his hero should be rescued from despair by Freud, whom Nazism has been so particularly eager to destroy. Yet the fact that Mr. Freeman's protagonist and *raisonneur* is confessedly ill makes it difficult for the reader to assess the validity of his opinions. It can work out that we forget Professor Schuman's condition so long as Mr. Freeman, speaking through him, thinks and says what we wish him to but that when he fails to record modern history as we would, we are disarmed by the knowledge that it is not Mr. Freeman but an admittedly sick man who is in error.

Actually, of course, we go through no such process of thought: we quite forget that Schuman is being psychoanalyzed. And if I purposely exaggerate the part this device plays in the narrative, it is only because it so well exemplifies Mr. Freeman's refusal throughout his book to commit himself on his opinions.

Never Call Retreat could scarcely be concerned with more highly controversial issues, especially in left-wing politics. Yet we are never sure whether it is Mr. Freeman's failure or Professor Schuman's that, for instance, the true relation between the Austrian Communists and Social Democrats is so carefully glossed over; and we have no certain way of knowing whether or not Mr. Freeman agrees with the wife and friends of Schuman who so unquestioningly endorse the role of the Communist Party in Spain. Schuman's liberalism protects him from having to take positions in action but the liberalism is also shown to be a weakness. It seems fair to assume that if Mr. Freeman's central character hears but one side of a story it is because that is the side Mr. Freeman wants the reader to read.

And it is not historical objectivity which is the sole victim of Mr. Freeman's evasiveness. The drama of *Never Call Retreat* is similarly undermined by Mr. Freeman's reluctance to announce where he himself stands. The best section of the novel deals with Schuman's years in a German concentration camp: it is a considerable feat to have drawn such a convincing picture of prison life without first-hand experience. And in this section Mr. Freeman develops and almost brings to a climax a story which is as close a study in the relation of men and principles as anything I know in current fiction—it investigates what happens to two comrades, a poet and a man of action, when they come together in the high-tension world of a prison underground. If Mr. Freeman had written his whole book on the level of courage and insight with which this story, so far as it goes, is conceived, he would have written a great book. But the point is that even this drama is not fully explored because that would be for Mr. Freeman to admit that revolutionary power can breed the same injustices and corruption as any other form of power. Having stated the problem, he shirks its resolution: his two characters die before their conflict can reach conclusion. This is a sad disappointment and the failure not alone of a single episode in Mr. Freeman's novel but of the book as a whole.

April 10, 1943

Two books published as novels in recent weeks, *Search for a Key* by Walter Duranty (Simon and Schuster, $2.50) and *A Time to Live* by Michael Blankfort (Harcourt, Brace, $2.50), are to be called fiction chiefly by virtue of the fact that their authors appear in them under fictional names. Mr. Duranty's book is such out-and-out personal history—it is about one Oliver Joby who is born in England, becomes a newspaperman, is lamed in an accident, becomes a foreign correspondent—that it is hard to understand why it was not frankly presented as autobiography, a form which would have more easily accounted for the sparseness of the narrative and more gracefully accommodated Mr. Duranty's excursions into anecdote and reflection. Less patently autobiographical and making more of a conventional fictional effort, Mr. Blankfort's book is so much a textbook of self-castigation that it is more case history than novel. But of the two books, Mr. Blankfort's is far the more interesting if only because it is so much sicker. While my first, and final, response to *Search for a Key* is dreary amazement that a person of Mr. Duranty's worldly experience can be so sophomoric, my first, and final, response to *A Time to Live* is acute dismay before so extensive a clinical footnote to the history of the radical movement among American intellectuals.

On the day Pearl Harbor is bombed Mr. Blankfort's Ernie Cripton, a young left-wing playwright, stands upon a peak in Hollywood as upon a cozy bed of hot coals, casting up the score of his moral failures. The trouble with Cripton-Blankfort is that, although he had been a devoted Communist fellow-traveler, he had never had the courage or faith to join the Party. But this is only the core guilt of Ernie's life; around it are circle after circle of related guilts—guilt because as a young boy Ernie had been afraid to go to his father's deathbed, guilt because as a young man he had had an income of $50 a week while others starved, guilt because he had continued to write plays instead of going to fight in Spain. Between Cripton and his hair shirt (or between Blankfort and *his* hair shirt: we can have little doubt that Blankfort speaks for himself through his protagonist) there is room for neither irony nor humor, nor yet for common sense. For instance, to his inability to substitute an act of Communist faith for his questioning mind, Cripton traces the death of his baby at birth—lacking confidence in the revolutionary future, Cripton had been unsure he wanted a child—and the death of his wife from leukemia, a disease in which the white blood corpuscles destroy the red! *A Time to Live* is a strange psychological document indeed, the most cheerless published evidence I have yet encountered of the frightening connection between self-torment and social conscience, and proof, if it be needed, that if there is little fictional good to be got from a writer's hatred of others, there is even less to be got from hatred of himself.

John Cheever's short stories, which for the most part have appeared in the *New Yorker* and which are even more talented than the average stories printed in that magazine, are now collected in a volume called *The Way Some People Live* (Random House, $2.00). To read them out of their usual reassuring context is an exceedingly frustrating experience, a bit like holding a conversation in a language in which one has been well-schooled but in which one is still not fluent. For even the best of Mr. Cheever's stories, such as "The Pleasures of Solitude" or "The Edge of the World," are strongly-worded hints rather than completely communicated statements. No doubt this is explained by the fact that even more than our novelists our present-day writers of short fiction not only choose inarticulate characters to write about but refuse to be articulate *for* them. It is an artificial limitation and wholly self-imposed, of a piece with the time-limitation in the contemporary short story. The sooner it is got rid of, the better for this branch of fiction.

Hervey Allen's *The Forest and the Fort* (Farrar and Rinehart, $2.50) is announced as the first in a series of six long early-American novels. Never having read *Anthony Adverse* I am unable to say how Mr. Allen's new venture measures up to that earlier best-seller but I can report that after a dull and self-conscious start, full of scholarly coyness, *The Forest and the Fort* is a conventionally engrossing story about an English boy who is captured by the Indians but in maturity rejoins his own people.

Surely the nicest title of the year is *You Can't Do That to Svoboda*. It appears on a little book by John Pen (Dial Press,

$2.00) which treats the worm-that-turned theme that is always so heartening both in fiction and in life, and especially endearing when the worm is a Slovakian station porter who turns against the Nazis.

Taking its text and title from *Paradise Lost,* Hiram Haydn's *By Nature Free* (Bobbs, Merrill, $2.75) is the story of a moody young man named Philip Blair who works in a dull office by day and at night labors on a monumental intellectual history of the nineteenth century, of Philip's relation with his wife, a fine and beautiful woman unscathed by two years at Bryn Mawr, with his father, a retired street-car employee (known only as Dad) who takes his baseball and his democracy with equal seriousness, and with his brother Harvey (love 'em and leave 'em Harvey), who had suspicious intercourse with the Nazis in South America before he returned to the suburbs of Cleveland to threaten the Blair way of life. An autobiographical novel in no obvious sense but simply because its hero is the usual sensitive young man whose sufferings may be supposed to be those of his author, *By Nature Free* is chiefly interesting as still another example of the significant change in this kind of fiction in recent years.

In reviewing Michael Blankfort's *A Time to Live* last week I made unhappy comment on its urgent self-castigation: according to his author, the trouble with Ernie Cripton was that, while Rome burned, he had fiddled away at playwriting and remained a doubting fellow-traveler instead of becoming a member of the Communist Party. The self-reproach that tortures the pages of *A Time to Live* is not special to Mr. Blankfort; his is merely an extreme instance of the bad conscience of this generation of novelists. Persuade a writer that anything in the world—politics, sociology, economics, religion—is expected of him *except*

29

literature and you can hardly expect him to practice literature without guilt. And it can be no surprise that it is in the autobiographical novel that self-blame is at its most stringent. While in the Twenties and even in the early Thirties it was the whole point of the autobiographical novel that society was responsible for the unhappy condition of the author-hero, ten years of "social consciousness" topped off by a new world war have reversed the situation: now it is the author-hero who is responsible for the unhappy condition of society. If he fails to meet his public responsibility as he believes he should, self-accusation sears his pages.

"Every man's law must first come from inside himself, from his learning to rule himself with freedom," says one of the characters of *By Nature Free,* and Philip Blair's struggle to make this law for himself, to lower his denominator and find some measure of domestic peace, is the major substance of the book. In another day this effort at self-understanding would have been a sufficient burden to lay on a hero but not today: the hero of *By Nature Free* must learn to rule himself with freedom not to make him more comfortable in the world but because it is his duty to society. "[All men] are equal in that they have a native capacity to learn how to govern themselves; they are free alike in their privilege to choose this course, which in turn alone leads to true liberty," Mr. Haydn's spokesman continues. "And only when these facts . . . are realized, will democracy cease to be a dream or a slogan or a joke, and only then will you walk on your hind legs like men."

Philip—it turns out—has misunderstood the nature of human freedom. He must therefore blame himself not only for the sufferings of his private life but also for all misery everywhere: since the fate of democracy rests on the proper integration of liberty and law in the individual, each time Philip is sullen with his wife he is undermining the democratic order! Ultimately sound as it undoubtedly is to grasp the fact that the relation between the individual and the state is a reciprocal one, surely to live with so exacerbated a sense of cosmic influence is scarcely to live at all even in the world of useful imagination.

Because Mr. Haydn so fashionably regards fiction as preachment and warning, and feels that his pen should be at the immediate service of society, the sum of *By Nature Free* is distressingly inferior to its parts, and the conclusion of his book is absurd—all his main characters are washed away in political symbolism, a sin against judgment that is particularly regrettable in the instance of Dad, who was by way of becoming a memorable portrait. One can only shudder for a society that would trade the genuine dignity of Dad falling asleep on the porch for the spurious dignity of his Lionel Barrymoresque mouthings of political folk wisdom.

As for two other novels I read this week, Jo Pagano's *Golden Wedding* (Random House, $2.50) suffers from being published so soon after Jerre Mangione's *Mount Allegro*—it is the same kind of Italian-American family reminiscence but less charming than Mr. Mangione's very charming story—and *White Ensigns* by Taffrail (Putnam's, $2.50) compares poorly with a predecessor, *East of Farewell* by Howard Hunt. *White Ensigns* is nevertheless an informative and dramatic record of life on both a destroyer and an armed merchantman, and should greatly appeal to the landlocked sailor. Its several chapters that deal with the evacuation of Dunkirk are fascinating hints of the whole narrative yet to be recounted.

May 8, 1943

While I have never been of the majority that considers the Sinclair Lewis of *Main Street* and *Babbitt* a major novelist, I feel sad to report of *Gideon Planish* (Random House, $2.50) that I found it unimportant, sloppy, even dull. There is something endearing about Mr. Lewis as a writer that checks an entirely objective estimate of his recent work—perhaps his boyish idealism of which he is so boyishly ashamed, or the fact that his fictional creations seem so clearly to be aspects of his own many-faceted personality that one feels that to turn on him is to take unfair advantage of what he has been naïve enough to tell us about himself. For obviously Mr. Lewis is all the leading characters in his novels, the admirable and not so admirable: Carol Kennicott and Babbitt and Martin Arrowsmith and Elmer Gantry and now Gideon Planish. This is at the heart of his fictional energy, this constant bubbling-over of his self-imagination. But it is matched by a compelling need to show himself up; and when an author is this insistent upon putting himself in an unfavorable light it makes a nice problem whether the reader should spare him the mockery he has not spared himself.

In *Gideon Planish,* which is in the debunking tradition of *Elmer Gantry,* Mr. Lewis's hero-villain is a young man who rises from a (highly unlikely) professorship in a small Western college to become the "organizator" of a series of questionable philanthropic and educational institutions. The war finds him associated with a group of plain and fancy fascists operating under the name of the Dynamics of Democratic Direction. Although Gideon Planish is no worse than a soft, stupid go-getter of easy virtue who is in love with the sound of his own words, with the encouragement of his wife Peony, whose rosy ruthlessness makes her the most attractive character in the book, he goes on to make a fairly good thing of America's aptitude for do-gooding. But long before Gideon has achieved his dubious destiny, Mr. Lewis has become much more interested in his associations than in Gideon himself: in love with the sound of *his* words, Mr. Lewis can no more resist the euphonious possibilities of a racket called the Citizens Conference on Constitutional Crises in the Commonwealth or the lurid potential of an organization called the Every Man a Priest Fraternity than Planish can resist spewing forth his balderdash. Ready to sacrifice any character or situation for his own fun, Mr. Lewis fills *Gideon Planish* with abstractions—of people called Bultitude and Blizzard and even Zeke Bittery and Bonnie Popick, and of situations among his abstractions of people. When he occasionally remembers that he is writing a novel and that a novel, being concerned with people, must be concerned with emotion and that emotion is best dramatized in conflict, he sets a conflict on top of a character like an undersized hat ready to be blown off by the first breeze; then he himself supplies a gale.

The result of Mr. Lewis's method is that no more than Elmer Gantry won a place for himself in our mythology as the archetype of religious racketeer will Gideon Planish survive as the type of philanthropic racketeer. If we say of someone "He's a Babbitt," as we never say of anyone, "He's an Elmer Gantry," and as I suspect we shall never say of anyone, "He's a Gideon Planish," it is because there was once a time when Mr. Lewis himself knew what he seems to have forgotten, that even weakness or error or villainy must be shown in its full humanity to do its job as literature and hold our imagination.

But whatever its faults, *Gideon Planish* is at least on the side of the rational and positivistic, and this is something to be grateful for in these days of always-increasing mysticism and mystification. Lion Feuchtwanger's *Double, Double, Toil and Trouble* (Viking, $2.75) is so rooted in mumbo-jumbo that it deceives itself in professing to cast the non-rational into the clear educative light of historical analysis. It tells the story of one Oscar Lautensack—he had his counterpart in life—a German practitioner of the dark sciences whose gift for mind-reading and foretelling the future brings him into the service of the Nazis during their rise to power. So long as he is kept in rein, Lautensack is useful to the Nazis as adviser to individual leaders, including Hitler, also as public exemplification of the mystical element in the Nazi philosophy and symbol of the supreme powers of the party. So far, so good for even the crassest materialist—until it turns out that Mr. Feuchtwanger himself believes in Lautensack's telepathic gifts; he would simply distinguish between their proper and improper use. Indeed, if I understand him correctly, what he is saying is that the powers of telepathy are of such public value that they must be preserved uncorrupted for the service of a *good* political ideal, a discrimination that considerably worries me for the future of his good political ideal. At any rate, it seems there will be a fellow-novelist whom Upton Sinclair can count on for company when the next Democratic Convention adjourns for a seance!

May 15, 1943

Charles Mills's *The Choice* (Macmillan, $3.00) is a first novel of talent. To be sure, it has grave faults of style. Its young hero, David Lennox, has too many "feelings": his emotions strain at the prose and some of the most crucial moments in his intellectual development are close to unintelligible. Then Mr. Mills is over-fond of quasi-poetical abstractions in language; sentences like the following are typical and wearing: "He sat for a long time, and he felt himself growing to the very limits of touch, beyond which was being. He felt a happiness such as he had never known before, for just beyond his sight, just beyond his understanding, was the perfection of all things, and in this time to know its being brought promise to its supremest fulness, and desire into a foretaste of peace." Yet despite such wordiness, Mr. Mills has an unusual ability to evoke scene, and an uncommon patience in the building of character. While in its prose *The Choice* suggests Thomas Wolfe, in its method of creating character it resembles Santayana's *The Last Puritan*.

With this conscientious salute to its author's gifts, I can go on to say that this quiet novel is also one of the most distressing books I have recently read. It is an archetypical document of Southern reaction: what other Southern writers reveal only unconsciously, Mr. Mills states boldly. Granted that violence, prejudice, myth-making, anti-intellectualism are everywhere these days, in the North no less than the South, the rankling bitterness that obsesses the South even these many years after the Civil War, and the defined myths and prejudices which always seem to be at hand to give form and direction to violence, make right-wing novels with a Southern background especially frightening to the liberal Northern reader. In most such cases, how-

34

ever, the reaction is likely to be almost entirely a response to cultural tone; and even when these cultural signs are present, to carry them to their logical political conclusion is often to be brought up short with the realization that it is not quite fair to formulate a political accusation on only cultural evidence. But *The Choice* is another sort of book in that it actually uses the word fascism and itself takes its hero to Italy and into close approving contact with Italian fascist leaders. For all his bias, Mr. Mills is a more than usually thoughtful person who understands the relation between the emotional tone of a society and its government. He is aware that ours is a world in which individual and group frustrations almost inevitably find their outlet in politics, and he is not afraid to name with approval even the most unappealing of political outcomes.

The outline of Mr. Mills's narrative is simple enough; the complexity of his novel, when it isn't due merely to overcharged language, is the internal complexity of his protagonist. David Lennox is the last aristocrat of Georgia. The beautiful pre-Civil War house in which he spends his early years becomes his symbol of the traditional way of life which has given place throughout the South to Yankee vulgarity. The best of contemporary Southern society is little better than its worst; in association with his peers David finds himself lonely as an exiled king. In fact, though he is an artist—he loves music and becomes a writer—his sensitivity even as an adolescent is not that of the artist but of the young prince. Eventually, like his father before him and like his cousin George, a cruel arrogant youth to whom he is exaggeratedly attached, David looks to Europe for a continuation of the old tradition and in Europe finds fascism, cure for the weakness of his lost America.

But not the least interesting part of Mr. Mills's story is that, having discovered fascism, David, unlike his cousin George, goes on to reject it in favor of religion. This is on page 400 of a 424-page book. Mr. Mills's princeling had always been a Catholic but, too much given to the search for other solutions, he had neglected the religious possibility. The choice of Mr.

35

Mills's title is the choice between fascism and Catholicism. As David finally (and this time not spinning words) puts it: "Either God rules or I am a fool not to place myself with the men who rule." His cousin George chooses fascism but although until the last twenty-four pages David has been with him among the men who rule, he makes a final quick switch from Mussolini to the church.

Twenty-four pages are of course very few in which to experience a personal revolution of any profundity, just space enough to apply a new complexion to an old face. It is nevertheless hard for me to suppose that Mr. Mills would intend his novel to establish this close affinity between Catholicism and fascism. But whatever its ultimate reading, and quite in spite of David's belief that he is so much alone, *The Choice* is worth study as an unusually forthright statement of Southern literary reaction.

May 22, 1943

Perhaps not in a class with Mickey Mouse or Donald Duck but in a class, say, with Andy Hardy, Rose Franken's Claudia is one of America's present-day minor institutions. At the age of twenty-five Claudia is the heroine of countless stories in the women's magazines, of a Broadway hit, of a radio serial and a trilogy of novels. The latest of these is called, simply, *Another Claudia* (Farrar and Rinehart, $2.50). According to its jacket, "what Mark Twain did for the small-town American Boy, Rose Franken has done for the American Wife." The comparison is not wholly exaggerated: if a potential Huck Finn lies hidden in even our most progressive-school little boys, a potential Claudia no doubt lurks beneath the surface of even the least Claudia-like of American women, ready to emerge if given a decent chance. Usually she isn't given permission, any more than the youngsters of my acquaintance would be allowed to come within a block of Nigger Jim, let alone expose themselves to grippe and athlete's foot by going without shoes. Nevertheless, as Huck belongs to the dream of American boyhood, so Claudia belongs to the dream of American wifehood: the young matron who reads *Claudia* may be no Claudia herself but she could wish to be, and as she grows older she may wistfully persuade herself that that's how things were when she was young.

For who wants to grow up, and here is Claudia a perpetual child yet enjoying all the privileges of maturity. No one could be better loved than Claudia by her David, and no one could be more charming or prettier and yet so unburdened by the responsibilities even of brains or beauty. This is indeed the stuff that dreams are made of. A baby herself, Claudia is the mother of two children, she is a wife but also a mistress, a dimwit but married to a man who is the soul of competence and earns a fine living—surely Miss Franken has mined a rich vein of female fantasy. It is true of course that book by book Claudia must grow older but how gently time lays its hand upon her and how lightly Claudia slips from under its touch! It is the "realism" of the Claudia stories that their author recognizes that *too* much immaturity is not entirely desirable in a grown woman and regularly provides Claudia with a fresh calamity to age her: Claudia's mother dies of cancer, a third baby miscarries, Claudia has a nervous breakdown. Still, what to someone less fortunately endowed would be a near-knockout blow is for Claudia no more than a new occasion to exhibit the wonderful resilience of childhood.

The important thing about Claudia is that she is so modern. In Miss Franken's heroine Hemingway has seeped down into the women's magazines: Claudia is a Connecticut Catherine Barkley. Gallant and sophisticated, she scorns cliché and sentiment, she can listen to four-letter words without a blush, and she talks about going to bed like a charming little hussy. But scratch the surface of Claudia's gallantry and you find a clinging vine, scratch the smart surface of her language and you uncover the eternal clichés of folk wisdom: Claudia's values are compounded of "feed the brute," "all men are little boys grown up," and "the hand that rocks the cradle rules the world." As for her sexual sophistication, there was the revealing moment in the play *Claudia* when a wandering gentleman thought Claudia knew what she was up to when she put on that lipstick and those pajamas. Poor David had to sock the guy, then explain that his wife was a sexual infant!

But perhaps even more significant than Claudia's relation with her husband is her relation with her servants and children—again so modern but so practical too. Some of Claudia's best friends are her maids: she understands that servants are human, understands it so well, in fact, that the current Jane, or whatever her name is, plans the meals, does all the cooking, bathes and dresses the children, mends, sees that the children have haircuts, and does the cleaning, all without visible help from Claudia. Or in her role of mother, Claudia understands what an error it is to sacrifice one's husband to one's children: Claudia makes no such mistake, she sacrifices her children to anything including the dogs. The new brittleness in child-rearing one might call the principle on which Claudia brings up her boys—the reaction to the reaction which, only so few years ago, was teaching us that children grow on love.

Indeed, all along the line this is the nature of Claudia's modernity: reaction to reaction. According to how you look at it, then, Miss Franken's creation is either one step ahead of the game or a cultural lag. For instance, it is 1942 and Claudia, whose husband is about to go to war, finds it adorably feminine to be ignorant of geography and cute about insurance. When she backs the car out of the garage, ripping off the door, deep in her heart she knows it will only make David love her the more—it makes men feel so superior that women are awful drivers! Claudia even avoids the beauty parlor except *in extremis* because men prefer their women "natural."

I nevertheless enjoyed reading *Another Claudia* much more than I've enjoyed reading what passes for serious fiction. The writing is simple and adequate. If there isn't much action, there's a good substitute: the sense of every page filled with the detail of day-to-day living. And after all, so few writers have anything to add to life, it is rather a relief to read someone who makes no pretense to doing more than mirror our suburban make-believe.

June 5, 1943

I am struck by the naïve frankness with which Jerome Weidman's *The Lights Around the Shore* (Simon and Schuster, $2.50) is being described as Mr. Weidman's first non-hard-boiled novel. It is exactly as if an optical company were to describe its new lenses as its first that enable the wearer to see with both eyes. For to say of a novelist that he is, or was, hardboiled is not a neutral description, it is an evaluation and not a flattering one. It announces of a writer that he is so handicapped that he is capable of seeing only those aspects of life which fit into a single, highly restricted line of vision.

But Mr. Weidman's own wish to free himself from his earlier limitations is something else again, and much to be recommended. In fact, the best to be said of *The Lights Around the Shore*—for it is a failure—is that it has an admirable intention and an excellent "idea." It is the story of a fifteen-year-old boy who is catapulted into maturity by the double experience of being taken out of his native environment and of discovering that the aunt to whom he is deeply attached is ready to sell him out for a dubious lover—a first-rate point of departure for a novel of psychological exploration. But people baffle Mr. Weidman. He intended his novel to be a mystery of the kind which so much attracted Henry James, in which the secret element is at last the clue both to character and action, but what he has actually produced is a novel which is full of pointless psychological obscurity or just plain error in human understanding.

Take Mr. Weidman's adolescent boy. Peter Landor is of

Hungarian parentage, not Jewish, semi-proletarian. His aunt has been in America only a few years; she earned the money for the trip she and her nephew take to Europe by working in a factory; the suitor whom she leaves behind is the proprietor of a candy store. These circumstances are plainly told us and they even have their place in the narrative. Yet Peter's origins play no part in the experience of a boy who is at the age when "class" is of poignant importance and in a situation, on an ocean liner, where he would necessarily be put to constant social test. For instance, he travels third class but he visits in first class with hardly a trace of unease—there is one brief flurry with a steward, one interesting (though more appropriate to a thirteen-year-old than a fifteen-year-old) interchange with another boy passenger. He shows no interest in the mechanics of the ship, in the complications of landings and boat trains, in the myriad novelties of arriving in a strange country. His unawareness of his surroundings is so extreme that when he returns to America and gives his high-school teacher his diary to read (another false note for if Peter is anything, he is a boy who would never expose himself by such a gesture), it comes as a surprise that anyone who had ever taught Peter should be disappointed that the diary is so bare. Is Peter supposed to be bright? Mr. Weidman fails to demonstrate it.

Or one examines other details of characterization, so many of them false or unconvincing: the matter of the aunt's hands, for example. The aunt's nails are scarred and shabby from factory work, she has to be shown how to care for them. But a young woman who would not know better than to let her hands betray her in this fashion would also betray her class in a hundred other ways which seem never to have occurred to Mr. Weidman—in her clothes, her speech, her table manners, even in the way she would receive the suggestion of a first manicure.

So then one wonders how a writer whose eye and ear are famed for their sharpness, as Mr. Weidman's are from his previous novels, could so have missed fire in this novel. And I think the cruel answer is that neither Mr. Weidman nor any other of the narrow "realists" of the hardboiled school ever does have an eye or ear to be relied upon. Like a general staff equipped with strategies to cover a series of possible military emergencies but with no knowledge as to when to pull out this plan or that, such writers have only enough talent to serve them within prescribed situations; in unforeseen circumstances they go down to defeat. We forget, in fact, how much of the "characterizing" supposedly supplied by these writers we ourselves do for them; how readily, once the button is pressed, we come up with suitable traits for the persons they are presumably depicting. The writer of detective stories—and the hardboiled novelist is of course symbiotic with the detective-story writer—has but to report of someone that he has a gold tooth in the front of his mouth and wears a striped vest with a heavy gold chain, and we at once fill in the rest of the psychological portrait, from his crude greed to his lascivious conduct with women and his sentimental attachment to his mother.

And of course the temptation to this kind of speed-writing is particularly marked when a novelist deals with racial minorities; prejudice itself is, after all, a form of speed-writing. In the past, when Mr. Weidman wrote about Jews, his ability to reproduce the rhythms of Jewish-American speech effectively substituted for the hard work of character delineation. In *The Lights Around the Shore,* when for the second time he writes about non-Jews and also attempts to write in a mode that demands that people have some measure of emotional substance, he proves how different it is to provide us with the recognizable paraphernalia of a "type" and actually to draw a character.

The White Face (McBride, $2.75), a first novel by Carl Ruthhaven Offord, a young Negro newspaperman, is worth study as a sociological report on one of the less-known aspects of the Negro problem, the activities of fascist agents in Harlem. On the principle of divide and rule, and taking advantage of the bad feeling that already exists between the Harlem Negroes and their Jewish landlords, shopkeepers, and domestic employers, fascist agitators are apparently finding Harlem fertile territory

41

for anti-Semitic propaganda. Mr. Offord's book may not be a good novel but it is a chilling account of something that is more than a footnote to the problems confronting us on the home front.

According to his publishers, C. S. Forester, author of *Captain Horatio Hornblower,* spent only a few weeks on a warship of the Royal Navy gathering the material for *The Ship* (Little, Brown, $2.50). He must have studied assiduously, for Mr. Forester's latest novel is encyclopedic in its naval knowledge. Of course, as in all the sea-battle stories of this war, in proportion as the technical information of *The Ship* is detailed and clear, the people are misty or oversimplified. This is perhaps an accurate reflection of ship life in time of war. Or perhaps it is even their salvation that people can put up the appearance of subordinating themselves to the giant machinery they serve.

June 12, 1943

A social-work novel, despite the fact that it is unsparing in its criticism of that profession, Caroline Slade's *Lilly Crackell* (Vanguard, $3.00) is the most estimable novel I have read this week. A story of America's lower depths, *Lilly Crackell* traces the career of a young girl raised in the squalor that is so apt to fringe American prosperity. When we first meet Lilly it is 1918; Lilly is a lovable child of fourteen, about to become the mother of an illegitimate baby. Twenty-four years later Lilly is the mother of six children and still the victim of almost unbelievable misery and privation. Mrs. Slade has not written an exciting novel or even a novel which is particularly imaginative. *Lilly Crackell* is a painstaking sociological report on certain aspects of democracy which we prefer to ignore for the duration. It is a salutary corrective to the assumption that because we are at war against fascism abroad, we have the right—perhaps even the duty—to close our eyes to the poverty and injustice within our own land.

Mrs. Slade's indignation that people like Lilly Crackell can exist in this country is of the slow-simmering variety that indulges neither author nor reader, and her candor is completely unsensational. She writes barely and factually with none of the "literary" overtones that make poverty good reading: it is unlikely that *Lilly Crackell* will have a fraction of the popular appeal of *Grapes of Wrath*. But the book is no less courageous: it takes courage to make explicit the meaning of the war for people who have never had a chance to be anything but a drain on society. When Lilly's four sons are drafted, their army allowance is her first promise of decent food and housing but it is a bitter promise: Lilly loves her sons, and their possible loss is a high price to pay for what may be but a temporary freedom from want. As for the boys themselves, they know nothing of what they are fighting for, and indeed why should they? All they know is that at long last they will have enough to eat and the medical and dental care they have needed so desperately. I have no particular fondness for fiction as reform, and there were even moments when I found *Lilly Crackell* tedious. But in the current flood of propaganda novels compounded of Hollywood-*Life* sentimentalized generalities, a book like Mrs. Slade's shines out in its old-fashioned zeal for decency.

At quite an opposite pole from Mrs. Slade's study in social responsibility is Edita Morris's highly individualistic first novel, *My Darling from the Lions* (Little, Brown: An Atlantic Monthly Press Book, $2.50). Mrs. Morris has published a volume of short stories but I am unacquainted with the earlier work. Her novel is set in Sweden where she was born, and has two heroines, the sisters Anna and Jezza, who tell their first-person stories in alternating chapters. Both girls are excruciatingly precious, and precious to themselves; self-love seems to be a concomitant of sensibility in women writers, and Mrs. Morris is one of those oh-the-aching-wonder-of-it-all literary women for whom a snowflake or a sausage is equally an occasion for ecstasy. Yet whatever my dislike of so much quiver, I have to admit Mrs. Morris's talent. Cumulatively, her sensibility loses some of its exacerbation and even begins to take effect; after the first hundred pages I found myself acutely aware of the charm of her village in northern Sweden, almost as nostalgic for it as if I had myself known it. And it is certainly no denigration of Mrs. Morris's gifts to say that she frequently invites comparison with better writers than herself: for example, her gallery of decayed gentlewomen—Anna and Jezza's aunts—is suggestive of Chekhov, and the spiritual stature which she can give to the life of privacy suggests Isak Dinesen.

Edita Morris is Swedish by birth but her experience has been cosmopolitan and she writes in English. *Ride This Night!* (Doubleday, Doran, $2.50) has been translated from the Swedish of Vilhelm Moberg. An apologue of present-day conditions in Nazi-occupied Europe, *Ride This Night!* is an account of a peasant revolt against feudal oppression in the days of Queen Christina. The outline of Mr. Moberg's novel is conventional enough: his hero, the sole member of his small farming community who has the courage to resist subjugation, loses his land, his friends, his sweetheart, and finally his life but dies with the knowledge that he has died for freedom. More interesting than this familiar story is Mr. Moberg's description of seventeenth-century peasant customs, especially his account of peasant superstitions. More than his right-mindedness, his fund of folklore makes tolerable the Knut Hamsunish bread-and-water, ox-and-plow rhythm of his prose.

Ayn Rand's *The Fountainhead* (Bobbs-Merrill, $3.00) is a 754-page orgy of glorification of that sternest of arts, architecture. What Ruth McKenney's Jake Home is to the proletarian movement, Ayn Rand's Howard Roark is to public and domestic buildings—a giant among men, ten feet tall and with flaming hair, Genius on a scale that makes the good old Broadway version of art-in-a-beret look like Fra Angelico. And surrounding Howard Roark there is a whole galaxy of lesser monsters—Gail Wynand who is Power, and Peter Keating who is Success, and Dominique who is Woman. When Genius meets Woman, it isn't the earth that rocks but steel girders. Surely *The Fountainhead* is the curiosity of the year, and anyone who is taken in by it deserves a stern lecture on paper-rationing.

Burdened by its uningratiating title, by the fact that it is a novel by a newspaperman (for we have little reason to think that journalism is a good training school for fiction), and even by a dust jacket whose quaintness is maniacally designed to drive away readers, Ira Wolfert's *Tucker's People* (L. B. Fischer, $3.00) is the surprise literary package of the season, the most thoughtful and talented novel I have read this year. Mr. Wolfert is correspondent for the North American Newspaper Alliance, a Pulitzer prize-winner in reporting, and author of *The Battle of the Solomons* but he turns out to be that rare creature, a newspaperman with a notable gift for creative writing. *Tucker's People* is an outstanding novel, the simple statement of whose theme—the numbers racket in Harlem—gives no hint of its emotional and intellectual scope.

Tucker's People is a study in gangsterism; its characters are racketeers, politicians, hangers-on, police, and their families. But this is no Damon Runyonesque novel of the underworld; Mr. Wolfert talks out of his head, not out of the corner of his mouth. He views gangsterism as an aspect of our whole predatory economic structure and at least by implication his novel is as much a novel of legitimate American business as it is of racketeering. Tucker himself had his start in industry as it exists with full benefit of the law: unemployed, he began as a scab, to progress through union racketeering and bootlegging to become czar of the policy game in Harlem. Leo, another of Mr. Wolfert's leading characters, owned a garage before he got caught up in numbers: he was an honest man who sold space, air surrounded by four walls. What Mr. Wolfert is saying is that gangsters are little different from their legitimate brothers, they have the same amount of principle and are driven by the same fears and insecurities, "cutting the world to measure as they can and cutting themselves to measure where they have to." Keep piling pressure after pressure upon people and inevitably you drive them to destroy themselves and one another. In such a society the distinction between right and wrong is at last a legalism.

But *Tucker's People* is not a thesis novel. There is no mention of economic or political theory, no slogan, no call to reform. In the sense that Mr. Wolfert is attacking the entire system of capitalism, he has of course written a "radical" novel, but it is in the sense that his method is the method neither of pamphleteering nor of rabble-rousing but the method of anatomizing society by anatomizing people that his novel is truly radical. Which comes first, a good society or good people? Mr. Wolfert makes no attempt to answer simple-minded questions. He is a diagnostician; he has no panaceas. He cuts through the whole bleary notion that all you have to do is drop the "Communist Manifesto" in the social slot machine and out will come a society of smiling Workers and Peasants. It is significant—indeed, it is of the essence of Mr. Wolfert's view of the unhappy condition of modern life—that his novel draws heavily upon the insights of psychoanalysis. The fact that his use of what he has learned from psychoanalysis is both too theoretical and clinical to serve the best purposes of fiction may diminish its effectiveness. It in no way invalidates Mr. Wolfert's modulated conception of the relationship between group and individual.

In these recent months of Russian victories on the battlefields there has been a spate of "radical" novels. As I think back on them, it occurs to me that the one thing they all have in common is the need of their authors to protest their own virtue. In one way or another the novels of Joseph Freeman, Ruth McKenney, Michael Blankfort are all of them long wails of self-justification: "I am in favor of the poor people," "I apologize for my own success," "I am in favor of justice," "I am honest," "I try to be good." Mr. Wolfert is not concerned with this kind of moral self-certification. He stays out of his book and in consequence, such is the fine paradox of art, he is everywhere in it, its best creation. Yet unfortunately, respect and fondness for the author of a novel, while so uncommon these days as to be startling, are insufficient substitute for respect and fondness for its characters. We understand Mr. Wolfert's racketeers and we feel sorry for them but there is no character in *Tucker's People* whom we love, and I do not think this is due simply to the difficulty of identifying ourselves with gangsters—after all, we are not Moors but we can identify ourselves with and love Othello. But perhaps Mr. Wolfert's inability to involve us in the fate of his people is not so much a flaw in his talent as the self-consciousness of a first novelist which will disappear as he continues to write fiction.

It is a wryly enlightening experience to read Ilya Ehrenburg's *The Fall of Paris* (Knopf, $3.00) in the same week with *Tucker's People*. Mr. Ehrenburg's account of the French defeat is a novel chiefly because it is inaccurate history. It is also a demonstration of the belief Mr. Ehrenburg shares with other literary people that the Communist Party is the only solution for the ills of the world and another instance of the vital connection between a writer's language and political purpose. Mr. Ehrenburg's vague, discontinuous, lifeless, impressionistic prose is an excellent instrument of his political partisanship. It so beclouds the sequence of historical facts that I doubt whether any but a reader very jealous for the truthful story of modern Europe would realize that in 530 pages on the history of France between 1935 and 1940 there is hardly a mention of Russia except as a flag on the horizon, and that apart from one oblique reference to a newspaper headline there is no mention of the Soviet-Nazi pact. According to Mr. Ehrenburg's report of the period, what happened in France is that while the French workers under Communist leadership clamored to destroy Nazism and die for France, they were sold out by the alliance of fascism and democracy. All his characters are puppets. On the one side, that of betrayal and reaction, they are the puppets of ambition, confusion, gluttony, and sex; on the Communist side they are the puppets of innocence, courage, self-sacrifice, and even virginity. To confound confusion, Mr. Ehrenburg intersperses his large cast of fictional people with several real-life figures— Blum, Laval, Daladier. These are intended, one must suppose, to give credibility to Mr. Ehrenburg's historical canvas.

The difference between *The Fall of Paris* and *Tucker's People* is obvious. Perhaps more interesting is a comparison between *The Fall of Paris* and Aldanov's *The Fifth Seal*. I remember that *The Fifth Seal* was thought by many people to be dead because it was anti-Soviet: certainly it was full of political despair. Well, *The Fall of Paris* is full of political hope. Also it is pro-Soviet. But it is one of the deadest books that has come to me for review.

July 10, 1943

With her second novel the author of *Young Man with a Horn* deserts the jam session for the life of the mind; what hot jazz there is in Dorothy Baker's *Trio* (Houghton Mifflin, $2.50) is off stage. Based on a theme dear to Henry James—the impact upon an innocent American of a complicated European—*Trio* is set in a Western university town among university people. It is even courageous with a certain amount of intelligent talk about the nineteenth-century poets. I find this a pleasant progression in a young writer, from jazz musicians to teachers of French literature, and I wish Mrs. Baker could have made the advance with a fully adventuring intellect. But it is precisely as a novel of the mind that *Trio* fails, and this despite Mrs. Baker's energy and craft. It is an enormously readable book, swift and tight, polished to the point of brilliance, and plotted with the kind of dramatic suspense which makes it impossible not to race to its end. And yet almost in the measure that we are seduced by Mrs. Baker's skills, we feel betrayed by the essential poverty of her thought.

There is enough "mystery" in *Trio* to make one careful about giving away the plot but I suppose it is all right to report that it is about two women in a homosexual relation, with trimmings. One woman is a cultivated Parisienne who is a professor of French literature, the other a young American graduate student whom the French lady has taken under her elegant bat-like wing. Then there is a young man who falls in love with the American girl. The ensuing triangle is capable of a variety of treatments but unfortunately Mrs. Baker's approach is considerably closer to Hollywood-Broadway than to James.

I mean this in several ways. First, it is Mrs. Baker's stated intention to mold her novel as closely as possible to the form of the drama: her story is told largely through action and dialogue and Mrs. Baker even goes so far as to divide her book into three parts, or acts, and to limit her cast to three leads and her scene to two sets. This constitutes a kind of novelistic suicide, and one wonders what virtues Mrs. Baker finds in the drama form that warrants the superiority she apparently attributes to it. Suppose it does add pace to a story; it also imposes an arbitrary and mechanical unity and robs a novel of the diversity which can be its peculiar charm. Then, and this is exemplified in all Mrs. Baker's characters, there would seem to be a blood connection between theater techniques and cliché notions of motivation and conduct. Mrs. Baker's people are Hollywood stencils: her young American girl goes through her harassing emotional experiences equipped with little more in the way of a characterization than a loose sweater, a string of pearls, and a lock of hair which needs constantly to be brushed back from her face; and her Ray MacKenzie, the young man in the triangle, is one of those sturdy independent types (he enters the story as a kitchen helper at a university tea) who turns out to be John Garfield without the sterling neurotic accent. In other words, for all that Mrs. Baker's book is supposed to be about educated people, actually it is about a Girl, a Villainess, and the Boy who meets the Girl. The French poetry which so much concerns the two women might just as well be the secret plans in a Hitchcock movie.

In fact, in many significant ways *Trio* recalls the films of Hitchcock: there is the same sense of the firm directorial hand slowly losing its grip, of the spacious opening so wide with promise and of the gaps closing without being filled, the same sense, at last, of having been cheated both intellectually and emotionally, of having had your nerves twanged; there is the same craftiness about craft and the same assumption that an interest in psychopathology is equivalent to a comprehension of motive and conflict. The trap of the over-slick story, especially the over-slick story of psychological horror masquerading as a story of psychological insight, seems to be a particularly bad one for a young writer to fall into. If it is Mrs. Baker's notable literary aptitude which tempts her into it, perhaps she should be assured that excellent novelists have for good reason been willing to rest in a less obvious technical proficiency.

August 7, 1943

In a curious fashion it is at once the achievement and the misfortune of S. I. Hsiung's *The Bridge of Heaven* (Putnam's, $2.75) that less than halfway through it I had forgotten it was a novel about China, written by a Chinese, and had begun to judge it as I would a Western novel. For clearly, in proportion as a novel is a good novel, it invites the creative participation of the reader. We all of us, however unconsciously, write along as we read; this participation is our stake in a work of fiction, and we instinctively turn away, bored or untouched, from the novel which doesn't invite us to share in its creation. Yet our participation is of course possible only when a novel deals with people who are culturally close enough for us to make some sort of identification with them. In the case of Oriental fiction such a wall of mystery separates us from the Oriental way of thinking that the identification is extremely difficult; the best that most Western readers manage is to approach a novel of China or

Japan as if it were a work of non-fiction: educational or quaint but not our kind of fun. Denied a share in the creative experience, we are robbed of our most reliable means of judging a novel and we cease to judge at all.

The Bridge of Heaven is notable as an exception to this generalization. Mr. Hsiung not only writes flawless English but, except for details of local color, his book might as well be about English, Americans or Frenchmen as about Chinese; a novel about the Chinese nationalist revolution which overthrew the Manchu dynasty, its psychological and ideational tone is so little special to China that, with the necessary changes of topography and names, it could be a routine report on revolution anywhere. Either Mr. Hsiung is unusually assimilated to Western culture or, what is more likely, the division between East and West can be more easily bridged than we had been led to suppose. And here lies Mr. Hsiung's misfortune: if judgment is restored the Western reader takes *The Bridge of Heaven* as he would its Western counterpart; reading it without fear or favor, he discovers that it is estimable and workmanlike but not worth getting excited about. Like any of the American novels on national themes which appear each season, Mr. Hsiung's novel is little more than a useful refresher in history.

In conscience I should perhaps add that this view runs counter to the copious opinions quoted on the dust jacket of Mr. Hsiung's book which compare Mr. Hsiung to everyone from Goldsmith to Dickens.

Another novel to which my response will probably be of the minority is *I Am Thinking of My Darling* by Vincent McHugh (Simon and Schuster, $2.50). Labeled an adventure story, Mr. McHugh's book is a fantasy of what would happen to New York if a large part of the population were suddenly infected by the virus of instinctive behavior. What happens is that people quit their jobs, money makes no difference, telephones go dead and elevators stall, women throw their skirts over their heads in the streets to pull down their girdles, and offer themselves to the hero in a number to satisfy the imaginings of the most incorrigible fifteen-year-old. Also the medical-research people have a field day.

Coming from someone who seems to be second only to Aldous Huxley as a delver into scientific mysteries, it strikes me as a disappointingly primitive notion of instinctive behavior. Of course an author is entitled to his fantasies, and if Mr. McHugh chooses to make his virus a microscopic bluebird, he must be allowed his Saroyan. Myself, I would have preferred a little less love-and-happiness and a little more of how people actually behave: it's more adventuresome. And something in me doesn't relish the marriage of city planning or biochemistry to hot jazz. But no doubt that's a prejudice.

September 4, 1943

Although it is usually as meaningless to separate the style of a novel from its story as to separate the way an artist lays his paint on canvas from the content of his picture, Enrique Amorim's *The Horse and His Shadow* (Scribner's, $2.50) is one instance in which the division can be made. The cheap muddy prose of this Uruguayan novel looms large between the reader and a powerful novelistic conception. Mr. Amorim wrote his book in Spanish and it would be easy to blame the bad prose on his translators—except that there is sufficient proof that the translation is faithful and that Mr. Amorim fancies his stylistic mannerisms. There is his habit of verbless sentences, whole paragraphs of them. There is his device of delaying necessary explanation: when a blind character is introduced, we are in his company for fifteen pages before we are told of his affliction. There is even the trick—or perhaps it is not a trick but a failure in skill—of skipping explanation entirely: what is the role, for example, of the well-driller, Hoffman, in this novel? Even after we catch on to, and are caught up by, Mr. Amorim's story, we must reconcile ourselves to puzzlement and irritation.

52

Like most good South American fiction, *The Horse and His Shadow* is a revolutionary novel but unlike the revolutionary fiction of our own country, it is subtle, fluid, deeply concerned with the drama of human relationships. The action moves between the *estancia* of Nico Azara, outside Montevideo, and the community of Polish refugees and poor natives who live on the fringes of Nico's lands. On the *estancia* itself there is every shade of political opinion. In addition to the peons at the one extreme, and the arrogant Nico at the other, there is Adelita, Nico's wife, an aristocrat of decent liberal opinions; there is Bica, her servant and illegitimate half-sister, who lives in lonely severity among the men ranchers; there is Marcelo, Nico's brother, sought by the government for his part in smuggling refugees into Uruguay. Mr. Amorim doesn't measure either the decency and courage or the weakness of these people by the familiar yardstick of their social-political views. If it is Marcelo who brings to the *estancia* the gift of the stallion, Don Juan, symbol of life-creating powers, and Marcelo who gives the stricken family of refugees permission to cross his brother's lands, it is also Marcelo who seduces Bica and then calmly goes on his way, leaving her pregnant. Again, Nico is the dark force of reaction in the book who, by refusing his neighbors access to the road across his fields, precipitates the tragedy with which the book ends; yet the stallion knows Nico for his master, and in the duel in which Nico loses his life, the horse allows his body to be used as a barricade by his owner, and Nico's death itself, for that matter, is a display of the kind of heroism which fiction likes to reserve for heroes. Even the poor people in Mr. Amorim's novel, the gauchos and the struggling refugees, are shown naked of grandeur in an amazing scene in which two of their number steal the services of Don Juan for a broken-down mare. What Mr. Amorim is saying is what is too seldom said in fiction these days, that it is by both the new and the old, by the mixture of good and evil, by the progressive and the retarding, that society must advance, and he says it in the only way fruitful for the novelist, through drama and even melodrama.

It is dangerous to use the larger animals symbolically in fiction. Unlike the stallion in D. H. Lawrence's *St. Mawr,* the horse whose shadow is so pervasive in Mr. Amorim's novel is saved from absurdity by being not only a sexual but an economic symbol, indeed an economic fact. This play between symbolisms, but also between symbol and reality, is an excellent complication in a novel of revolution. It almost makes us forgive Mr. Amorim's wretched writing.

By now you will have been assailed by the avalanche of promotion extolling the virtues of Betty Smith's *A Tree Grows in Brooklyn* (Harper, $2.75). I am bewildered by so fervent a response to so conventional a little book. Like the heroine of her first novel, Miss Smith was born and raised in the Williamsburg section of Brooklyn. But we would not have to know this in order to recognize that the story is largely autobiographical. Women authors in particular have a way of looking upon their childhoods as if the process of growing up were an experience reserved for people who will one day write a book about it, and Miss Smith even falls into the common error of forgetting that it takes time to learn the language of their future literary sensibility—at sixteen, even at eleven, her Francie Nolan thinks with the mind of the mature Betty Smith. I quote at random:

She began to understand that her life might seem revolting to some educated people. She wondered, when she got educated, whether she'd be ashamed of her background. Would she be ashamed of her people; ashamed of handsome papa who had been so light-hearted, kind, and understanding; ashamed of brave and truthful mama, who was so proud of her own mother even though granma couldn't read or write; ashamed of Neely, who was such a good, honest boy? No! No! If being educated would make her ashamed of what she was, then she wanted none of it.

Such are neither the thoughts nor words of an adolescent girl. They are the effort of a literary grown-up to exhibit herself as an adolescent girl.

Because Francie Nolan is poor, Irish, a Catholic—perhaps,

too, because there's a drunkard in the family—I have seen *A Tree Grows in Brooklyn* compared to the novels of James Farrell, to Miss Smith's advantage. This saddens me for the condition of fiction reviewing and for Mr. Farrell, whatever may be his shortcomings as a novelist of stature. To be sure, Francie Nolan's story is more cheerful than Danny O'Neill's and makes a more popular commodity. But cannot popular taste be allowed to find its level without its audience being encouraged to believe that a "heart-warming" experience is identical with a serious literary occasion?

September 18, 1943

A mad, bad, and dangerous book, Allan Seager's *Equinox* (Simon and Schuster, $2.75) is fiction's most recent attempt to practice psychiatry without a license. Received as a conscientious study in incest, actually it develops from a not unpromising idea—and a very good first chapter—into a penny thriller in morbid psychology, on the intellectual level of a Boris Karloff or Peter Lorre movie. In fact Verplanck, Mr. Seager's psychiatric detonator who makes the incest explode, is more than half our old friend the Mad Scientist of the comics and Hollywood; his lineage can also be traced back through Spandrell of *Point Counter Point* to des Esseintes of Huysmans's *A Rebours*. Start experimenting for experiment's own sake and you seem to end up with a man-eating shark.

It's a father and daughter in Mr. Seager's Oedipus situation: a young middle-aged newspaperman comes home from Europe on the eve of war and sets up house with his seventeen-year-old daughter. For the father his new home is a protection from the world; for the girl, fresh from a convent school, it is a romantic ideal of domestic love. But along come malicious friends who mouth the ugly word "sex," and father runs to Verplanck for advice and help. This is the moment Mr. Seager has been waiting for; indeed throughout the book you have the sense of an author lying in wait for his characters. Verplanck, an amateur psychiatrist, devotes his life to destroying people by his "scientific" understanding of them. He keeps elaborate case records on his friends. He marries a woman so that he can give her a neurosis which he will be able to follow from its onset—all very serious, sinister and fantastic. Verplanck too says sex, with the full weight of his psychiatric authority. The girl commits suicide.

When I call *Equinox* dangerous I mean it simply: there is public menace in the representation of Verplanck's scientific authority. Although Mr. Seager is careful to call him an amateur, Verplanck is also an M.D. and has been psychoanalyzed— his analyst is mentioned by name, Stekel. Also, the ethical practice of psychiatry is at no point offered in contrast to the profession practiced by Verplanck. Psychiatry being, to the popular imagination, the most suspect of sciences, this propagation in fiction of one author's morbidities is an extreme of irresponsibility.

October 2, 1943

In her latest collection of short stories, *The Wide Net* (Harcourt, Brace, $2.50), Eudora Welty has developed her technical virtuosity to the point where it outweighs the uses to which it is put, and her vision of horror to the point of nightmare. Of course even in her earlier work Miss Welty had a marked tendency toward stylism and "fine" writing. She liked to move toward the mythical. She had a heart for decay and an eye for Gothic detail. But she also had a reliable and healthy wit, her dialogue could be as normally reportorial as Ring Lardner's, and for the most part she knew how to keep performance subservient to communication: she told her story instead of dancing it, and when she saw horror it could be the clear horror of day-to-day life, not only the horror of dreams. There was surrealist paraphernalia, if you will, in a story like "The Petrified Man": the falling hair of the customer, the presence of the three-year-old boy amid the bobbie-pins and sexual confidences of the beauty parlor, the twins in a bottle at the freak show, even the petrified man himself. But compare to "The Petrified Man" the story "Asphodel" from Miss Welty's current volume, with its Doric columns and floating muslins, its pomegranate stains and blackberry cordial and its "old goats and young," and you will recognize the fancy road up which Miss Welty has turned her great talents.

The title story of Miss Welty's new volume is its best but not typical. An account of a river-dragging party which starts out to recover the body of a supposed suicide but forgets its mission in the joys of the occasion, "The Wide Net" has elements of a tour de force but it has more communicated meaning than the rest of the stories in the book, and best fuses content and method. Of the six other stories, "Livvie" is the only one which I like at all and the only story, in addition to "The Wide Net," which I feel I understood. Yet despite its obscurity the volume has tremendous emotional impact. But this seems to me to be beside the point. The fear that a story or a picture engenders is often in inverse proportion to its communicated content: witness the drawings of children or psychotics, or most of surrealist art. Miss Welty employs to good effect the whole manual of ghostliness: wind and storm, ruined buildings, cloaks, horses' hooves on a lonely highway, fire and moonlight and people who live and ride alone. But her evocation of the mood of horror or dream has become an end in itself, and if, for each story, there is a point of departure in narrative, so that I can report, for instance, that "First Love" is about a deaf-and-dumb boy who falls in love with Aaron Burr, or that "Asphodel" is about a tyrannical half-mad Southern gentlewoman, or that "A Still Moment" is a legend of Audubon, the stories themselves stay with their narrative no more than a dance stays with its argument. This, indeed, is the nature of *The Wide Net:* it is a book of ballets. Even the title piece is a *pastorale macabre.*

And it is my belief that to make a ballet out of words is a misuse of their function. I dislike, because it breeds exhibitionism and insincerity, the attitude toward narrative which allows an author to sacrifice the meaning of language to its rhythms and patterns. The word "sincerity" has lost caste in the criticism of serious writing, which is unfortunate. We live in a crafty literary period in which what aims to be art but is only artful is regularly mistaken for the real thing. If, describing something which exists outside himself, an author says "Look at me" instead of "Look at it," there, in my opinion, is insincerity. The test of sincerity is wasted, however, in the sphere of popular art where criticism has sent it; most popular art is nothing if not sincere, and where it is not, it is usually because it is aping the manners of its betters. In these new stories Miss Welty's prose constantly calls attention to its author, away from her object. When she writes, ". . . Jenny sat there . . . in the posture of a child who is appalled at the stillness and unsurrender of the still and unsurrendering world," or "He walked alone, slowly through the silence, with the sturdy and yet dreamlike walk of the orphan," she is being falsely poetic, also untrue. How does the walk of an orphan differ in its sturdiness and in its dreamlike quality from the walk of a child with two parents? How would one explain "unsurrender" to a child, and wouldn't a child be appalled precisely by the *surrender* of the world, if the concept could reach him? This is the sin of pride, this self-conscious contriving, and it is endemic to a whole generation of writers since Katherine Mansfield, especially women writers.

Certainly somewhere between Chekhov and Katherine Mansfield the short story went off its trolley. I think it is Miss Mansfield who must be help accountable for so large an infusion of subjectivism and sensibility into the short fiction of our day. As I say, in Miss Welty's case subjectivism takes the form of calling attention to the author by her fine writing. In stories for a magazine like the *New Yorker,* which happily has no taste for fine writing, the form it takes is more subtle: the calling of attention to an author for his fine moral perceptions. This is a point I shall develop next week in discussing several other current collections of short stories, including those of Sylvia Townsend Warner.

I have spoken of the resemblance of Miss Welty's stories to ballets. In this connection I am reminded of the painter Dali and through him of the relationship between the chic modern department store and much of modern fiction—one day I should like to trace what I see as a direct line of descent from Miss Mansfield to Bonwit Teller. Although one has always the suspicion that Dali works with his tongue in his cheek, Miss Welty's dedication is unquestionable: this should be said at once. Still, the cultural kinship between the two is striking. Both Dali and Miss Welty are mythologists, creators of legend, both take their metaphor from dreams and yet are devoted naturalists, and each has a mother-country—Dali, Spain; Miss Welty, the Natchez country—whose atmosphere and superstition permeate their work and whose confines are determining beyond the power of travel or maturer experience to enlarge them. But more suggestive than such similarities is their common service to what amounts to a myth of modern femininity; for if it seemed a strange day for both art and commercialism when Bonwit Teller engaged Dali to do its windows, actually it was not as revolutionary as it looked. In the making of modern myths, the American department store has been well abreast of the American artist. The chic department-store mannequin is one of the great metaphors of our time, the display of merchandise in our department stores one of the great abstractions—though based upon naturalism—of our art. More fundamental, we recall the slogan created a few years ago by Bonwit Teller, "Have you that cherished look?" and we realize that it was the department store which stated most unmistakably (so unmistakably, indeed, that the slogan had to be dropped) the modern woman's self-loving dream. Here, that is, in all its economic nakedness is the narcissism, the mythologizing of female selfhood, which finds so strong a support in current female writing, including Miss Welty's.

59

There is now running in the magazines an advertisement for a Schiaparelli product, "Shocking Radiance," the illustration painted by Dali. "Shocking Radiance," it appears, is four oils—for the body, the face, the eyelids, and the lips—and to promote its sale Dali has painted a Venus rising from her shell, attended by a trio of sprites, one of whom pours a libation on the breast of the goddess, while another holds before her the mirror of her self-regard. Even at the sad risk of caricaturing Miss Welty's stories, I suggest a study of this Schiaparelli-Dali advertisement to recognize the *reductio ad absurdum* of the elements in Miss Welty's latest work which have no place in so serious and greatly endowed a writer.

October 9, 1943

In writing last week about Eudora Welty's latest volume of short stories I said that somewhere between Chekhov and Katherine Mansfield the short story had got off its trolley. I suggested that it was Miss Mansfield who was in large part responsible for the exaggerated subjectivity which has so variously corrupted modern short fiction. The line of descent from Miss Mansfield to Miss Welty may not always be easy to trace: the family resemblance is more a matter of carriage than of likeness of feature. In Sylvia Townsend Warner the heritage is easier to see. Less talented, also less ambitious but more typical of her literary generation than Miss Welty, Miss Warner is an accomplished practitioner of her craft. Twenty-eight of her stories, many of them familiar from the *New Yorker,* are now gathered in *A Garland of Straw* (Viking, $2.50). They are an interesting sampling of the thin brew of sensibility which has been our chief nourishment in English and American short fiction since Miss Mansfield separated the flesh from the bone of Chekhov.

I use the word sensibility in a frankly pejorative connotation;

obviously, sensibility under control is as necessary to a writer as an ear to a musician. But just as, in the case of Miss Welty, too much subjectivity manifests itself in too great a preoccupation with fine prose, in Miss Warner a too great subjectivity manifests itself in overdependence upon the author's private and special awarenesses. And this is what I mean by an excess of sensibility: the delusion that in a work of fiction an author's fugitive insights will carry the full weight with which they are charged in the writer's own experience. They never do. Instead, they reduce the stature of a story to the size of the smaller elements that compose it.

And this is peculiarly unfortunate because one of the commonest of the small elements in overly-subjective fiction is the author's emotion of superiority to his environment and to his fellow creatures. I seem to recall that many of Miss Mansfield's stories, too many, were stories of pity; although she might have wished to project her sensibility more widely, even in her most objective efforts she never succeeded in raising her work above the private context in which it was conceived. The first modern writer to look for salvation almost wholly in her pride of insight, Katherine Mansfield perpetuated a mood for the short story from which we have to turn back to Chekhov to remember that there's nothing in the story form which in itself demands the substitution of the fragmentary and allusive for the broadly conceived and fully stated.

Sylvia Townsend Warner lives in a more socially conscious world than Miss Mansfield. Many of her stories are concerned with politics, war, and "issues." One nevertheless has the impression that the bigger the issue the smaller and more personal the symbol by which Miss Warner communicates her indignation, and that the cause itself is finally secondary to the triumphant play of Miss Warner's sensitivity around it. For instance, a story called "Apprentice," in intent one of the very serious stories in *A Garland of Straw,* deals with the way Nazism can corrupt people. "Apprentice" is set in occupied Poland and is the story of a little girl who lives under the protection of a

61

German *Gauleiter*. In the midst of starvation Lili has plenty to eat, and she elaborates a wonderful game in which, standing above the public road, she dangles bits of food on a string for the starving passersby to jump for. But one young Polish boy resists her temptations, and Lili becomes maddened with the need to break his independent spirit. On a particularly cold day she dangles a cinnamon bun before the boy; he is so hungry that he jumps for it, and Lili jerks the string out of his reach just as the boy falls dead of cold and hunger. Thinking, "It must be really terrible to die like that," Lili pulls up the bun and eats it.

For me, a story like this defeats its purpose. In her concern to assert the rightness of her own feelings Miss Warner luxuriates in scorn of the child Lili and as a result Lili becomes an incredible little monster instead of a credible young girl. And in consequence of Lili's monstrosity the whole of Miss Warner's indictment of Nazism is reduced to a self-serving contrivance.

Of course, not all of Miss Warner's stories reveal so marked a discrepancy between purpose and method. Some are merely sketches or anecdotes ("The Trumpet Shall Sound," "To Cool the Air"), some are frankly fragmentary ("Rainbow Villa," "Setteragic On"). But the least of them mingles with the most ambitious without the reader being aware of a disturbing difference in kind because they all of them subdue their larger communication to the fleeting triumphs and self-affirmations of their author's creative moment. Although Miss Warner is willing to be more humanly fallible than Katherine Mansfield could ever let herself be, and although her prevailing temper is neither ecstatic nor pitying but acidulous, her stories are unmistakably fledglings from *The Dove's Nest*.

I use Miss Warner as I did Miss Welty, in exemplification of a literary tendency. In fairness I hasten to point out that, whatever my criticism, these writers exist in a class quite apart from most of the writers represented in a collection such as Martha Foley's *The Best American Short Stories, 1943* (Houghton Mifflin, $2.75). Miss Foley, still flogging the dead horse of the popular-magazine story over whose grave she should long ago have said her requiescat, illustrates a more "living form of tale-telling" with selections from Vicki Baum, Kay Boyle, Rachel Field, Jesse Stuart, and other such supposed bringers of life to fiction. True, she also includes a typical story by Eudora Welty ("Asphodel") and a typical and good story by Delmore Schwartz ("An Argument in 1934"), which, though I much dislike the Eudora Welty story, certainly belong in a volume intended to confer distinction. And she reprints John Cheever's "The Pleasures of Solitude," a small piece which nonetheless has enough substance to bear several readings. Perhaps, indeed, no editor could have done better in covering the range of available material. But I could wish that Miss Foley were herself less satisfied with it.

The Night of the Summer Solstice and Other Stories of The Russian War (Holt, $2.50) is Mark Van Doren's selection of seven comtemporary Soviet authors in representative short fiction dealing with war themes. It would be hard to find a volume of stories farther removed from the subjectivism I have been describing in American and English fiction: these reports of the fighting in Russia are so untouched by the personalities of their authors that any one of them might have been written by the author of any other. But if there is relief in impersonality, it is only for the moment: all too soon we realize that an excess of self-effacement is as unfruitful for fiction as an excess of self-celebration. These stories, which record the misery and courage of the Russian struggle, far from continuing the great tradition of the Russian short story, are Soviet poster art.

October 30, 1943

The season's fiction continues to be undistinguished and this reviewer continues to cherish the pious hope that it is the war—the loss of talent to the services and the confusion of the times—that accounts for the poor quality of the new novels.

Margery Allingham is one of England's most successful detective-story writers. Now, as Margery Allingham Carter, she has written her first non-mystery novel. *The Galantrys* (Little, Brown, $2.50) is the biography of a certain James Galantry, half gipsy and half gentleman, and it is also the story of a changing society, the period in English life when the established order of the eighteenth century was giving way to modern industrialism. But although Mrs. Carter, like so many of the English detective-story writers, is notably well-educated and not ashamed of it and, in her hero's struggles to cope with his complicated heredity, has the material for a perfectly plausible psychological study, she sacrifices the realities both of fiction and social history to an eccentric interest in genetics. She is obsessed with the science of breeding. Drawing most of her lessons from animal mating, she regards all human character, not only James Galantry's, as if it were as susceptible to hereditary determination as the character of a horse. The result is neither convincing nor funny, just odd, especially the last section of the story in which Galantry has a vision of his descendants right down to their roles in the present war.

Still, there is one good reason, and it is closely related to Margery Allingham's past reputation, why *The Galantrys* cannot be completely dismissed as no more than the indulgence of eccentricity: Mrs. Carter's prose, which is startling in its intelligence and wit. No one who has not been deadened by contemporary writing can fail to respond to the sweet pleasure of such a sentence as "No one spoke ill of her, everybody loved her absentmindedly," or of this description of a rural performance of Richard III: "The play was Cibber's version, of course, but even that consequential little hack could scarcely hurt it, nor could the woman who played Queen Margaret and muffed her lines in the very midst of her envy." That Orville Prescott,* in an otherwise accurate estimate of *The Galantrys,* should refer to its style as "highly mannered" and censure Mrs. Carter for her

* Daily book reviewer of the *New York Times.*

habit of commenting on her characters as she goes, because "modern readers are conditioned to a different tradition, where characters may speak for the author, but not the author for the characters," indicates how willingly modern critical judgment has assisted in the damming up of one of the life-streams of fiction.

But since it is indeed our present-day preference that our fictional characters speak for their authors instead of the other way around, why, one wonders, do so many of our novelists choose spokesmen of the least possible stature? As example, Albert Halper's new novel, *Only an Inch from Glory* (Harper, $2.50), locates itself as far below any level of literary glory as Mr. Halper could manage and still keep a typewriter beneath his hand. Of his four main characters, all Greenwich Village failures, not one has the energy even of colloquialism, let alone of ideas. "She knew I was her friend, her loyal friend, and I'd be her friend for life no matter what she did or what happened to her," says the painter-failure of the sculptor-failure.

"So she let me hang around her and take her out. She wouldn't let me spend much on her, either. She knew I was making only twenty-five dollars a week. Besides lending small sums to her fellow students down at school she subsequently pressed ten- and twenty-dollar loans upon me, when I was out of work afterwards. It hurt my pride at first, but I soon realized she was generous with everybody; and it's hard to explain but I sometimes felt that the root of her generosity was a desire to get back at her mother."

Mr. Halper's prose is so slack with humility that it can say nothing about failure except that it exists and is pitiful.

At a considerable geographic remove from Mr. Halper's book yet equally typical of our present-day failure of fictional verve is Wallace Stegner's *The Big Rock Candy Mountain* (Duell, Sloan, and Pearce, $3.00), a 515-page story of life in the West in the first decades of this century. Theoretically preferable though it may be, hard work without inspiration turns out to be little more fun than humility without effort. Mr. Stegner's novel

65

is detailed, careful, utterly respectful of the world it describes. Where Mr. Halper abdicates before his characters, Mr. Stegner gives them every last ounce of his strength. Yet the result, if not exactly muscle-bound, lacks the resilience of fictional life. *The Big Rock Candy Mountain* is a novel of the American dream, most of its action centered in the rambunctious Bo Mason, a big, restless, amoral hero-villain who sacrifices his wife and family to his unprincipled ambitions. (It might incidentally be noted that whether as frontiersman, robber baron, or gangster, this type of hero-villain is becoming alarmingly frequent in current fiction.) By far the best sections of Mr. Stegner's book are his pleasant evocations of little-boy life in the country, one of which you may already be familiar with from its publication as a short story.

Vardis Fisher's *The Mothers* (Vanguard, $2.50) is a historical novel of American pioneer days. A party of travelers—it includes, for our popular satisfaction, a couple of vicious Germans—sets out to reach the green fields of California; although most of the group perish en route, a few hardy souls endure the unendurable tortures in order to reach their destination. *The Mothers* is more exciting reading than Mr. Stegner's story or Mr. Halper's or Mrs. Carter's but it is not a sincere novel in intention or execution though it will no doubt make a sincere movie. I regret that Mr. Fisher broke off his account of the beginnings of man, started last year in *The Darkness and the Deep,* in order to switch his mechanical Freudianism from the ape world to the world of modern history since even his persisting prejudice in favor of women becomes less authoritative, if no less gratifying, when it continues into a period with which we are more familiar.

According to his publishers, Hans Habe's *Kathrine* (Viking, $2.75) is concerned with the life of an unconventional woman tangled with the destiny of a nation. I expected Mata Hari and was disappointed. After its first pages of watered-down Colette, Mr. Habe's novel is a dreary, overcharged portrait of a still-beautiful cocotte—she was known as Kathrine the Great—who is trying to marry her daughter to the son of her lover. Kathrine's lover happens to be an airplane manufacturer and the war happens to be threatening. This gives Mr. Habe an opportunity to have his fling with the fall of poor France.

Out of the Silent Planet by C. S. Lewis (Macmillan, $2.00), the diabolically clever author of *The Screwtape Letters,* is a well-written novel about a journey to Mars. Since I am sadly without taste for fiction about life anywhere except on earth, I was unable to finish a book that was recommended to me by friends whose judgment is otherwise unimpeachable.

November 20, 1943

Despite the destructive efforts of the critics—and even the *Times Book Review* allowed itself an unaccustomed field day of happy irony—Ilka Chase's *In Bed We Cry* (Doubleday, Doran, $2.50) is a novel inevitably slated for large sales. In the first place, it deals with a segment of contemporary life infinitely inviting to wishful thinking: its world is the world of zebra stripes, bounded on the north by Cartier and on the south by Carnegie (Hattie, not Hall). In the second place, it talks about sex—oh, how it talks and talks!—in just the right voice to tickle the ears of people who would be horrified by out-and-out pornography. The gentility of its sexual accent is, in fact, one of the things that especially interests me about Miss Chase's upper-bracket bohemia. Just as Devon Elliott, the dainty little tycooness of the cosmetic industry who is Miss Chase's heroine, can be blandly ruthless in her business dealings at no cost in manners or adorableness, she can move from bed to bed and still be a lady. The daughter of a college professor, Devon speaks French, knows a Picasso from a Chippendale, and even has friends in Washington. The upper-class libido is as well-anchored in literacy as it is cushioned by wealth.

I could wish that Miss Chase had been more specific than she is about the spending of Devon's millions. I would have enjoyed studying the cost-sheets instead of being left to wander wide-eyed through an untagged paradise of Madison Avenue decorating and English butlers, champagne buckets and snacks at Voisin's. I could snare only two cold-cash items: on Beekman Place a plausible gift of roses costs $35 and at the Fifth Avenue salon of Devonshire House a good account is someone who spends ten thousand a year on her cosmetic upkeep. (Don't look now, darling, but isn't that a tumbril?)

The central conflict of *In Bed We Cry* is between sex and science: Devon's husband is tired of mixing beauty preparations and wants a laboratory of his own in which to experiment with a cure for burns. But Miss Chase's auxiliary problems are more suggestive. Did you know, for instance, that in one important section of metropolitan society the big matrimonial challenge is to find a man who doesn't drink? Another problem is that more and more men are finding it impossible to match the incomes of their wives, and Miss Chase says that after the war it will be even harder for women to balance their beds with their budgets. Political compatibility has also to be taken into account, what with the war and Roosevelt—Devon wonders about the political background of her refugee lover; she herself has strong feelings about the Nazis since they broke into her Paris salon and stole her secret formulas. Indeed, on the whole subject of refugeeism east of the Avenue Miss Chase is thought-provoking. "Not all refugee Europeans were automatically desirable," she explains. "Recent arrivals especially were so hell-bent on charming rich American women and trying to show up American men as poor lovers that their overzealousness made them ridiculous."

In Bed We Cry is a mine of such nuggets. But no doubt this is to read it the wrong way. Miss Chase did not intend her novel as a social, even a revolutionary, document but as a purer form of entertainment.

Like *Darkness at Noon*, Arthur Koestler's new novel, *Arrival and Departure* (Macmillan, $2.00), is essentially a novel for intellectuals, by which I mean that it is directed to that section of society for which the rise and decline of the radical movement, in its broadest aspects, is the central social-political fact of these last decades. This is not to say that it lacks dramatic interest, or that it is particularly difficult to read, but only that its drama is largely philosophical and its suspense more a matter of wondering where the theoretical cat will land when it stops jumping than of concern for the human fate of its hero. While this may not diminish its fascination and even, given the emptiness of current fiction, make it something of a literary event, it necessarily deprives it of the emotional overtones and wider reference of the very best novels. Even the fact that Mr. Koestler deals with psychoanalysis and devotes a large part of his novel to the description of a case of hysterical paralysis, though it may increase the popular appeal of his book, does so, as it were, under false pretenses. Psychoanalysis is only the new armor in which Mr. Koestler has chosen to dress science for its old battle against faith.

Faith wins but the manner in which Mr. Koestler conducts the fight—and by my reading of the book *Arrival and Departure* is more fight than novel, however disarmed and disarming its author may appear to be—is as tricky and unconvincing as it is brilliant. Mr. Koestler is investigating the problem of the relation between neurosis and conduct, specifically the relation between unconscious guilt and the radical impulse. He tells the story of Peter Slavek, a middle-class intellectual and dissident Communist who has suffered terrible physical tortures in his service to the radical cause. The European war has begun, and Peter has escaped from his own (unnamed) country to Lisbon (also unnamed), where he intends to join the British forces. While he waits in Lisbon for his papers, he has a brief love affair with a girl, Odette, who is awaiting passage to America. Peter, too, is offered the possibility of escape to America, and respite from the old struggle. But his devotion to the political cause for which he has suffered is in such conflict with the desire to follow love and find peace that, not knowing which way to move, he "resolves" his conflict by becoming paralyzed in one of his tortured legs. It happens that a family friend, Dr. Sonia Bolgar, a psychoanalyst, is in Lisbon. She cures Peter of his paralysis by uncovering the childhood roots of his need for martyrdom and by showing him that his devotion to the cause of the weak springs from guilt at having "accidentally" killed the younger brother of whom he was jealous. Having regained his health, Peter is now free to seek personal freedom and follow Odette to America. But at the last moment he rejects this escape. Just as he had originally planned, he goes off to fight against fascism with the British.

Now at first glance—and accepting the identification of revolutionary activity with anti-fascist activity as an expedient, literary or political, which for present purposes we need not pause over—what Mr. Koestler seems to be saying is that a revolutionary can be psychoanalyzed and still continue to be a revolutionary, a proper and useful thing to say. For "revolutionary" we might substitute "painter" or "priest" or "mathematician," and I daresay psychoanalysis would itself be the first to thank Mr. Koestler for exempting it from the wearisome accusation that it destroys the volitional nature of human activity. But then what shall we make of Mr. Koestler's fable of Pythagoras which is intended to remind us that if Pythagoras had been analyzed and shown that his interest in triangles was an obsession with his wife's fidelity, he would never have discovered the Pythagorean proposition? Actually what Mr. Koestler is saying with this book is quite the opposite of what its general movement promises. His hero is not a political idealist who also happens to be a neurotic; he is a neurotic whose guilts are shown to be the source of his political fervor. Yet when the guilts are presumably removed, Peter continues to function according to his old political pattern and not, apparently, on any new basis. The only difference between "his first crusade which had ended with his breakdown on Sonia's couch," and the second, to which he departs at the close of the novel, is that "the first time he had set out in ignorance of his reasons; this time he knew them, but understood that reasons do not matter so much."

In other words, Mr. Koestler, at pains to recognize neurosis and to grant psychoanalysis its healing powers, ends up by saying, *not* that Peter, cured of his neurosis, is free to act unneurotically, but that Peter, with the knowledge that he is neurotic safely under his belt, is free to continue to act neurotically, which is tantamount to saying that at least in political conduct our motives make no difference. Or, to put it another way, while Mr. Koestler seems to give determination and volition each its due place in human activity, actually he refuses to make any value distinction between determined conduct and volitional conduct.

This is an unfruitful attitude in a novelist. But as I have said, Mr. Koestler, for all his impressive talents, comes to fiction not as a novelist but as a polemicist. His book is an elaborate structure of arguments fashioned to support his mistaken assumption that psychoanalysis is at odds with revolutionary activity. To the revolutionary mind even at its most dissident, Freud persists as the arch-enemy, and Mr. Koestler's method of combat is first to take the enemy into camp and then help him commit suicide. Nor is his antipathy to psychoanalysis disclosed only in these broad errors of reasoning which I have suggested: while appearing to be utterly fair to the analytical side, in detail after detail he does his best to prejudice the reader against it. Thus, he grants Dr. Bolgar the ability to cure Peter of his gross paralytic symptoms but also shows her as a person with "roots in the air" and no social principles—quite as if rootlessness were a prescribed psychoanalytical position—and he also makes her a nymphomaniac Lesbian. And her only patient other than Peter to whom we are introduced is a Nazi whom she has "adjusted" to Nazism! One cannot help inquiring why it is that if analysis is so little a threat to the revolutionary impulse as in theory Mr. Koestler maintains, he goes to such lengths to discredit it.

And I suppose that with this much unease and sophistry behind us we should be prepared for the almost desperate mystical note on which Mr. Koestler concludes his novel. Having given us "scientific" proof that it is emotionally sound to be a radical, Mr. Koestler finds it necessary to reject the science which, he believes, questions this right in favor of an imperative taken from religion. *Arrival and Departure* ends on a statement of faith—a poor little bastard-of-pragmatism kind of faith, but presumably enough to support action. "If one accepted a faith, one should not ask because of what—the 'because of' should be taken for granted, beyond questioning. He who says 'because of' will be open to disillusion. He has no firm ground under his feet. But he who accepts in spite of his objections, in spite of the imperfections which are manifest to him—he will be secure." It is in these weak but willing words that Peter Slavek sums up what we must take to be Mr. Koestler's position as he continues in the political struggle.

December 18, 1943

As I began James T. Farrell's *My Days of Anger* (Vanguard, $2.75), the fourth and final volume of the Danny O'Neill series, I was at once struck by how vividly Farrell's characters had remained in my memory from my reading, some years ago, of no more than a single one, the first, of the Danny O'Neill novels. Danny's father Jim (now dead), his mother Lizz, his cranky and wonderful old grandmother, his Uncle Al who worships education as a holy mystery, and his drunken Aunt Margaret—all Danny's family had stayed with me with uncommon clarity. I found myself contrasting this with the experience I had had when I reread John Dos Passos's *U.S.A.* Surely I am not the only reader who has difficulty remembering the people in Dos Passos's novel, and it occurred to me that perhaps the reason we forget them so quickly is that while Dos Passos gives them intellectual understanding he gives them no love. This is quite the opposite of Farrell's relation to his characters. Of the two writers, Dos Passos has the more various and dramatic imagination; indeed, it is Farrell's great weakness as a novelist that his people have so little dramatic possibility—he seems unable to let them grow up and have their life in the big world. But he has the more generous heart: his characters endure in memory because of the affection he gives them.

Of course, in the measure that the material of Farrell's fiction is autobiographical, his love is self-love. Perhaps it is embarrassment in the face of his long fictional obsession with his own past that in fact accounts for the gruffness with which each of his re-visits to the autobiographical subject is received by certain critics. But even granting that Farrell's love of mankind is love only for that section of mankind from which came his own life, there are few contemporary writers who have the power to trace their source and growth with such closeness of observation and in such disciplined prose. For some reason in the years since I last read one of his novels I had got the impression that Farrell was a careless writer, quite as if, being like Dreiser a realist, he shared Dreiser's stylistic slovenliness. The truth is that Farrell is a meticulous craftsman, choosing both incident and language with care and skill. The contradiction between the apparently uncontrolled flow of his narrative, and the rapidity with which novel follows novel, and the judiciousness with which each scene is chosen for its place in the larger pattern of the story is actually a paradox of his work. There is another paradox which relates to Farrell's obsession with his past: although his energies are so consistently directed to autobiography, his basic objectivity and his refusal to intervene on behalf of Danny O'Neill's author could serve as a lesson to many

73

writers who would condemn him out of hand for his excessive self-concern.

My Days of Anger covers the period 1924–27, the years in which Danny comes to young manhood. He earns his own living, studies at the University of Chicago, breaks with Catholicism, and, perhaps most important, makes his first eager steps as a writer. O'Neill-Farrell is moving away from the family group and testing its values; and because he is young and soon to be an artist, the education of his mind and feelings is the education of his taste in poetry. In literature he finds meaning for the environment in which he was raised, and in the promise of literature the promise of the righting of its wrongs. At the end of the novel, his grandmother dead, Danny is leaving for New York and he thinks: "His people had not been fulfilled. He had not understood them all these years. He would do no penance now for these; he would do something surpassing penance. There was a loyalty to the dead, a loyalty beyond penance and regret. He would do battle so that others did not remain unfulfilled as he and his family had been." In other words, it is on a call to battle, at once touching in its naïve inadequacy and moving in its personal passion, that Farrell concludes his portrait of the novelist as a very young man.

But literature is not made from calls to battle, and it is one of Farrell's grievous errors not only to think that it is but also to see even his literary problems as a continuing conflict between two clearly opposed sides. On the one side is truth, on the other lies. And since he knows that he tells the truth, he thinks that whatever someone else wants him to say is untruth. Thus in *My Days of Anger* Danny is studying with a professor of creative writing, a not very subtle caricature of the academician. "You want to be a realist," says this thin voice of criticism. "But is it realism to say that all life is unhappy?" The professor goes on to take the young author to task for omitting a "glimmer of hope" in his stories. Danny replies, "I didn't make unhappiness. I didn't invent Chicago. I'm only trying to describe Chicago as I know it." In other words, Farrell interprets any criticism of his work as an objection to its unpleasant truthfulness. It may well be that some unimportant section of opinion—it would be the same opinion that acclaims *A Tree Grows in Brooklyn*—is this unworthy of his consideration. But Farrell gravely deceives himself if he regards all adverse criticism as if it were essentially without seriousness. For clearly his pleasantness or unpleasantness is beside the point of his ultimate success as a novelist. The people he writes about could be rich and beautiful instead of poor and woeful and superstitious, and he would still be open to criticism for the limits within which he has held his imagination. One of the best things about Farrell may be his capacity for love but even love, and certainly all the accuracy in the world, cannot compensate for the lack of action, plot and—especially —variousness in his novels. He seems to believe that to intensify an experience by dramatic invention is to falsify it, but this is as if, telling the story, say, of Othello, he thought it more truthful to record a lifetime of Othello's emotional insufficiencies and racial inferiorities than to introduce an Iago to escalate Othello's uneasy innocence into violence. In fact, his rigid refusal to allow his characters movement in the world has a significant resemblance to the loving-cruel family authority which crippled all the O'Neills and made it necessary for his grandmother to die before Danny O'Neill could leave Chicago.

January 8, 1944

Gontran de Poncins's *Home Is the Hunter* (Reynal and Hitchcock, $2.50), although not so direct in its romantic appeal as *Kabloona*, the same writer's account of his stay among the Esquimos, is still one of the notable books of recent years, shining out of the mist of most current writing with the full light of M. de Poncins's remarkable personality. To read the books of M. de Poncins is to be unusually aware of their author: he seems at once very worldly and very internalized, monastically intense in spirit. One has the impression of an intelligence peculiarly of the French aristocratic tradition, and indeed *Home Is the Hunter* is a reconstruction—or a commemoration—of the almost feudal background against which, we can guess, M. de Poncins was himself bred. It is published as fiction but it is not strictly a novel. Rather, it is both elegiac poetry and penetrating sociological research into a culture which was already vanishing glory when the author was a small child before the first war.

M. de Poncins's fictional device is to tell the story of Jean Ménadieu, for forty years a servant of the d'Ombres family, who in his old age returns for a few days to the d'Ombres estate. Moving from room to room in the old château, pausing over all the objects which hold his affections and memory, Jean re-creates the history of the d'Ombres family and his own life in his long years of service; through the old man's eyes we see the change between past and present as the movement from a world thick with meaning to a thin and barren modernity. There was a time when both masters and servants accepted their responsibilities, when for a servant like Jean there was a religious dignity in service and, for his masters, no greater satisfaction than in the fulfilment of their duty to their tenants and to the estate itself. But now even in rural France that time has passed; the old values have disappeared and modernity has supplied no adequate replacement. A broken pot, a bit of string, an old brick, anything that belonged to the château, had once been something to be permanently cherished because, having been useful, it was always beautiful. The easy prodigality of the present generation sums up for Jean, and for M. de Poncins, the emotional barrenness of modern living.

And in another day a servant could feel that he too had a beauty in his life because he was useful. If to contemporary readers Jean seems too good to be true, that only proves M. de Poncins's point, that to the present-day world a devotion like Jean's has become unrecognizable. And if it has also become undesirable, if, steeped in egalitarianism, we are offended by the extreme of self-abdication with which Jean devotes himself to his masters in order to achieve his sense of purpose, then we can guess that M. de Poncins would ask us what it is that democracy, shorn even of religion, has offered Jean in substitute for humility and service.

I am very sorry but not surprised that *Home Is the Hunter* has been dismissed as a statement of political reaction. Issuing in a poignant assertion of values which have disappeared from modern life, it can of course be all too easily read as an anti-democratic document, and this despite the fact that M. de Poncins's complex and subtle intelligence quite comprehends the price that his old society often paid for its virtues. Democracy makes a bad mistake to shut itself off this promptly from criticism like M. de Poncins's by giving it an unpleasant political label: culture no less than nature abhors a vacuum, and democratic culture, fiercely on guard against encroachments from the right, calling them mystical or religious, on the one hand, or degrading to the individual, on the other, lets itself be insufficiently aware of the mysticism and the degradation of the individual which invade it from the left.

In the same week in which I read *Home Is the Hunter* I read Ben Field's *The Outside Leaf* (Reynal and Hitchcock, $2.50). A novel about Connecticut tobacco farming, it is, if you will, as much a document of the cultural left as M. de Poncins's book is of the right. It would be difficult to find a more telling argument in support of M. de Poncins's indictment of modern culture than this manifesto of "progress." *The Outside Leaf* is the story of a young man, Moe Miller, who at the age of twenty takes over the running of his father's tobacco farm. More interested in the Talmud and in people than in success, the father has failed with the farm but Moe cares nothing about the Talmud or family affection, nature, or anything except his work, to which his devotion is more extreme than Jean's devotion to the d'Ombres family. Moe believes religiously in tractors, farm implements, and sweat—indeed an inordinate amount of sweat drips through the pages of this book; it is Mr. Field's test of reality from which any sign of inner or outer grace would be a seduction. I can

77

recall no novel I have read as a reviewer that has as repellent a hero as Moe Miller but Mr. Field thinks of him not as a dangerous monomaniac, but as heroic. At the end of the book, against our most fervent hopes, he gives him a very nice wife as reward for his subhumanity.

There are certain things to be said in commendation of Mr. Field's book: it is written with effective sparseness, it takes as much trouble with its secondary characters as with Moe, and it is encyclopedic in its knowledge of tobacco growing. But these are negligible virtues compared to its horribleness as a statement of how the progressive novelist defines a good and meaningful life. *The Outside Leaf* is certainly more in tune with the times than *Home Is the Hunter;* it will never be attacked as reactionary. But in substance what it is saying is that the less man tempts the spirit and the closer he approximates the mindless power of the machine, the more he reinforces the values that we should desire in a democratic society.

Against so frightening a threat from the left we could do worse than reexamine the values M. de Poncins finds in an outmoded social tradition. It seems to me to be simple and wrong to assume that in order to preserve certain old values, we must necessarily move backward in our political and economic process and plans. This is itself reactionary and none the less dangerous because it now so regularly supports presumably liberal thought.

February 12, 1944

John Hersey is a *Life-Time* correspondent with our invasion forces. His novel, *A Bell for Adano* (Knopf, $2.50), is our first fiction of the American government of Italy, occupational history written while it was still little more than a gleam in Amgot's eye. But the very speed of composition of Mr. Hersey's book gives it what interest it has because, writing quickly, Mr.

Hersey has written out of a deep reservoir of folk-idealism and popular assumption. This is not to say that *A Bell for Adano* is an unconscious book any more than most movies, also created out of popular assumption, are unconscious. It is as possible for me to believe that a person who has had the education and experience necessary to get a correspondent's job on *Life* naturally thinks of Americans or Italians in the simple way that Mr. Hersey appears to in this novel as it is for me to believe that the Hollywood scenario writer who wrote *Joe Smith, American* naturally thinks of Americans as Joe Smiths. The contrivance of simplicity is one of the things that may set my spine tingling in a movie, especially in a lesson-in-democracy movie, but it also leaves a bad taste in the mouth because I feel that I have been taken in. I feel the more taken in, indeed, the more these popular assumptions have some basis in truth.

There seems to me to be a good deal of truth in Mr. Hersey's picture of an American. In fact, *A Bell for Adano* might accurately be described as the Platonic ideal of Americanism, of which the American reality is an active approximation. Its hero, Major Joppolo, is a compendium of easily recognized national characteristics. Joppolo, the American occupation officer of the little town of Adano, thinks for himself, works fourteen hours a day, is realistic about taking help where he can find it, is gentle from instinct and ruthless on principle, respects authority where it earns respect and, where it is unworthy, countermands it at whatever risk, knows how to play with the church, has sex but knows how to control it, loathes protocol and red tape, and first and always is a man of heart who understands that a town full of Italian peasants has more need for a bell than for American sanitation; when his M.P.s get into a drunken orgy and smash up the house in which they are billeted, instead of sending them to the guardhouse he invokes the memory of their mothers. So convincing is Mr. Hersey's portrait of the American as an administrator that we even come to think it a national characteristic that Joppolo should be of Italian parentage and live in the Bronx.

Obviously, folk idealism of this kind is its own good clean fun. What offends me is its being put forward as all of his truth by someone in a position to boast a more complicated view of things. When Mr. Hersey says in his Foreword that only men can guarantee the future, men like Major Joppolo, I tend to agree with him; for all its limitations the Joppolo incarnation of American democracy at work isn't a bad star to be shooting for in these practical days. But when, also in his Foreword, he uses Hollywood-naïve prose like this, "Major Victor Joppolo, U.S.A., was a good man. You will see that. It is the whole reason why I want you to know his story. . . . Major Joppolo was Amgot officer of Adano, and he was good," I know that Mr. Hersey's ideas, like his prose, have undergone a process of conscious falsifying and of purposeful simplification.

March 4, 1944

The Hunted by Albert J. Guerard (Knopf, $2.50) has rather more to say than most current novels. It is even good enough to make one wish it were better. Mr. Guerard writes about the kind of people of whom he seems to have experience, he is knowledgeable, and he tells his story by means of dramatic action. Perhaps one of the defects of his book is an excess of drama: there is surely an over-contrivance of plot which makes even his title too obvious. The main theme of *The Hunted* is the fate of a young singing waitress who marries a decadent poet-professor and comes to live in a narrow New England college town. To this Mr. Guerard subjoins the story of a young fugitive from the law, a strange figure called the Bomber. At first, for the sake of sensation, both the professor's wife and the Bomber are taken up by the less reliable college element, but eventually—even inevitably—this disreputable society conspires with bigoted respectability to betray and hound the two outcasts. Mr. Guerard's psychological girl-hunt, in other words, is melodra-

matically underscored by his physical man-hunt, and the inter-
weaving of the two narratives reveals the potential violence that
lies behind what might otherwise be thought of as mere social
snobbery. The trouble is that Mr. Guerard's man-hunt over-
states his girl-hunt, and the girl-hunt reduces the terror of the
man-hunt. The doubling of motifs works out to weaken the
impact of each.

It is also a weakness of Mr. Guerard's book that, for all the
author's obvious sympathetic interest in people, its leading
characters are finally not very interesting. But this is a common
failure in fictional people, and probably as little susceptible of
explanation, except in terms of the creative chemistry, as the
failure of perfectly plausible people to hold our interest in real
life.

The Hunted is nevertheless impressive because Mr. Guerard
has something of considerable importance to communicate
about American social psychology at the level just below political action. His picture of American college fraternity life—its
anarchy, its sensation-seeking, and its sexual cruelty—is more
than a little disturbing and very convincing. We are used to
social horror in novels of the South. The existence of a compar-
able gentlemanly degeneracy in other parts of the country has
yet to announce itself very loud in our fiction though the fact
that it exists comes to us by way of hearsay, certain newspaper
stories, and the intuition we often have of a peculiarly native
devil lurking beneath our more arrogant humors. Mr. Guerard
has the good sense not to weaken his novelistic case by naming
the likely political outlet for this kind of anarchic energy but
sections of his book are as frightening as the sound of marching
feet in early Hitler Germany.

March 18, 1944

Although neither its theme nor its setting is new to fiction, Lillian Smith's new novel, *Strange Fruit* (Reynal and Hitchcock, $2.75), is a newly moving and unusual book. There is something extremely comforting in the singlemindedness with which we are in the habit of approaching the "Negro problem," but Miss Smith is anything but comforting or singleminded. In her hands the Negro problem turns out to be not only the problem of the South but, by implication, of all modern society. To say that *Strange Fruit* anatomizes a small Georgia town at the end of the last war is to regionalize and to particularize in time a social study which is applicable to any number of other American communities and moments, and to say that Miss Smith's book is concerned with racial conflicts is to ignore her knowledge that in the degree that race is set against race, man is set against himself. *Strange Fruit* is so wide in its human understanding that its Negro tragedy becomes the tragedy of anyone who lives in a world in which minorities suffer; when it ends in a lynching, we are as sorry and frightened for the lynchers as for the victim. Indeed, we are terrified for ourselves by the realization that this is what we have made of our human possibility—a rare effect for a problem novel to produce. Yet Miss Smith's novel is no more than a problem novel; it is simply an uncommonly good one.

Of all race situations I suppose the situation of miscegenation is the touchiest. Even the liberal Northern imagination shrinks from the question, "Would you want your sister to marry a Negro?" and I think it took special courage and passion for Miss Smith to hang her novel on the main thread of the love of a white boy and a colored girl. However, Tracy Dean is not the usual scion of Southern aristocratic blood running thin; he is the son of the rather nice white doctor of the town, and if he is weak, it is because it served his mother's complicated emotional needs to make him so. Nor is Nonnie Anderson the conventional high-spirited Negro girl; she is college-educated and refined, by *her* mother's excessive pride, beyond the point where she can ever hope to find a workable way of life in a bigoted society. Perhaps people such as these are doomed even apart from the difficulties that inevitably rise in the path of their marriage. They never do marry; Miss Smith knows they never could marry. Actually she never says they should marry. Yet as their love story unfolds, the issue forces itself upon us: why in the world can they not marry? What is this difference in color which is admittedly no bar to love but so unassailably a bar to marriage? And even our vaunted Northern liberalism begins to look unpleasantly like hypocrisy.

Indeed, the prime merit of Miss Smith's novel is that it refuses to give quarter to an easy tolerance. It would be a very complacent Northerner who could take solace from the fact that *Strange Fruit* is a novel about the South. Sam, Miss Smith's Negro doctor, is at pains to explain that there are some nice white people in Maxwell, Georgia, too; among them he specifies Mr. Harris, owner of the sawmill and one of the town's most substantial citizens. Well, Mr. Harris is a liberal and he risks his life to try to save the Negro who is being lynched. But Mr. Harris pays wages which are below union scale and some of his workers are of the lynching party. He is also strong in support of a church which not only blinks lynching but considers itself above saving black souls in the same revival tent with white. *Strange Fruit* concerns itself with contradictions within individuals, and also within the social group, which have their parallels above the Mason and Dixon Line and in fields other than those of racial conflict.

Just as the town of Maxwell is divided between its colored and white sections, Miss Smith's story is divided between its white and colored characters, but it does a better job with its white people than its Negroes. In conflict with each other, or in family or affectional relationships, her Negroes carry psycholog-

83

ical conviction but when Miss Smith undertakes to give them individual character they fall into stereotypes. Apparently with the best will in the world it is impossible for a member of the dominant social group to imagine the way of thinking and feeling of a people who for so many generations have been taught to hide what they think and feel.

March 25, 1944

The Silence of the Sea by Vercors (Macmillan, $1.00) is a tiny book, scarcely longer than a short story, with a dramatic genesis and history. We are told that it was written in Nazi-occupied France in the fall of 1941, published in that country by an underground publishing organization called Les Editions de Minuit, and then smuggled to England, where, translated by Cyril Connolly, it was brought out under the title *Put Out the Light*. We are further told that it is the first in a series of French underground publications which are to be known as "Les Cahiers du Silence." The name Vercors is of course a pseudonym.

Naturally one comes to such a volume much prejudiced in its favor. We know that many of the distinguished writers of modern France are still living in that country; whether or not the author of this story is someone with whose work we are familiar, we are eager to greet any work that has survived the occupation. But unfortunately *The Silence of the Sea* falls far short of our expectations—perhaps, indeed, only the greatest short story could live up to so dramatic a birth. It is sophisticated in conception and sure-handed in the writing but its interest is notably political rather than literary.

Told in the first person by a cultivated Frenchman—it is indicated that he is a writer—the story describes the developing relationship between himself, the niece with whom he lives, and a German occupation officer billeted in their home. The German, in civilian life a composer, is handsome and cultivated; he is sensitive to the hostility of his unwilling hosts and even respects it. He never intrudes into the part of the house in which they live except for a short visit each evening, when he knocks on their sitting-room door—only to enter without being asked. Then while the old Frenchman sits on one side of the fireplace sipping his coffee and the niece sits on the other with her knitting, both of them coldly silent, the officer talks to them of his life and ideas. It develops that he is in love with French culture, the culture represented by the long rows of books that line the room in which he is so unwelcome. He sees the conquest of France as a marriage between the beautiful soul of France and the strong body of Germany, and he even carries this image to the point of describing the native betrayers of France as the disreputable matchmakers of an inevitable and fruitful union. And as he talks it becomes clear that the Nazi officer is purposefully addressing himself to the young niece, symbol of the French spirit, and that his charm and passion are beginning to have a profound effect upon his listeners despite their hostile silence. But one day the officer goes on leave to Paris and when he returns his hosts realize that the evening intrusions have ceased. We watch them wait in increasing tension for the accustomed knock at the door. Finally it is heard again: for the first time the Frenchman calls loudly, "Come in," and even adds, "Sir." The German is markedly disturbed; he has come to explain his absence. In Paris he had visited German headquarters and had had a shattering experience: he learned that Germany intends to subdue French culture for a thousand years, not to woo it as he had imagined. Under such circumstances he can no longer serve as an occupation officer and he has applied for military duty; he has come to say goodbye. At this news the niece at last raises her eyes to the German and addresses him. In the attitude of a deserted lover, she utters a tortured farewell.

The ambiguity of such a story is apparent even in this broad outline; if we also take into account details which I haven't space to report here, *The Silence of the Sea* is thoroughly puzzling, susceptible of many interpretations. But to me what Vercors seems to be saying—and if I am correct in my reading, his book is one of the thoroughly disconcerting documents, if not of the war, then of an aspect of contemporary intellectual life—is that if Nazism would only promise to preserve French culture, it could or would or should be acceptable to the French. By French culture he means purely and simply French art, the good French literature over which the officer ranges as he stands before his host's bookshelves.

There are no people in Vercors's narrative except the characters I have mentioned and one or two people to whom the officer refers; there are no *French* people other than the narrator and his niece. By implication there is no starvation or exploitation or murder or forced labor in the train of Nazism, there is only the outraged dignity of the spirit of high French civilization. By further implication there is no importance in the power exercised by a political system over the multitudes of uncultivated people, there is even no connection between a nation's culture and its uncultivated people. The intellectual class, this is to say, lives in a social vacuum, with but one significant commitment: to itself. By my reading, *The Silence of the Sea* is such an extreme of special pleading as to be a *reductio ad absurdum* of the case for the intellectual's valuable place in society.

And this, in fact, is the merit of the book, that it is a story based in a point of view pervasive in important sections of our intellectual life and that it allows us to see the political folly to which the logic of its position must lead. There is little to distinguish the isolationism-in-thought of *The Silence of the Sea* from the isolationism-in-thought of those of our intellectuals and artists who insist that they have no share in the running of government or in the making and waging of wars. But have they then no share in the outcome of government and wars? If not, there can be no reason why they shouldn't welcome any political system, even fascism, so long as it allows them to function, and what a bitter irony this is, for if there is one thing that

86

would horrify them it's the accusation that they are reactionaries. In their reverence for the internationalism of art, in their lack of respect for the political units which are nations, and in their lack of concern for the forms in which society is cast, they find warrant of their liberalism, even of their radicalism. But perhaps a story like *The Silence of the Sea* will remind them of the degree to which cultural privilege is capable of being as strong an arm of political reaction as hereditary social privilege.

April 1, 1944

So far as I know, Frederic Wakeman's *Shore Leave* (Farrar and Rinehart, $2.50) is the first novel of this war to concern itself with the effects of the war on our actual combatants. The action of *Shore Leave* takes place in January, 1943, when many of our Pacific fighters were already seasoned veterans. It reports the emotional state of four navy fliers sent to San Francisco on medical leave. Mr. Wakeman's four pilots are all, in varying degree, heroes. Although they come from different parts of the country and different backgrounds, they are bound by their passion for flying, by their intimate knowledge of death, and, most of all, by the unbridgeable chasm separating them from the civilian population. They are nearer home than they have been for many months yet none of them has the desire for reunion with family or old friends. They share a desperate restlessness: the only way to spend their leave is to settle down to the serious business of drinking and the serious business of nonserious lovemaking. *Shore Leave* is a first report on our newest lost generation. It can be read as this war's spiritual parallel to Ernest Hemingway's World War I.

But there is this not unimportant difference: there was no earlier Hemingway on whom the early Hemingway could model himself whereas Mr. Wakeman follows not only Hemingway himself but all Hemingway's followers. Without a new war, the hard-drinking, tough-loving way of life has for some time now been crystallizing into the whole view of life of a large section of our fiction, a fact which is not to be missed in reading Mr. Wakeman's novel. I am not suggesting that *Shore Leave*, because it is familiar, is necessarily inaccurate in its observations—it may be that even in respect of its hangovers, World War II is merely a frightening repetition of World War I. Perhaps the influence of Hemingway persists into the fiction of the present war because Hemingway caught so much of the lasting truth of modern war. But Mr. Wakeman could, I suspect, have written this book, minus only its service stripes, long before Pearl Harbor. We are told he is an advertising-radio man in civilian life, and certainly this is fundamentally the same old advertising-radio novel of psychological disorientation and spiritual unrest with which we have long been acquainted—of the relation between Hemingway and this literary-fringe view of things one has indeed always wondered whether it is a case of art imitating life or life imitating art.

The more I read short stories, the less rewarding I begin to find the form except in the hands of really great writers. Surely the talent in the ten stories that make up *The Common Thread* by Michael Seide (Harcourt, Brace, $2.00) would count for far more in a novel than in this collection of short pieces—good as are his heart, eye and ear, the form in which he works seems always to be stopping him short of what we feel he is capable of knowing and saying. But there is one other element to account for a reservation of praise: the poor-Jewish background of these stories seems inevitably to make pity one of their dominant emotions. True, Mr. Seide's pity embraces all the characters in all his stories while in most Jewish-American fiction, and in short fiction generally, it is the I-person who absorbs the author's sympathies. Yet wherever there is an overcharge of pity there is likely to be an under-supply of action and drama, and more movement in the world and less mood would make for a significant improvement in *The Common Thread*.

Mr. Seide not only writes wonderful dialogue but what we

could call his basic prose is also excellent. But he has a bad habit of parentheses (such a tempting habit!) into which he likes to drop bits of fancy writing, and far too often, even outside the parentheses, he destroys a first-rate passage by straining for effect. A sentence like the following, of which the fourth to eighth words should have been sternly rejected, is typical both of Mr. Seide's peculiar gift and his pursuing weakness: "An old woman hunched fatly against the freeze shuffled past him with her herring smell, uttering toothlessly that the world was much too small for her."

April 15, 1944

Reviewing Eduardo Mallea's *The Bay of Silence* (Knopf, $2.50) in the *New Yorker* of March 18, Edmund Wilson brings to our notice the important fact that in translation this novel by one of Argentina's foremost writers has been cut by some hundred thousand words. Although it is of course unforgivable if this alteration was made without Mr. Mallea's permission, I am afraid I cannot go along with Mr. Wilson in the generous assumption that it is ruthless cutting which makes the difference between a successful novel and a "puzzling" and "unsatisfying" one. It is annoying in the extreme to be given a book in which characters disappear while they hold the center of the stage, but ignoring the gaps in the narrative and judging *The Bay of Silence* by the 339 pages we are given, or any one of them, it is my guess that Mr. Mallea's novel might have been twice as frustrating rather than twice as rewarding if it had been twice as long. While I agree with Mr. Wilson that Mr. Mallea's book "has a tinge of distinction," I find persistent evidence of an inherent vagueness of thought which can scarcely be blamed on either translator or editing. I recall a similar quality in "Fiesta in November," the novelette which is Mr. Mallea's only other work to have been translated into English.

This amorphousness or indirection or inconsequentiality, whatever one might call it, is most apparent in the political discussions that make up such an important part of *The Bay of Silence.* Mr. Mallea's hero-protagonist—the story is told in the first person—is an Argentinian writer who passionately loves his country and devotes himself to finding the way in which Argentina can throw off both its corrupt native leaders and corrupting foreign influences and assert its best strength. In his twenties the young man hopes to achieve this goal through a left-wing magazine called *Enough.* In his thirties, somewhat wearied but still hopeful, he puts his political energies into fiction. But from the dozens of conversations between Mr. Mallea's protagonist and his friends, and from the endless thought-passages of the writer himself, we grasp only the vaguest political direction, never a distinct line of political purpose or argument. The people in *The Bay of Silence* are notably well-informed but they speak at a tangent to sense; for example, a newcomer to *Enough* wishes to write some articles for the magazine on the theory of the coup d'état and Mr. Mallea sets forth his subject for him in the following words: "He wanted to comment on Curzio Malaparte, to go back to the days of the Florentine Republic and attempt an interpretation of Dante Alighieri"—an odd, muddled, and pretentious enterprise, if ever there was one. But Mr. Mallea presents it as simply the way in which well-educated people naturally speak and think.

This style of thought, or what passes for thought, is not peculiar to Mr. Mallea among contemporary writers who concern themselves with the political scene, and this is another reason for not blaming the cloudiness of *The Bay of Silence* on its editing or translation. It is what makes Aldanov's *The Fifth Seal,* at least in its non-satiric sections, read like an allegory to which we have lost the key, it is persistent in Jules Romains—who would wish to undertake a redaction of the political soliloquy in the first chapter of the latest volume of *Men of Good Will?*—and it contributes to what makes one so angry with Ilya Ehrenburg's *The Fall of Paris* or Hans Habe's *Kath-*

rine. In fact, the inability to grasp and state a political point appears to be so endemic among social-political novels which come to us from abroad that we are tempted to look for an explanation either in the times or in the issues on which they focus. Yet American and English books of the same period and species, whatever their other faults, seem not to suffer from this one; the novelists of the English-speaking countries are apparently able to speak to *some* point if not always to the right one. It is an observation I record at full risk of the charge of Anglo-Saxon chauvinism!

In both length and conception, *Dangling Man* by Saul Bellow (Vanguard, $2.50) resembles an extended story rather than a novel. It is the diary of a young man who has been classified 1-A, has given up his job and made all his preparations for going into the army, and then waits month after month for his induction. It explores, that is, the strange period in a young man's life when he has given up his normal habits and responsibilities but has not yet had his new habits formed for him or his responsibilities taken over for him by an outside agency. Thrown back on his own resources Mr. Bellow's dangling man finds that he has none, he has only exacerbated nerves. The raw emptiness which he faces reflects the raw emptiness of contemporary life.

Mr. Bellow is talented and clever and he writes with control and precision. But *Dangling Man* is not the kind of novel I like. I find myself deeply opposed to novels of sterility—or, rather, to small novels of sterility. It is not that I think fiction should be blind to the badness or horror of certain aspects of modern life, or that it should refuse to despair, but simply that I demand of pessimism, more than of affirmation, that it have a certain grandeur. I have never understood why it necessarily follows from the loss of political hope—and it is at the core of the unhappiness of Mr. Bellow's young man that he is a disillusioned radical—that one must see human nature as robbed of drama and variety, and even the physical world as non-dimensional. Art is a wonderful bootstrap by which to raise life above this mean level.

Although *The First Lady Chatterley* (Dial Press, $2.75) is only a first version of the famous novel which D. H. Lawrence wrote three times before he achieved the book he wanted, it is announced on the jacket as "an original and hitherto unpublished novel," quite without mention of *Lady Chatterley's Lover,* and it is delivered to the public with a happy air of overthrowing Lawrence's own judgment as to which version of the novel merited publication. Esther Forbes, who helped bring the manuscript to light, writes in her foreword: "Obviously he was a born novelist before he grew a beard, read Freud, and set himself up as the Prophet of sex." This single statement, as vulgar as it is patronizing, serves to indicate the fundamental difference between the first and final drafts of the Lady Chatterley story, and the reason why many readers will wish, like Miss Forbes, to disconnect the two versions of the book, with their preference all in favor of the first. Sex, Lawrence's kind of sex, is perhaps even less popular today than when Lawrence published *Lady Chatterley's Lover.* What he called the book-talking, book-thinking people prefer the class struggle, and the first version of Lawrence's novel buries in class conflicts the sexual theme which he would go on to proclaim in full voice.

In broadest outline the two versions of the book are not dissimilar. In each Lawrence is telling the story of a woman who is married to a paralyzed husband and falls in love with a gamekeeper, but there is a drastic revision of detail and a profound shift in emphasis between the first and final texts. It is fascinating to read *The First Lady Chatterley* as the first step in the evolution of Lawrence's difficult idea. In several ways the first version is "artistically" superior to the third version: it is more economical, more visual, and wittier; it is also considerably less cruel. But it not only subordinated, it distorted Lawrence's sexual message and therefore had to be discarded.

The evolution of Lawrence's idea is best traced in the evolution of the gamekeeper. Even the name of Constance Chatterley's lover is different in Version 1 and Version 3. In the first draft Mellors is Parkin, an out-and-out proletarian, small, peppery, and ugly, uncouth to the point of cloddishness; when he loses his job at Wragby because of an ugly squabble with his estranged wife, he becomes a truckman in Sheffield and a Communist. That is, the choice of sexual fulfilment would require Lady Chatterley to give up every educated taste and established value in her life. In *Lady Chatterley's Lover* the gamekeeper is made personable, and if he is not a gentleman by birth, his sensibility gives him an air of breeding. His use of the local accent is not necessary, it is symbolic protest; his gamekeeper's profession is also a symbol, of the lonely man. Mellor's place in the social structure is conceived as classless, and it is his role not to threaten the security of the Chatterley class but to represent the power of sexual knowledge and completeness.

Now, on the surface this transformation of Parkin into Mellors has the unpleasant look of snobbery: certainly the promotion of the gamekeeper from a private to a lieutenant in the last war is hard to take. And we have evidence from his other writings that Lawrence was not untouched by snobbery. But he was a peculiar kind of snob: attracted by the upper classes as a man of his mixed background might well be, he was at the same time fully aware of their dead ruthlessness. Conversely, although Lawrence had a tendency to romanticize the lower classes, he refused to blind himself to *their* deadness and their resentful idolatry of their masters. So double a vision of society is an invitation to satire, and indeed there are moments in *The First Lady Chatterley,* such as Constance's visit to the gamekeeper's friends, which are almost Shavian. Satire was at odds, however, with the passion in Lawrence's temperament, and as he worked on the Chatterley novel he evidently came to see that the class situation was confusing the sexual issue. The transformation of Parkin into Mellors is the transformation of the Lady Chatterley story from a Shavian problem novel which asks the unanswerable—and pointless—question, "Is the whole world well lost for the sake of sexual fulfilment?" into a thesis novel which asserts Lawrence's passionate conviction that without a healthy sexuality life is meaningless and can turn vicious. The rewritten gamekeeper also saves Lawrence from the fatal error he was always on the point of making, of supposing that sexual neuroticism is a blight to which only the upper classes are subject.

And the transformation, from the first to the third versions, of the character of Mrs. Bolton moves in a similar line of sexual logic. In the early draft Chatterley's nurse is only a harmless gossip, a woman who, because she had once had a marriage of sexual happiness, is capable of great generosity toward Lady Chatterley. But in the final version Mrs. Bolton is not the passive object of Chatterley's infantile sexuality; she herself finds a complex and rather malign gratification in her unhealthy relationship with her paralyzed master. It is a cruel, disturbing portrait based not alone in sexual insight but in an understanding of the subtle way in which social motive can intertwine with sexual motive. Just as, in the developing study of the gamekeeper, Lawrence rejected class simplicities for human complexities, so also, in the development of the character of Chatterley's nurse, he rejected sentimentality for a frightening reality.

I do not think that in the ordinary terms by which we judge novels *Lady Chatterley's Lover* is a great novel. I think it is a great failure, as a thesis novel is very likely to be, even at its best. Certainly its cruelty diminishes its quality as a work of art and even as a text. For instance, I have never understood why Lawrence had to paralyze the husband of Lady Chatterley. If Clifford were physically normal, his sexual inadequacy would be less melodramatic and much more relevant to ordinary life. And although Lawrence tries to show us that Clifford's paralysis is only the physical counterpart of a deeper inner crippling which antedates the war, the fact that he *was* a war victim necessarily makes us sympathetic to him, or at least makes us wish to protect him against Lawrence's relentless pursuit. Indeed, all along the line the book is marred by an unforgivingness of judgment, quite as if people are to be condemned for weaknesses which they themselves would happily be rid of. It is almost as if Lawrence were fighting a *personal* fight against their tragedies.

Yet the lesser cruelty of *The First Lady Chatterley* is not enough to compensate for the lesser insight. If the novel in its final form is in many ways horrible, it is still the novel Lawrence had to write, a fierce truth toward the end of a lifetime spent in search of truth however unpleasant. One thinks of Lawrence writing his heart out with all his novels, and in no case perhaps more than with *Lady Chatterley's Lover,* and one wonders whether to be sadder for him that the Chatterley story was once read just for its dirty words or that it will now be read in this earlier version because there are scarcely any dirty words at all.

May 20, 1944

After finishing Anna Seghers's new novel, *Transit* (Little, Brown, $2.50), I thought I had better read *The Seventh Cross,* Miss Seghers's previous novel which was so well received when it appeared in 1942. It seemed to me impossible that a book of the quality of *Transit* could have been preceded by a book worthy of the critical acclaim that greeted the earlier novel. Either Miss Seghers's abilities had startingly diminished between books or *The Seventh Cross* had been mis-estimated.

It turns out that neither of these conjectures was entirely correct or, rather, that both are correct in some part. While *The Seventh Cross* is a better book than *Transit,* the connection between them is not wholly remote. And perhaps I too would have been more impressed by it if I had read it before instead of after *Transit.*

With *Transit* in mind, Miss Seghers's earlier novel strikes me as one of those books which flowered because the soil in which it was planted had been so richly prepared. We all like nothing better than to witness a defeat of Nazism, and Miss Seghers's intensely dramatic narrative of an escape from a concentration camp excited ready and strong emotions. Because in his flight the hero of *The Seventh Cross* moved through a varied landscape and touched many people's lives we were quick to translate a varied experience of suspense into a deep and various human experience, and because he pitted himself against large hostile forces we accepted the illusion that the author grappled with large literary materials. But actually *The Seventh Cross* is no more than an adventure story on an unusually high level, and it even occurs to me that were we to change the political allegiance of its hero—as, say, in the movie *The Invaders*—we would not be tempted as we are to read more artistic significance into it than it in fact achieves.

Of course it is no a priori fault in a novel that it takes advantage of our political sympathies; we should just take this into account in judging it. And similarly we should take into account the possible disadvantage of writing to an already prepared audience. In *Transit* Miss Seghers suffers from being out of line with established feeling. She is writing about refugees, and most of us have strong feelings of sympathy for the people whom Nazism has made homeless wanderers. But Miss Seghers deals with refugees so unsympathetically that at least one reader's sentiments were much violated.

Technically *Transit* is even more skilful than *The Seventh Cross* because it is more closely knit. It is the story of a young man, the narrator, who escapes from a French labor camp before the German occupation and makes his way to Paris, then to Marseilles. In Paris he accidentally comes into possession of the papers of a German writer named Weidel who has committed suicide, and in Marseilles he falls in love with Weidel's beautiful wife. Like all the refugees crowding Marseilles, Mme Weidel and the doctor-lover with whom she is traveling are caught in the awful maze of transit visas, exit visas and steamship accommodations, and it develops that the narrator, by using his false identity, can expedite Mme Weidel's departure. But he is infatuated with her and wants to keep her near him. Since he doesn't learn until very near the close of the book what the reader has guessed all along—that although Mme Weidel has been estranged from her husband she still loves him—he feels no scruples about delaying the moment when she will depart with the doctor. While the woman he is supposed to love roams the streets and cafés frantically searching for her husband, the narrator never confesses to her that Weidel is really dead and that it is only his own use of Weidel's papers that has spread the report that he still lives and that he is in Marseilles. And even at the end, when he has learned that she still loves her husband, he lets her leave believing that she is about to be reunited with her husband on board ship.

This is the cruel joke of a plot of Miss Seghers's new book, and if *Transit* is more than its plot, I fail to recognize it—unless, indeed, the "more" is the embroidery of scenes among Miss Seghers's minor characters. These are the refugees whom the narrator meets daily in the cafés and consulates and steamship offices; Miss Seghers's treatment of them is something between ironic superiority and sneer. The narrator himself, it is pointed out, has no desire to get out of the country. His willingness to remain in France is given no political explanation but it is shown to be a kind of affirmation of life in contrast to which the effort at departure of the other refugees is a weakness or negation. This is a new and thoroughly unpleasant slant on a tragic situation.

I have said that the connection between Miss Seghers's first and second novels is not very distant. It is to be traced, it seems to me, through Miss Seghers's political partisanship. In *The Seventh Cross* the author makes frank confession of her Communist preference. *Transit* has no expressed political bias yet it is rooted in the Communist belief that means are justified by the ends they serve. The "end" in *Transit* is not political but personal, but the hero pursues his love as he would no doubt

97

pursue his political objective, with ruthlessness, cunning, and small regard for truth—though his author thinks of him as a good person. Miss Seghers's novel, that is, can be read as a rather frightening statement of the outcome in personal morality of a political morality which never stops to question the methods it employs.

June 10, 1944

Rex Warner's *Return of the Traveller* (Lippincott, $2.00) is chiefly interesting for the fresh evidence it brings of the difference between the way the war is being written about in England and over here. I have several times commented on the refusal of American fiction to discuss any of the political, social, or psychological realities of this war. Ideologically the war plays about the same role in our current novels that a storm plays in murder mysteries: it is something noisy going on outside the house to add to our indoor tensions. But this is not the case in England, where, probably because of a different cultural tradition or perhaps only because the walls between the outdoor and indoor worlds have been blown in, all classes of novelists dare at least to nibble at the real issues. And now it appears that even in the matter of titles we on this side of the Atlantic show our disposition to evasion: Mr. Warner's book, published in England under the blunt name *Why Was I Killed?* arrives here labeled for a more delicate taste.

Mr. Warner is best known in this country for his *The Wild Goose Chase* of some years ago, a Kafka-like fantasy. In *Return of the Traveller* Kafka is gone but fantasy persists: the return to earth of a dead soldier provides Mr. Warner with the basis of a philosophical research into the possible justifications for the present war. Appropriately, the research starts among a group of people gathered at the tomb of an unknown soldier— Mr. Warner's philosophical microcosm includes a priest, an upper-class English patriot, a self-seeking member of the English lower-middle class, a socially-conscious intellectual, an emotional woman pacifist, and a refugee, each of whom first argues his attitude toward the war and then, in flashback, reveals the source of his opinions in his personal and family history. Each of the revelations is illuminating but no one in the group except the priest can give the soldier a satisfactory answer to his question, "Why was I killed?" For it happens that, dying, the soldier himself had had a double vision—of the battlefield and of the sunny valley of life—and among the people the soldier is canvassing only the priest has also had this vision. What Mr. Warner means by this double vision is the tragic view of life, a view of life that includes a view of death—but here Mr. Warner's mystical syntax becomes muddled. I take his last chapter to be a plea for a kind of political theism: good politics must be based on a tragic view of life and a tragic view of life depends on a belief in something which can encompass both life and death—which is to say, God. As Mr. Warner's priest would put it, only God is big enough to surpass all the conflicting ideas which have been presented to the returned soldier, and only God can organize all of mankind into brotherhood. And only in brotherhood is there hope for the future of mankind.

The religious proposition is decidedly in the air these days and one should perhaps have been prepared for Mr. Warner's turn in this direction. But the modern intellectual comes to religious faith disconcertingly well-armed with the arguments of the world and in consequence the forthrightness with which Mr. Warner presents the positions which he finally discards threw me off the religious scent for much of the way. In the light of his religious conclusion, however, even the truths Mr. Warner announces in passing lose their validity. There may be those for whom the attitude in which *Return of the Traveller* issues is consoling. Myself, I find it useful neither in formulating the hope that we can avoid future wars nor in comprehending this one.

Three new novels by women have me wondering about my

sex: such a field day of villainy I haven't come across in many a fictional moon. *No Mortal Fire* by Elsa Valentine (Simon and Schuster, $2.50) is a detailed account of the incredible doings of a young woman of Nazi leanings but it seems to me that the Nazi tie-up merely gilds this lily. *Insurgent Summer* by Charlotte Aiken Yarborough (Harper, $2.50), a first novel not without talent, has it in for a publisher—understandable enough, I hear, but it surely should have been held within more convincing limits. Fanny Sedgwick Colby's *The Apple Must Be Bitten* (Scribner, $2.50) has it in for virtually the whole race of man, divorce lawyers included. It all seems vaguely unwholesome.

June 24, 1944

Usually where there is a low degree of emotional tension in a novel we expect to find false feelings, and when a story is told as easily as James Norman Hall tells his new story, *Lost Island* (Little, Brown, $2.00), we are unprepared for any serious content. But the conjunction of technical smoothness with false emotions or the lack of ideas is by no means inevitable. As a matter of fact, in fiction, and even more in the movies, a great many of the smooth commercial jobs strike me as having more validity than the knotty "art" jobs. Nowadays, a display of seriousness is likely to be only a display of our newest emptiness. Emotional tension has itself become a commercial trick.

Certainly *Lost Island* has the mark on it of a hand practiced in writing for a large unselected audience. (You will recall Mr. Hall as half of the famous *Mutiny on the Bounty* duo.) I find it much more serious, however, than such a patently "serious" novel about the war as, say, John Hersey's *A Bell for Adano*; it seems to me to spring from deeper feelings. The story is simple: it is the brief account of the life and death of a South Sea island. We need the island for a Pacific air base; in a week we destroy the fruit of generations of peaceful living. Yet obviously, if the United States didn't take the island, Japan probably would; and as between America and Japan, or as between democracy and fascism, there is no question in Mr. Hall's mind. On the other hand, there is the island itself, with its beautiful quiet life. It has not only one of the few indigenous cultures left in the world but it is inhabited by people who are incapable of understanding the issues for which they are sacrificed; they don't even understand the world on a map. The fact that they are victims in a cause bigger than themselves scarcely makes them any the less victims.

I think Mr. Hall makes it clear that the tragedy of the island is perhaps only a small one. But it is absolute and implies a very large tragedy. For what *Lost Island* is saying—and strongly, too, though its voice is so evenly pitched—is that it is a strange world we have contrived in which we have to destroy civilization in order to try to preserve it.

September 16, 1944

I have been surprised at the dearth of novels on a theme which I should have thought would be particularly appealing for war-time fiction, the predicament of wives whose husbands have gone off to war. Yet now that one has finally arrived, Hannah Lees's *Till the Boys Come Home* (Harper, $2.50), I admit even greater surprise at its content. Without literary distinction, Miss Lees's novel is important as a study in what the middle-brow American reading public can take, or at least be offered, in the way of realism. In manner, *Till the Boys Come Home* might well have appeared in one of the large-circulation women's magazines: it has no overtones or references beyond itself and asks little of the reader. But if its matter is similarly acceptable to a wide popular audience this country has gone further in recent years than we commonly suppose. For Miss Lees's novel is remarkably free of the expected sentimental and patriotic clichés, and in sexual matters it is unselfconsciously courageous. In *Till the Boys Come Home* bravery without intelligence is the object only of scorn. The good sportsmanship of an army wife is shown to cover a wide streak of bitterness. Also, female sexuality achieves the authenticity and stature of a nuisance. Even the name of the novel's heroine strikes a new note in popular realism: she is not Sandra or Michele but Sophie.

Miss Lees angles her story boldly by making Sophie a victim of the male urge to adventure rather than a victim of the draft; she is the wife of a doctor who has chosen to go to war. She has a job and two small children to occupy her, she has no financial worries, and she has a close circle of women friends in the same boat as herself; in other words, here is a heroine who should be admirably equipped to meet the popular ideal of home-front sturdiness. Instead, Sophie comes very near to going to pieces. A normally emotional person, she wants to share her life with another adult whom she loves. A normally sexual woman, she finds her enforced celibacy unendurable. By the time her husband comes home Sophie is full of resentments, guilts, and confusions.

And this is to speak of only the heroine of the story: the minor characters are in equally unorthodox bad shape. Except for Julia, Sophie's priggish sister who has been created by idealizations of the service wife and who is shown to be correspondingly stupid, even vicious, all Sophie's friends either have similar experiences or, like Kate, sustain the absence of their husbands so well because they never loved them in the first place. We gather that the boys who come home to Miss Lees's world will encounter emotional situations such as usually lie beyond the range of any but the best fiction.

But it is not in this broad outline, heterodox as it is, so much as in the nature of its details that *Till the Boys Come Home* is especially interesting. Neither Sophie nor any of her friends is under any illusion about the political future of this country; they recognize the possibility not only of another war but of American fascism, and Miss Lees is very clear about the incipient fascism of the most heroic of her war wives. Or, quite without any intention of sensationalism, Miss Lees describes with extraordinary frankness the sexual substitutes for a husband which are available to the women left behind. Or *Till the Boys Come Home* is illuminating on the subject of war babies: it tells us that women become pregnant, or want to become pregnant, before their husbands go overseas not because they wish to preserve the image of love but in order to keep themselves out of sexual mischief and because pregnancy is so absorbing.

According to its dust jacket, the author of *Till the Boys Come Home* was educated at Vassar and the University of Colorado and is the wife of a physician. This is no doubt a fairer way to define the intellectual and emotional area of the novel—to describe it, that is, as the work of a mature young woman of decent education, married to a doctor—than to try to describe its possible audience. For it is in Miss Lees's generation and class that certain political, social, and domestic attitudes which are good have begun to take firm root, perhaps eventually to disseminate throughout our culture. Even Miss Lees's psychological insights bear the stamp of her training, age, and professional connection. It may be a section of society not notable for its humor—there is something almost grim in the fervor with which Miss Lees insists that a child sucks its thumb for its own good reasons—but it serves as liaison between theory and practice and has the potentiality of performing an invaluable educative function. Recently there have been several instances in which the women's magazines have recognized their educative power and broken through the old sexual taboos to tell small but difficult truths. One can guess that these steps in progress are directly to be traced to the influence of young writers and editors of the same cultural cast as Miss Lees, with perhaps no special artistic gift but with the same seriousness and conscience.

For all the virtues of the shorter pieces in Katherine Anne Porter's new collection of stories, *The Leaning Tower and Other Stories* (Harcourt, Brace, $2.50)—and I shall speak of them presently—it is the long title piece of the book which claims our enthusiasm and confirms Miss Porter's high literary reputation. Miss Porter's new novelette is not only the best thing she has herself written but it is by any measure one of the finest of modern stories. It may in fact have been an error to combine in one volume this novelette, which is such a sizable achievement, with the rather fugitive sketches which precede it. The large work so overshadows the small that we tend to forget that even at its most fragmentary Miss Porter's writing is full of things to give pleasure.

"The Leaning Tower" is a remarkable literary-political document, not unrelated in method to Thomas Mann's story of the German inflation, "Disorder and Early Sorrow." It is a story about Hitler which never mentions Hitler except as the unnamed subject of a photograph in a barber shop. It is an analysis of political forces without political analyses. It is a chapter of history which still manages, as literature, to stand outside and above history. Miss Porter is telling us about Germany in 1931, about the emotions that prepare national violence. Her narrative device is to follow an impressionable young Texan, who in the first freedom of maturity carries out the romantic resolution to visit the Berlin he had heard about from a childhood friend, as he becomes more and more frightened by the creeping awfulness of pre-Nazi German life. Nothing much happens to this Charles: he checks out of his hotel, he has his hair cut, he looks for lodgings, he becomes acquainted with the other tenants of his boardinghouse and celebrates New Year's Eve with them, but the eyes of Charles become the eyes of an ideal documentary camera. Miss Porter's story has neither action nor drama, in the usual sense, but slowly borrows all the brooding drama of its time and place; in Miss Porter's Berlin of 1931 every house, every room, every piece of furniture or crockery is a portent of a dreadful consummation. I think the underwritten climax of "The Leaning Tower" constitutes its sole mistake in literary judgment; impression has mounted on fierce impression until our sense of a necessary explosion is almost unbearable. Even as readers we require some of the ranting and roaring that in actuality climaxed this German story.

If space were available, a score of masterly details in Miss Porter's novelette could be dwelt on: its proportioning and pace, its genius of visuality, the elegant use that Miss Porter makes of colloquial language, the use to which she puts Charles's childhood attraction to the little German boy, the choice of a Pole as one of Charles's Berlin circle, the focus upon the Heidelberg scar of another of the lodgers, the endless avenue of horror which Miss Porter can open up by a dozen sentences of description of a hotel keeper and his wife, the instinct that led her to create the half-world café which is the scene of a Berlin New Year's party. In view of its achievements, it becomes unimportant that "The Leaning Tower" has one weakness in conception, the character of its protagonist. Much in the picture of Charles is beautifully handled, especially his litmus-paper quality as a stranger in Germany, disconnected from the familiar even in language; but as an artist Charles is obscure and disconcerting. Granted that he is less an artist than he is young and American, the question is allowed to intrude upon us whether he is a good artist or an artist as Hitler was once an artist. There seems to be a suggestion of the latter; but then, if she intends the parallel, Miss Porter would be introducing a chauvinism which, highly as she values the American spirit, is miraculously lacking from the rest of her story, for she would be saying, in effect, that the American temperament responds to frustration very differently from the German, a racial generalization whose truth is only devoutly to be wished for.

As for the shorter pieces in *The Leaning Tower,* although

there is always the danger in writing as conscious as Miss Porter's, and particularly in very brief fiction, that carefulness will move over into preciousness, Miss Porter avoids this pitfall of the too wary. Taste is her instrument rather than her nemesis. There is as much vigor as there is precision in her language, and this in itself distinguishes her among present-day women writers, most of whom are so desperately given to breathy effects and soft figures of speech. In "The Source," for instance, Miss Porter writes the following sentence in description of cleaning-up day on a Southern farm: "Every mattress cover was emptied of its corn husks and boiled, every little Negro on the place was set to work picking a fresh supply of husks, every hut was thickly whitewashed, bins and cupboards were scrubbed, every chair and bedstead was varnished, every filthy quilt was brought to light, boiled in a great iron wash-pot, and stretched in the sun; and the uproar had all the special character of any annual occasion." Prose like this is not only in the best American tradition, from Mark Twain to Hemingway, but typical of Miss Porter's constant effort to keep her eye on the object.

Yet a faint perfume of sensibility does linger around Miss Porter's shorter stories, despite their vigorous objectivity, and I am puzzled to know whether this is because of their abbreviated length or their subject matter. I have often written about the limitations of short fiction: it is an unsatisfactory medium, allowing insufficient room for the play of the imaginative intellect and rather too much room for the display of personality. And even in Miss Porter the little gem of a piece reflects more of the light of its author than of the world. But on the other hand, Miss Porter's subtle self-extension in these sketches may not be a result only of their small compass, it may derive from their common theme. With one exception all the shorter pieces in *The Leaning Tower* are re-creations of what we can take to be Miss Porter's own childhood; and there seems to be a peculiar difficulty these days in writing about such early memory without making of oneself too sensitive and cherished a case. Perhaps even as sturdy and educated an attitude to fiction as Miss

Porter's is not proof against the special feelings about children that now prevail in our culture.

September 30, 1944

There is no doubt that Jean Stafford, author of *Boston Adventure* (Harcourt, Brace, $2.75), is a remarkable new talent. This is not to say that her first novel is a completely satisfying experience but that Miss Stafford brings to the writing of a novel an uncommon endowment; I would find it hard to name a book of recent years which, page for page or even sentence for sentence, is so lively and clever. By the light of any one of the incandescent moments of *Boston Adventure,* it may turn out that the book as a whole is strangely disappointing, reminding us that in the final analysis no amount of skill as a writer substitutes for the total novelistic power. But for its manner and for the way it stands up to the literary job, Miss Stafford's book unquestionably demands a place for itself in the best tradition.

The tradition which Miss Stafford has most lovingly studied is quickly apparent. Written in the commentative first person, half a re-creation of childhood and half an anatomy of "good" Boston society, Miss Stafford's novel scarcely hides the influence of Proust, and although often, in the chapters which deal with Boston, *Boston Adventure* might be criticized for being too obviously derivative, in its first half Miss Stafford has beautifully assimilated the lesson of the master to her own needs. Indeed, the early section of this book could be put forward as a telling argument against our modern tendency to disavow our literary heritage. Even the most original writer is bound, after all, to lean on the past, and the test of a new novelist is not in how much he depends on the already established but in what model he chooses and what use he makes of it. When we say unhappily of certain modern novels that they have been influenced by Steinbeck, it is not the fact that *an* influence is at work that we regret, it is the fact that this influence is not of the best; and we do not dismiss the followers of Hemingway simply because of their discipleship but because despite a good model they are themselves second-rate. Miss Stafford chooses an excellent teacher and is herself a worthy pupil. For much of its way her novel, like a child in relation to its parents, is able to assert its individual vitality in the degree that it acknowledges its sound connection with its antecedents. The dignity and flexibility of manner that Miss Stafford would seem to have learned in her apprenticeship to Proust is perhaps the most important single element in what we must now call her own literary gift.

We have been given many stories about miserable childhoods and many novels about poverty and sordidness but the first half of *Boston Adventure,* in which Miss Stafford describes the girlhood of her Sonie Marburg, is something quite new in awfulness. Sonie's father disappears, her mother is insane, her brother dies after a short life of Dostoevskian horror; virtually from babyhood Sonie is the financial and moral mainstay of her family. The meanness of Sonie's family life is so extreme and the girl's competence so precocious that they would seem to strain credulity, yet Miss Stafford not only convinces us that the Marburg world is possible but manages to give it grandeur. Neither the autobiographical taint to be found in novels even as good as those of James Farrell, nor the note of self-pity and sentimentality which sounds such disturbing overtones to stories of distress like *A Tree Grows in Brooklyn,* mars the first half of *Boston Adventure.* But unfortunately in the second section of the novel, where objectivity might have been thought to be easier of attainment than in the childhood portions, Miss Stafford loses her clean distance between author and narrator.

At eighteen Sonie has been taken to live in the home of a Boston lady named Miss Pride. With this shift in scene *Boston Adventure* breaks down into an alternation between a sharp-eyed but essentially not very significant or original social report and a highly subjective, almost hysterical self-study. Sonie, who as a child was never too big for her little boots despite her precocity, suddenly steps into the large boots of Miss Stafford herself. Her insights into the manners and morals of Beacon Hill strike me as being as improbable for a girl her age as the poise and finesse with which she accomplishes her feats of social adaptation would be unlikely for a girl of her background. The drama of childhood exhausted, Miss Stafford would seem to be unable to create a valid drama of maturity but instead is reduced to introspection, that inadequate literary substitute for action and conflict. And this failure of dramatic imagination at the point where the protagonist of Miss Stafford's novel reaches maturity suggests the autobiographical as its earlier section does not because it is as if the author were now saying: "And so my childhood ended and here I am grown up. What more would you have happen to me than that I should become a thinking person, the person preparing to write this book?" The novel of development regularly reveals the close connection of author and protagonist by just such recourse to internality when the protagonist comes of age.

I speak of Miss Stafford's inability to create a valid drama of maturity. I realize, of course, that in the second half of her book she has tried to create drama of a sort: there is a long episode centering in Miss Pride's niece. But this niece is a secondary character in the novel, and Sonie, who engages our chief interest, is never convincingly involved in the niece's predicament; in fact, it is Sonie's isolation that finally keeps *Boston Adventure* from being the completely satisfying novel we think it will be. Miss Stafford has nevertheless so much style and energy and intelligence in this first book of hers that one has much hope for her future as a novelist. She is a new writer to be read and applauded.

Come war or come paper-rationing, there is never a dearth of novels about female love. The best of them are still written by men. Indeed, so long as women write about themselves and their love as they nowadays do, they should be grateful that neither in life nor in literature do men always take them at their word. The picture of women, especially in our most talented and ambitious female fiction, is enough to scare any normal man out of his wits. It should also be enough to scare at least some women back into theirs.

Even more than our men writers, our women writers, especially when they deal with their sexual emotions, have a way of filling the world with themselves alone and of exploiting fiction to promote their own follies and grievances. Substituting intensity for understanding and confusion for valid conflict, they produce almost without exception one-character books in which the one character is the author and the book is more case history than fiction.

Christina Stead's new novel, *For Love Alone* (Harcourt, Brace, $3.00), is accurately named: it is an unusually obsessive study. It tells the story of the crucial years in the life of a young woman who is supposedly seeking an object for her deep powers of affection. Teresa Hawkins is a highly charged Australian girl who falls in love with a perverse devil of a young man, makes inordinate sacrifices to follow him to London, and there becomes properly disillusioned with him. Maturity begins for Miss Stead's heroine when she finally achieves her first mating, with a generous, warm-hearted older man. The outline of the narrative is thin and familiar. What makes Miss Stead's novel an interesting variation on a familiar theme is the baldness with which it states the resolution of its sexual problem.

For it is the irony of most novels about women's fatal urge to love that they regularly turn out to expose, all unconsciously, women's fatal inability to love, and in Miss Stead's novel this irony is even broader than usual. After having spent four years and almost 450 pages in the quest for someone on whom to unload her beautiful burden of affection, the heroine of *For Love Alone* requires only a few weeks and a chapter or two of consummation to reveal that she has been seeking not a lover but her own personal power. As Teresa herself puts it: "How had she advanced in a few months from the idea that no one would love her to the assurance that she could *control* two men?" (She is on the verge of taking her second lover.) The italics are mine but, believe me, the approving emphasis is the author's. A few pages later Teresa will talk of her desire to "master" men. *For Love Alone* ends with its heroine not only set for a life of conquest but firm in the knowledge that sexual power is the purest female poetry. The quest for love is little more than the grim business of collecting (shall we call it?) scalps. The desire to give and receive affection turns out to be the desire to become the proprietor rather than the property.

The language of property is Miss Stead's own. In the course of the education of Teresa Hawkins *For Love Alone* has many sound things to say about the economic motive in the relation of the sexes. This is to be expected, since our revolutionary sexual literature is necessarily well-grounded in classic economic argument. Nor are we surprised that for a large part of the book Teresa is victimized by an unworthy man; even revolutionary literature still likes to rattle that old skeleton. Less expected and also more interesting are Miss Stead's use of so young a heroine and her pungent comments on the cruel pressures which our society puts on a girl at the age of marriage.

Teresa is not yet nineteen when we first make her acquaintance but Miss Stead shows her to be quite frenzied with sexual desire—and this seems to me to be a healthy defiance of the present-day convention which permits sexuality to married women (or children) but not to very young women. By the evidence of most of our novels we apparently still feel the need to keep within the strict bounds of propriety the activity and even the fantasy of the young girl who is in the market for a husband.

But Miss Stead's heroine defies convention not only by being fully developed sexually at her tender age; she is also improperly outspoken in her fear of spinsterhood. I know no novel, including the novels of Jane Austen, which reveals as frankly as *For Love Alone* the frantic need young women have for a husband and the brutal hypocrisy with which society surrounds their efforts to find one. Most women novelists are unwilling to make the admissions that Miss Stead makes for her sex. Even Jane Austen put up a wall of satire against our temptation to accuse her of sharing with her characters their desperate longing for matrimony.

There are other accomplishments in Miss Stead's novel which I am afraid I have neglected in favor of its significance as a sexual document. Somewhat in the manner in which Elizabeth Bowen so wonderfully re-creates the color and smells of an English seaside resort in *The Death of the Heart,* Miss Stead remarkably re-creates the raw vulgarity of Sydney, Australia, and its suburbs; the latter are much like a World's Fair after the fair is over. Then, although the general tone of the novel is far too *exalté* for my taste, Miss Stead is capable of disturbing the rarefied air with flashes of downright intelligence and wit. And simply in the matter of prose she often has a salutary carelessness and gives the impression of rightly being much more concerned with what she has to say than with how she says it. It is a misfortune of our culture that a talent like Miss Stead's should be at the service of so much ardent confusion.

November 11, 1944

It would surely be understandable if novelists were so humbled or emotionally paralyzed by what it means to fight an ascendant fascism that they avoided the subject. But apparently no reality is too big for the truly unimaginative. Novel after novel dares to cope, as if it were all in the day's work, with material that one would suppose could be touched—and then but touched—by only the greatest talent, working at a sufficient historical remove. There is no end to the books that on the basis of good-will or anger put themselves forward as reliable, or at least adequate, re-creations of the anti-Nazi struggle inside Germany itself or in the conquered countries.

It is hard to say which of the various schools of anti-Nazi fiction I find most distasteful. There is the frankly blood-letting school whose curriculum of beatings and tortures is as well-established as its syllabus of heroism. Or at the other pole there is the school of liberty-loving idyll-ism which, though subtler, is almost as dismaying: these are the novels which weave a rainbow of poetry about the resistance to German domination of a small country or "small" people. And between these extremes stretches the whole long train of vehicles for comfortable ideals and vicarious courage, for unconscious cruelty and conscious political virtue.

This week I have read two anti-Nazi novels, Lord Dunsany's *Guerrilla* (Bobbs-Merrill, $2.50) and Albert Maltz's *The Cross and the Arrow* (Little, Brown, $2.75). Although each of them conforms to an established pattern, neither is as excessive of its kind as other novels I could name. I don't intend that the brunt of my general remarks be borne solely or wholly by these two examples.

There is no reason to have expected better than I got from a new Dunsany book. *Guerrilla* is thin, abstract, allegorical, "poetical." I guess it is about Greece but Dunsany calls his oppressed country The Land. When the Germans come to The Land, the People take to the Mountain to fight for Freedom. There is a young hero named Srebnitz, and Dunsany writes: "Whenever Srebnitz smiled he was thinking of his rifle that he was going to get and take away to the Mountain. The Mountain and its bright freedom, and the free men whom he would meet there, filled his mind as flowers are filled with sunlight." Lyricism such as this is the idiom of a young boy just a few pages after his mother and father have been murdered virtually before

113

his eyes. In the measure that Dunsany is remote from human feeling he is engaged by special boyish knowledge: he is pedagogically concrete about how to light fires, hide behind bushes, and outmaneuver an enemy. *Guerrilla* is an excellent boy-scout guide to the joys of outdoor living and dying.

Another manner of effort—a very much better one, if we must grade them—is Albert Maltz's *The Cross and the Arrow,* a novel set within Germany and concerned with the breakable link in the chain that thinks itself so strong. A certain Wegler, of hitherto sound Nazi record, suddenly lights a fire to guide English fliers to a hidden German factory. In the interval—act two of a three-act novel—between Wegler's insurgent moment and his death Mr. Maltz explains his hero: this way of conceiving a novel is not one that I particularly like but it is of course permissible. It depends for its success on the author's ability to create quick excitement and plausible character. Although *The Cross and the Arrow* is not without excitement, it is of a sort that makes me feel used, as if I had been made to keep a deathwatch over someone with whom I had no vital connection. Its characters alternate between unconvincing simplicity and equally unconvincing complexity.

December 2, 1944

I often wonder why of all forms of criticism book criticism is most wary of the popular, most fearful of being thought insufficiently discriminating. Class lines are much more firmly established in presumably serious book-reviewing than, say, in theater criticism. Where even our most serious drama critics will give as much attention to a *Voice of the Turtle* as to a new production of *Hamlet,* a similar catholicity on the part of the book critic puts him in danger of losing caste. One result of this literary emphasis on the "serious" is that the fiction reviewer constantly concerns himself with work that calls itself important but is only pretentious, and by-passes modest novels that have their own validity. The pretentious writer comes to feel that he has only to pamper his stylistic or thematic solemnities to achieve literary stature, while the more modest writer, ignored by the intellectual world, is encouraged to out-and-out commercialism.

I am aware of being myself prone to this snobbery: readers of this department may recall that in one recent instance the fact that a book was a Literary Guild selection kept me, by my admission, from reading it for three months. Yet as I glance over my reviews I find that I am more apt to respond with warmth to novels of no marked ambition than to fiction which deals badly with demanding materials. This is not because I prefer modesty to grandeur. Obviously I would rather have a big literary experience than restrict myself to the minor pleasure of small jobs well done. But I find no necessary correlation between the desire to create an impressive literary work and anything that approaches the achievement of this ambition. On the contrary, in current fiction the corollaries one is most likely to encounter are between big ideas and befuddlement and between modesty and the ability to provide at least a certain small satisfaction.

For instance, among the books I read this week there was a novel, *Behold Trouble,* by Granville Hicks (Macmillan, $2.75), who is a writer of defined intellectual position, and also a novel called *Where Helen Lies,* by Margaret Lane (Duell, Sloan, and Pearce, $2.50), of whom I had never heard. The theme of Mr. Hicks's novel is the psychology of a conscientious objector; the theme of Miss Lane's book is a not very important marriage crisis—I suppose, then, that I ought properly to recommend to your notice Mr. Hicks's more "significant" effort before Miss Lane's minor domestic narrative. But the truth is that Miss Lane's book not only more successfully accomplished what it set out to do; it also gave me more pleasure. Nor is my point especially invidious to Mr. Hicks: I admit a similar preference as between Miss Lane's book and the volume of stories *Crab*

Apple Jelly, by Frank O'Connor (Knopf, $2.50), described as the Irish Chekhov, or again as between Miss Lane's book and the collection of short pieces *Dear Baby,* by William Saroyan (Harcourt, Brace, $2.00).

I was much confused by Mr. Hicks's *Behold Trouble*—the reason is perhaps best suggested by a quick synopsis. It is the story of a conscientious objector whose draft board decides he must go to a work camp. But almost at the same moment that Mr. Hicks's Pierre Mason learns of this decision the rumor reaches him that an FBI man is in his rural neighborhood. Certain that this is a sign that the government is after him, Pierre goes haywire; he notifies the local paper that the FBI can come and get him, arms himself, and prepares to shoot it out. After firing, in his panic, on an innocent girl of the district, Pierre takes to the woods, where eventually, after involving the whole community in disaster, he is killed.

What Mr. Hicks means to communicate with this story bewilders me. Except as a study in insanity Pierre is incomprehensible, yet there is reason to doubt that Mr. Hicks considers him entirely insane; and manifestly he cannot be undertaking to say that all conscientious objectors are mad. On the other hand, if the purpose of *Behold Trouble* is to suggest that human impulses are compounded of many conflicting elements and that pacifism hides its own unconscious aggression, Mr. Hicks has scarcely done artistic, psychological, or political justice to this valid observation. Several of the minor characters of *Behold Trouble* are cogent and attractive, and altogether the novel has a high degree of rural verisimilitude. But these virtues do not compensate for a basic fuzziness of intention.

The Gaelic idiom works its magic on us all. There is an Irish lilt to the dialogue and an Irish color to the scenery of Frank O'Connor's stories, even at their most melancholy, which, because it gives them a dimension of the exotic, also proposes literary dimension. But emptied of local color, the stories in *Crab Apple Jelly* are for me without the weight that others have felt in them. I find them sweetly sad, sadly suggestive, or even at moments a touch frightening, but never more than in the way of the skilfully rendered pastiche.

One of the pieces in William Saroyan's *Dear Baby,* "The Hummingbird that Lived Through Winter," contains the following sentence: "The mature hummingbird itself is so small that the egg must be magnificent, probably one of the most smiling little things in the world." The first half of this sentence illustrates the best of Saroyan, a truly poetical simplicity of spirit. Its second half reveals him at his worst, in all the sweet goodness which accounts for so much of his success. We live in frightening and pious days, in which the more we recognize evil the more we wish to be assured that virtue is as original as sin. And Saroyan goes a step farther even than most of our memoirists of sweet youth: he actually arrests the mature world at the level of childhood which, while a comforting act of fantasy, is also a debilitating one.

I surmise that Margaret Lane is an Englishwoman not only because of the English-Irish setting of her *Where Helen Lies* but because, in my reading, the English appear to have a corner on these civilized little books which, though they may not provoke thought, never insult the intelligence. Miss Lane's novel is the account of a seemingly happily married man who suddenly decides to return to an earlier love. The story is slight but the idea that started Miss Lane's book is rather beside the point of a novel whose merit is its quiet literacy and its retiring but never-failing good sense.

December 16, 1944

Having, with *I, Claudius,* made a popular thing of the Roman Empire, Robert Graves has turned his attention to the English seventeenth century and given us *Wife to Mr. Milton* (Creative Age Press, $2.75), a fictional study of the Cromwellian wars and of the domestic life of John Milton. Mr. Graves's new novel

117

is an interesting, very readable book but a highly disconcerting one. For it is not a neutral exercise of the historical imagination. Erudite and a great respecter of historical exactness in matters of language, social behavior, and the like, Mr. Graves is no respecter of historical persons. In *Wife to Mr. Milton* he has not only a political but a personal ax to wield: this is in large part a hatchet-job on the memory of Milton. By the time King Charles has lost his head, one of England's greatest poets has lost as much prestige as Mr. Graves can deprive him of.

The Milton of Mr. Graves's novel is vain, tyrannical, pompous, priggish, ambitious, repressed, repressive, and absurd; by some accident he manages to retain a gift of sonorous verse and prose to serve his opportunism. It is perhaps an excess of zeal that the blurb writer for *Wife to Mr. Milton* calls the poet "Cromwell's Dr. Goebbels"; Mr. Graves himself, in the foreword to his novel, says no more than that the post-war Cromwellian order was what we would now call "undisguised fascism" and that lovers of democracy should be warned against Wordsworth's "Milton, thou should'st be living at this hour." But readers of Mr. Graves might as profitably be warned of the unfairness of the circular argument by which Mr. Graves supports a political conclusion with a highly conjectural personal picture and then confirms his personal conjectures by means of his political conclusions. Written in the first person—the narrator is Mary Powell, wife of the poet—*Wife to Mr. Milton* is offered as reconstruction of Milton's first marriage, and Mr. Graves creates so chicly sympathetic a portrait of Mary and so unremittingly hateful a portrait of Milton that the reader has to be unusually resistant to suggestion not to believe that here is an incontrovertible interpretation of authenticated domestic fact and not to conclude that where there was this much private smoke, there must have been a very malodorous public fire.

But Mr. Graves's novel is not only an ungenerous personal enterprise made to serve an unworthy political purpose. It is bothersome on yet another score. Like Oscar Levant on "Information Please," I, too, confuse Mary, Queen of Scots, with

Katherine Hepburn, and Christina of Sweden with Greta Garbo, and years from now, should I be asked why the first Mrs. Milton ran home to mother, in all likelihood I will revert with the authority of an original scholar to Mr. Graves's bridal scene out of "What Every Young Husband Should Know." Historical fictions must learn to recognize their special responsibility to people like myself, so long on unhappy memories and short on learning.

March 10, 1945

There has been a small spate of novels by newspaper correspondents. In recent weeks four have come my way—*The Troubled Midnight* by John Gunther (Harper, $2.50), *It's Always Tomorrow* by Robert St. John (Doubleday, Doran, $2.50), *Return to the Vineyard* by Mary Loos and Walter Duranty (Doubleday, Doran, $2.50), and *The Open City* by Shelley Smith Mydans (Doubleday, Doran, $2.50)—and they have started me pondering, among other things, why so much of a point is made of the inability of reporters to write fiction. For if by the ability to write a novel we mean no more than the ability to compose a story, there is no evidence that newspapermen have any more difficulty than other mortals in achieving this mild distinction, while if we mean something more, the ability to write a good novel, then the profession of the author is irrelevant—the incidence of creative talent in the journalist's trade is no more interesting or significant than the incidence of creative gift in any other field.

But on the other hand—and I am not being paradoxical—of the four novels I have been reading, two, Mr. Duranty's and Mr. St. John's, are worth discussing only because they are by newspaper people. While Mrs. Mydans's novel and Mr. Gunther's are not good books, we pass this judgment without reference to the way their authors earn their livings but we cannot read either Mr. Duranty's novel or Mr. St. John's without being struck by their lack of the very power we look for in trained journalists: an understanding of the political events with which they are professionally concerned.

For instance, in *Return to the Vineyard* Miss Loos and Mr. Duranty deal with the theme of the resettlement of a devastated European village. It is a subject to which one would suppose that someone of Mr. Duranty's experience would bring a degree of political insight, yet except for the single perception that after the war it may be difficult for the peasant populations of the liberated countries to get the aid of the occupation authorities in resuming their lives exactly as they were lived before the war, Mr. Duranty contributes not at all to our comprehension of what is bound to be an enormous problem. *Return to the Vineyard* turns out to be a *Swiss Family Robinson* of post-war reconstruction climaxed by a ridiculous sequence of Hollywood gangsterism.

Yet Mr. Duranty—I know nothing about Miss Loos—for years played a major role in forming American opinion on a very important political reality indeed, the Soviet Union. It was through his eyes that millions of us saw the workings of the Five-Year Plan, the Moscow trials, the Russian purges. To judge by this sample of his thinking on the subject of post-war Europe, how are we now to evaluate the reliability of Mr. Duranty's reporting?

The case of Mr. St. John is even worse; much worse. Miss Loos's and Mr. Duranty's novel has at least a serious point of departure but *It's Always Tomorrow,* the story of a newspaper correspondent who falls in love in Poland, loses his love but finds his soul in Hungary, Rumania, and France, and finds a new love and a strengthened soul in England, is from start to finish pointless, exhibitionistic, vulgar. I have never read Mr. St. John's *From the Land of Silent People* or listened to his broadcasts; this first-person narrative is my single experience of his work. It would be hard to convince me that the mind that deals in the primitive politics of *It's Always Tomorrow* could ever

120

under any circumstances give me a political fact or interpretation that I would now trust.

The novels of Mrs. Mydans and Mr. Gunther do not raise this question of their authors' professional authority and perhaps this is because, in the case of Mrs. Mydans's *The Open City,* the narrative stays close to actual experience and, in the case of Mr. Gunther's *The Troubled Midnight,* the pages of political discussion with which the trivial narrative is larded are sufficiently thoughtful to be reassuring. *The Troubled Midnight* is about the love life of a young American Lend-Lease worker in Constantinople; its possible allegorical intention—the young woman chooses for her love among a Nazi, an Englishman, and an American—is not supported by its quality of fantasy. *The Open City* is an account of what it was like to be interned by the Japanese and it might better have been told as simple fact than as such simple fiction. But if neither book is a notable act of the imagination, both of them at least allow themselves to be judged as acts of the imagination and not merely as evidence of their authors' inadequacy in their profession.

For sufferers from late-winter grippe or other complaints which might be alleviated by a good light novel, I recommend *Miss Dilly Says No* by Theodore Pratt (Duell, Sloan, and Pearce, $2.50).

March 31, 1945

When, some weeks ago, instead of writing about a certain novel at the usual length I confined my review to the statement that I had been able to read only 200 of its 600 pages and these with only the greatest self-discipline, it was protested that this represented an evasion of my reviewer's duty. To be sure, the protest was not widespread but even a mild flurry of disapproval surprised me. For to my thinking there is no more responsible method of book-reviewing than honestly to declare, if the occasion warrants, that a book is too dull or opaque to finish. If a case-hardened reviewer can't penetrate a novel, why should she suppose that other readers will be able or want to? It even seems to me to be a generous method of report: it spares an unreadable book the circumstantial indictment which is earned by bad books that are at least readable.

At any rate, protest or no protest, I follow the same procedure with Alex Comfort's *The Power House* (Viking, $3.00). Because of its author's place among the younger British intellectuals, *The Power House* claimed my attention. It was not able to engage it. I read the first two dozen pages three times without having any notion of what I was reading; then I made several firm attempts to break into the story at a later point of its development, each time without success. This report must therefore stand for the whole of my review.

On the other hand, there is Frederic Prokosch's *Age of Thunder* (Harper, $2.50), which I could perhaps wish I had not been able to finish since to complete it was only to confirm my suspicion, arrived at after the first chapter or two, that I was pursuing a well-charted path through a miasma. Mr. Prokosch's novel may present no difficulties from sentence to sentence; its prose, fancy though it is, is sufficiently navigable so that I can recount every incident and index every character. It nevertheless raises the unanswerable question of what Mr. Prokosch had in mind when he conceived it.

In *Age of Thunder* a young man has been dropped by parachute into occupied France with a mission to uncover the point of disaffection in the underground. After this reasonable start there follows a series of incidents which are not only unconnected with each other but in themselves connected with reality only as a dream is. The young man joins a party of secret travelers to Switzerland: we are not told why the journey is made or why the characters behave as they do in its course. There are accusations of darkest treachery which are neither confirmed nor dispelled. The group swells and diminishes without purpose; when two of its members, including a Negro who especially activates his author's gift for inappropriate adjectives and adverbs, are murdered, we know of their death only what is to be learned from a corpse. The young man wanders into a hotel and is visited by a grim Hollywood type who strangely reminds him of someone named Robinson, but who is Robinson? Who, in fact, is the grim Hollywood type? Even when the hero is arrested by the Gestapo—oh, most corporeal of incidents!—he is dismissed with a philosophical talk and a cigarette. And so on, through four nights of far-ranging fantasy in which, among other adventures, Mr. Prokosch's young man is housed in a castle, eats campfire spaghetti with a party of Italians, discusses love with a euphonious trio consisting of an Arab, an Annamese, and a Macedonian, and is wounded among a garrison of comrades. We are understandably relieved when, the Alps sighted, we are told that the hero's mission has been accomplished.

Age of Thunder is not presented as a surrealist novel but I suppose that if we must have a category in which to put it, that does as well as any: Mr. Prokosch's book combines recognizable details and dream conception in orthodox surrealist fashion. Whatever its aesthetic or philosophical intention, in actuality it is a narrative without sequence, interspersed with conversations more fabulous than enlightening. I still hold to my unfashionable opinion that fiction doesn't approximate poetry by turning its back on sense.

John O'Hara has a new collection of short stories, *Pipe Night* (Duell, Sloan, and Pearce, $2.50), with many of which you may be already acquainted from the *New Yorker*. They are worth looking at again. For whereas a great deal of our short fiction loses by being published in book form, Mr. O'Hara's pieces gain in intensity and even achieve a kind of cumulative seriousness. I am also freshly struck by their craft, their precision, and their economy of means, all of which should teach a lesson to the vague and garrulous.

Despite the fact that William Maxwell's *The Folded Leaf*
(Harper, $2.50) is unusually easy and gratifying to read, it is a
difficult book to write about. For it carves out such a seemingly
minor literary task for itself—to tell the story of the friendship
of two boys through high school and college—that one hesitates
to burden it with the kind of "importance" to which its author
would appear to be indifferent. Yet it not only goes about its
work with a precision rare in current fiction; it also manages to
evoke much larger meanings than show on the surface. The
source of this suggestiveness is of course its style. Style is latent
content, and there is an uncommonly rich content hidden beneath the modest overt statement of Mr. Maxwell's novel.

The prose of most current fiction is either excessively and
falsely simple, or it is prodigal without discipline; in either category the dimension added by style is likely to match the size of
the author's ego. The author of *The Folded Leaf* stands in the
most useful possible relationship to his material, in full control
of his characters and situations but not merged with them. Because he is free to comment on the fates of the characters in his
story, we have the advantage of his intellect as well as of his
imagination. In the degree that he keeps his personality clear of
his people, he achieves a true distinction of personality. Thus,
the scene of a high-school fraternity initiation not only is reported for its full worth as narrative but also provides the occasion for a very pleasant essay by Mr. Maxwell on the anthropol-
ogy of such rites. Or often Mr. Maxwell will point out, lightly
but sharply, the pattern of circumstance in which his characters
have been caught. This commentative function is obviously a
proper function of the novelist; all the great writers of the past
assumed it eagerly. But very few present-day novelists can keep
enough distance from their material to regard the free play of
mind as a privilege.

The Folded Leaf is divided into many small chapters, each concerned with a moment of significance in the lives of its characters, and Mr. Maxwell is at his best when these moments are physically seen. The initiation ceremony which I have mentioned is outstanding in the book, but there are any number of lesser scenes—in Spud and Lymie's college rooming-house, for instance, or at Spud's boxing work-outs, or at a college spring riot—which have an almost fragrant authenticity. Mr. Maxwell has a remarkable quiet gift for observation; his record of Middle Western American life in the Twenties adds up to a more useful social document than he was perhaps conscious of. But in the last third of the novel, when, because the story must be brought to a climax and conclusion, Mr. Maxwell concerns himself with only emotional developments, he becomes spare and even unconvincing. The scenario of *The Folded Leaf* inevitably requires that at the end of the book Spud and Lymie be brought to manhood. But to assume that people are mature and competent simply because they have reached a point where maturity is asked of them is to contrive for fictional people an outcome constantly denied us in life. The resolution of *The Folded Leaf* is shadowy and fortuitous. I question the independence which Lymie is supposed to have found so suddenly, and I look to the future of Spud with an uneasiness which his author gives no sign of sharing.

It is perhaps unfair to measure Stephen Seley's *The Cradle Will Fall* (Harcourt, Brace, $2.00), a first novel, against Mr. Maxwell's practiced writing, but Mr. Seley's novel is also a story of American boyhood in the Twenties and, like Mr. Maxwell, the author of *The Cradle Will Fall* is modest in his literary intention. But here all similarity ends, for from title to conception to prose *The Cradle Will Fall* is a novel that puts no distance at all between author and subject. Mr. Seley is everywhere in his story and in consequence his story has little life of its own.

Not the least significant result of Mr. Seley's self-indulgent presence in his book is the fact that the chief emotion it generates is that of pity. While *The Cradle Will Fall* hints that its central character deserves better than this limited response, it denies him the dignity to demand it. Its rather primitive psychoanalytical delving, so markedly in contrast to Mr. Maxwell's procedure which is simply to picture the behavior of a character and let us draw our own psychological conclusions, preconditions the reader's response and guarantees an identification between reader and central character such as exists between the central character and its author.

It is also interesting to contrast Mr. Seley's novel as a social document with Mr. Maxwell's. Mr. Seley is at a good deal more pains than is Mr. Maxwell to recapture the iconography of his time: we are told much more of what songs were sung, what cars were driven, what values were booming. Social documentation of this kind loses both point and savor, however, when it is used more to surround or "place" character than to create it.

May 5, 1945

I am not sure I know who the ghostly lover of the title of Elizabeth Hardwick's *The Ghostly Lover* (Harcourt, Brace, $2.50) is. It might be the shadowy young Southerner—is Kentucky the state?—who appears early in the story to offer Miss Hardwick's heroine a questionable love which he later backs up with the money for a year's study at Columbia. Or perhaps it is the equally shadowy but more commonplace youth whom Marian meets in New York and whom she contemplates marrying in order to have a point of security in her rootless life. More likely, it is Marian's mother, Lucy, one of the most elusive parents in fiction, for whom Marian lives and dreams in a curiously inverted child-mother relationship.

Of course the appropriateness of a novel's name is not necessarily of moment in judging the novel: if I begin my review of *The Ghostly Lover* with a statement of my confusion about its title, it is only as token of my larger confusion in regard to Miss

126

Hardwick's book. For by any of the usual tests *The Ghostly Lover* earns a poor score: it lacks drama or even a coherent story, few of the characters are given their narrative due, there is no unity of rhythm in the prose, and much of the book is dull reading. Yet, and however paradoxical strong praise may seem after such strong indictment, it gives sporadic evidence of more talent than a dozen current novels which can boast all the manifest skills which Miss Hardwick's book lacks.

I often think that the chief path being followed to the destruction of the modern novel is that of an excessive sensibility. The ability to clothe fastidious insights in fastidious language has become our modern stock-in-trade, and by Miss Hardwick's talent I most emphatically do not mean the sentences and paragraphs of fine writing of which *The Ghostly Lover* has its fashionable share. Indeed, I mean precisely the opposite, the quite fierce creativeness of which Miss Hardwick is capable when she leaves off being concerned with pursuing insight to its last pointed syllable. Although the general tone of *The Ghostly Lover* is the twilight tone of sensibility, it has a way of suddenly bursting into the full crude light of a rare imaginative intensity. Scattered through Miss Hardwick's book are perhaps twenty or thirty pages that would be remarkable from the most mature writer. There is the amazing moment, for instance, when Marian's grandmother, a delicate, invalid Southern gentlewoman, is all at once revealed as mesmerized in her dream of the possibility of violence between the sexes, or the scene between Marian's mother and a Negro rifling her refuse cans which has more bleak concentration of terror than almost any scene I have ever read out of the South. And there is the conception of Lucy's relation with her husband, Lucy's need to find the land beyond land where she can finally absorb all of her husband's masculinity into herself without the intrusion of any other human relationship. These are the moments in which Miss Hardwick passes beyond, say, Eudora Welty at her beginning best, to come close to the slashing courage of D. H. Lawrence.

It is worth noting that the inspiration for these grand occasions seems to be the South. When Miss Hardwick moves her heroine to New York, *The Ghostly Lover* is no longer either somnolent or flashingly brilliant, it is merely accurate. Although, to me, Miss Hardwick's social observations are only conventionally interesting, in the opinion of her publishers her picture of a graduate women's dormitory at Columbia is the especially distinguished portion of her novel, and I am afraid there will be enough others to agree with this judgment to tempt Miss Hardwick to forfeit her larger powers in favor of what should be only their tool or adjunct. D. H. Lawrence, too—I adduce him again since I have once already—had the reportorial gift in abundance. He learned to subdue it to the intensity of his larger vision.

In the reviewing vocabulary "promising" is the word to use of first novels. So far as I can recall I have never used it, and not only from the wish to avoid the laziness of jargon but because I have never felt the propriety of projecting a present merit into a hypothetical future performance. Yet in the case of Miss Hardwick, the disparity is so great between her talent and a kind of romantic literary mediocrity—the high points of her novel are so really high as well as so much higher than what surrounds them—that it is only in the light of a possible future fulfilment of Miss Hardwick's gifts that the book impresses itself upon me. Still, I hesitate even here for in order to bring her talent to fulfilment Miss Hardwick has a tremendous task ahead of her: she must learn to make her prose her servant rather than her mistress, she must put her powers of observation in the service of her powers of imagination, she must find stories big enough to allow her imagination its full intensive play. Nothing in *The Ghostly Lover* tells me whether its author has the understanding or energy to choose this course.

May 12, 1945

Since I myself was caught by the teasing name of Helen Haberman's *How About Tomorrow Morning?* (Prentice-Hall, $2.50), I suppose I should warn you at once that it has little to do with the content of the novel—about as much, say, as the name of a cold cream has to do with *its* content. Mrs. Haberman's book is about the advertising business; its heroine, Tina, of the doll-like body and the giant energies, makes $40,000 a year promoting Caress Cosmetics before she goes amateur in favor of cooperatives. No doubt we must think of Mrs. Haberman's title as an advertising slogan, the application of promotional talents like Tina's to the merchandising of fiction. The biographical material supplied by the author for the dust jacket of the book is also worth study as a demonstration of the advertising approach to the creation of literature. Here are the last lines of Mrs. Haberman's intellectual history:

And books! Emerson and Arnold and Wordsworth, the college loves, and in the last few years Henry James, volume after volume of James.

The intake growing bigger and bigger all the time and not enough outlet in the neat, tight pieces of advertising copy. Sublimating it with photography for years. Then bursting out with the great big lush luxurious form. The novel. The most fun of anything I've ever done. The big uncensored fun.

Unhappily *How About Tomorrow Morning?* turns out to be neither uncensored nor fun: it was clearly not the intention of the author to disclose as much as she does of herself and her sex, and if we are to take the book at all we must take it seriously, as a social document. Because Mrs. Haberman's novel avoids the royalist excesses of Ilka Chase's *In Bed We Cry,* the operatic excesses of Ayn Rand's *The Fountainhead,* and the excesses of infantilism of Rose Franken's Claudia stories, it has an uncommon awful authenticity as a portrait of the modern female

129

psyche. The fact that women novelists are held to speak for their sex as men novelists never are is manifest evidence of the extent of the "woman problem." Nevertheless *How About Tomorrow Morning?* is the last book in the world exempt from this typicality. In fact, at the moment I can think of no better single exhibit of the mind and spirit that forms and is formed by the higher-tensioned women's magazines.

In the first place, there is the quality of its sexual narcissism. A current advertisement addressed to women bears the legend, "You have never been so pretty." This effectively sums up the attitude toward herself of Mrs. Haberman's heroine. When Tina wrinkles her nose in that adorable way of hers, when she looks in the mirror to be so childishly pleased with what she sees, life imitates the advertiser's art with an embarrassing fidelity. Similarly, Tina's emotional plight is expressed in the clichés of duty and self-fulfilment that support and surround the advertising in women's magazines. I have been told that furniture, table settings, clothes and suchlike are described in careful detail in popular fiction addressed to women in order to focus their attention on *objects* and thus make them more receptive to advertising. No such conscious process is of course involved in *How About Tomorrow Morning?* but the emotional symbols it employs unmistakably betray the commercial association. When, for instance, Mrs. Haberman wishes to suggest the nervous breakdown threatening her heroine, she has Tina constantly thwarted in her efforts at interior decoration. Also her servants are discontented, and she neglects entertaining the people who could be of use to her doctor-husband.

At twenty-three Tina earned $10,000 a year. Advanced to $15,000, she is bitter because male chauvinism still refuses her her right to see the clients, to be on the contact front. She conquers this obstacle in her career by taking her agency's chief client as her lover: she achieves the contact front, and her earnings increase apace. But having profited to the extent of an East River town apartment, a home in the country, and the means to maintain both, she discovers that in the process she has lost her soul. While visiting in New Hampshire she has a nervous collapse and is nursed back to health by a refugee doctor.

It is this healer of body and soul who introduces Tina to the salvation of cooperatives. Throughout the book cooperatives have been the deep motif of idealism sounding against the thin tinkling music of success in the crass world of advertising. Tina throws up her job and decides to devote herself to the national cooperative movement. Immediately the old bounce reasserts itself; before you can say "Sweden" Tina has begun to apply the techniques for selling cosmetics to selling social progressivism—and we are assured that when cooperatives pall, there will always be a cause for which Tina can use her advertising genius. This is obviously the point at which Mrs. Haberman speaks most unconsciously but most contemporaneously for her sex, for what she is saying in substance is that the realm in which competitiveness and egoism operate has only to be a socially good realm for the competitiveness and egoism not to matter. She is also saying—though if she were made aware of its reactionary implications I dare say she would be uneasy—that if you remove the obvious money drive from female careerism, you remove the source of all emotional conflict. One wants to remind Mrs. Haberman of that older salvation of the well-placed woman, philanthropy. The circle has come full swing, even though Lady Bountiful wields a typewriter instead of a wicker basket.

What price, one asks—Mrs. Haberman herself forces the question—Emerson, Arnold, and Wordsworth, and volume after volume of James?

May 26, 1945

With no new novels that press for review, I have the opportunity to return briefly to John Hersey's *A Bell for Adano*, which has just been announced as the Pulitzer prize-winner for fiction. I have been rereading Mr. Hersey's book, to find it even more primitive than I had remembered. This much-admired story of the American occupation of an Italian village is written in a prose redolent of the primer; it defines political good and evil in terms that make good and evil unmistakable to a school child. There is Major Joppolo who stands for democracy: he is the kind of man who sees to it that simple Italian villagers are given a bell. And there is General Marvin who stands for a possible American fascism: he is the kind of man who has a mule shot because it blocks his arrogant path. The squeeze of lemon in a concoction that would otherwise be too bland for even our present tastes is the temporary victory, at the end of the book, of the Marvin force over the Joppolo force but this triumph of evil, we feel sure, is only momentary; we put down *A Bell for Adano* with the comfortable conviction that although democracy has been momentarily deprived of its job, its good deeds live after it and its eventual victory is inevitable. Mr. Hersey's political fears are a fillip more than they are a warning. They never suggest a valid and useful complication of ideas or feelings.

Of course we are not surprised that the Pulitzer committee has again chosen a novel that can scarcely give pleasure to people who take literature seriously. One has only to look back over the fiction awards of other years to recognize that what would be surprising would be to see the award go to a work of distinction. But this year's choice seems to me to be particularly striking for what it tells us both about the political direction of our present-day literary thought and about the quality of our political thought. For not only the general success but the critical prestige of *A Bell for Adano* indicates to what extent our literary judgment serves our political partisanship: a novel need only agree with our politics to be a good novel. And nothing better proves than the success of Mr. Hersey's novel that in the degree that we are disturbed by the confusions and contradictions of actual events, we deny or discourage any complication of our political ideas and emotions.

In her "Notes by the Way" last week Margaret Marshall

quoted the lesson Yeats's father taught him, that ideas rob a man of his nature and make the blood thin. A large part of the anemia of our current fiction must surely be due to the soft political idealism which is its major inspiration. There is even the anomaly that it is our literature of affirmation and fortification that is fast becoming our new escape literature. It seems to me that a not too perverse case could be made for the thesis that the detective story and the romantic love story, all the fiction that we commonly think of as an evasion of reality, actually if unconsciously bring us into closer connection with reality than our "healthy" didactic literature. In any event, at its worst our old-fashioned escape literature frankly substituted for reality instead of befuddling us about it.

June 23, 1945

If Walter Van Tilburg Clark's new novel, *The City of Trembling Leaves* (Random House, $3.00), proved to be at all to my liking, I had intended, before writing about it, to read *The Ox-Bow Incident,* his highly esteemed first novel. But the 690 pages of Mr. Clark's present book—it is the detailed story of the boyhood and young manhood of one Timothy Hazard of Reno, Nevada—strained my endurance to the point where no consideration of critical thoroughness could persuade me to pursue this highminded course. *The Ox-Bow Incident* has been described to me as a tightly-knit dramatic narrative, very much in contrast to the loosely-constructed undramatic *City of Trembling Leaves,* and it has even been suggested that in actual composition the second novel may be the earlier work. Be that as it may, I am content to let it rest that *The Ox-Bow Incident* was all it was said to be and that it is only on Mr. Clark's new novel that my opinion diverges so sharply from majority opinion.

I find little virtue in *The City of Trembling Leaves* and a myriad of all too familiar modern vices, of style and thinking and feeling. It is a novel of boogie-woogie *Weltschmerz,* an anatomy of the melancholy that seems to flourish in the shadow of the bandstand. I have often referred to the influence of hot jazz on current fiction: the more novels I read which are written in the rhythm and vernacular of hot-jazz addiction, and geared intellectually to the level of popular music, the more my distaste for the jazz idiom in literature crystallizes into solid prejudice. This is certainly not to attack popular music, or to voice a low estimate of people to whom jazz is more important than it is to me. It is simply to take a firm position against treating the novel as if it were generated as far below the head as, I gather, hot-jazz music is. And if it will be protested that jazz is an art, though a popular one, with its own discipline and cerebration, then I, in turn, will protest that its discipline and cerebration are not of a kind which artists in literature borrow to good purpose.

Here is a sample of what I mean by the jazz idiom of *The City of Trembling Leaves.* It is the closing passage of a letter in which Mr. Clark's hero discusses *The Education of Henry Adams:*

So I told Adams one more thing, in order that I should re-member it myself. "Adams," I said, "your trouble, after all, wasn't that you wanted too big and too soon. You really wanted the past, Adams, and not enough to go around. You didn't want out, Adams; you wanted in."

And I asked him one last nasty question.

"Adams, weren't you in love with a stained-glass Virgin?"

Mr. Clark's protagonist has already discredited Adams by call-ing him to account for not properly appreciating Lincoln and by paralleling a thirteenth-century peasant contemplating the stained-glass Virgin and a twentieth-century boy gazing in awe at a new motor car. Surely this is a style of thought which, if not bred in the murky atmosphere of the jazz hangout, would no-where else be more readily taken for a mind-at-work. Nor do the high Nevada mountains to which Mr. Clark flees from the dark smoky places purify his thinking; they only embarrassingly halt it. To one reader, Mr. Clark's novel has a way of being at its least elevating when it reaches for the highest peaks. This is also true of Timothy Hazard's symphony—he is a serious composer as well as an inspired player of jazz—which reads on paper like nothing so much as a Hollywood dream of musical stupendousness.

The point is, I'm afraid, that no novel is bigger than its people and that Timothy Hazard and his associates, although they are considered by their author to be persons of dignity and standing, are third-raters. This is not as apparent in the first half of *The City of Trembling Leaves,* when Tim is still a boy and his biography is chiefly a morbid, protracted shadow-fight with sex, as it is when Tim and his friends grow up and their sentimental maunderings are presented as mature struggles for salvation, their beery bitterness as a tragic commentary on the life of the artist. "You and I tasted the worm with the nipple, Hazard," one of Timothy's painter friends finally puts it and there is no one even to whisper whatever it is that registers the next degree of the maudlin and platitudinous after "corny."

I read another long book this week, Mary Lavin's *The House in Clewe Street* (Little, Brown: Atlantic Monthly Press, $3.00), 530 pages. Miss Lavin's novel has none of the inflated quality of Mr. Clark's book; indeed it has none of the obvious contemporary vices except wordiness, and Miss Lavin's words, although far too many, are almost excessively tempered. *The House in Clewe Street* is what is called, I think, an estimable book, a three-generations portrait of an Irish small-town middle-class family, done with sympathy and sobriety but crying aloud for the editorial scissors. Even as a change from the self-indulgence of most current writing, it is not worth getting excited about.

Robert Henriques, author of *No Arms, No Armour* and *The Voice of the Trumpet,* has a new novel, *Home Fires Burning* (Viking, $2.50), about the post-war world. It is a theme we may expect to see explored frequently in fiction, now that hostilities cease. But as a matter of fact, Mr. Henriques's story doesn't even await the termination of battle to set the wheels of domestic trouble whirling: victory is still only in sight when he faces his England with the difficulties of adjusting her fighting population to her civilians, her civilians to her fighters. Jane, a war nurse and a nice girl, reunites with her childhood sweetheart, David Sloane, a distinguished writer before the war and a distinguished war-time soldier until he'd been shot in the leg and head. The leg wound has healed but the head wound has laid bare another side of David's personality: a brain concussion turns a seeming liberal into a dangerous fascist—it is of course the point of Mr. Henriques's book that the returning troops are potential fascist material. But happily at the end of the story a sounder political thinking than David's is shown to prevail, that of David's unglamorous brother, Robert, and of Bill, the natural leader of the four returned soldiers with whom Jane has taken up on a railway platform. Of this symbolic quartet (they remind us of the drifting spirits that people a Prokosch novel), only another head-wound case is willing to follow David. We are made to understand, however, that even the mentally ill will also eventually prefer the direction of the Roberts and Bills of England to that of the Davids.

Even so brief a synopsis of *Home Fires Burning* should indicate its proper democratic intention and its not very fresh approach to a persisting political concern. Programmatic fiction is not to my taste, and even less attractive are the fancies of prose and the tangle of time-sequences which are supposed to suggest complications of thought which aren't actually there. And Mr. Henriques's representation of the mood of homecoming soldiers happens not to coincide with my own observation of their emotional temper: it is not at all my experience that the returned soldier is lawless and bitterly antagonistic to civilians. On the contrary, he strikes me as being modestly eager to resume his place in the world he left behind. But if it is easy for me to suppose that what I have myself observed is inaccurate, my imagination of this divergence is not fortified either by Mr. Henriques's particularizations or his implied generalizations.

November 17, 1945

Christopher Isherwood's *Prater Violet* (Random House, $2.00) is not only a short novel which is yet the most completely realized new novel I have read in a long time but it is also a charming novel which yet reverberates with important meaning. In contradiction of the present-day order of literary things, it is a book written in the author's own person but it is without ego. It is a novel about movie writers but it is also a novel about the life of every serious artist. It is a book without a political moral yet a profound moral-political statement. It is gay, witty, and sophisticated but it is wholly responsible. It is even a novel by a member of the coterie known as the younger British intellectuals but neither a coterie novel nor a novel nurtured in the shadowy recesses of the worried intellect: it is about intelligent attractive people living familiar interesting lives.

The story of *Prater Violet* is deceptively slight. The time is 1934, the place London. Isherwood is invited to write the scenario and dialogue for a musical movie of old Vienna, about a flower vendor in love with a disguised prince. The director who has been engaged for the film is a Viennese, Friedrich Bergmann, a man "with the face of a political situation, an epoch . . . the face of Central Europe," and with a Central European sense of political realities. To Isherwood's considerable daze at finding himself involved in doing the dialogue for *Prater Violet*—the novel's title is taken from the film—is added the rich confusion of daily intimacy with this collaborator: Bergmann is a person of large proportions, voluble, weak, vain, robust, deep-feeling, dramatic, amusing, devoted, loving, and lovable. In the midst of the shooting of the movie, the newspapers report the Vienna uprisings. Bergmann and Isherwood have their emotions about the fate of Austria and their emotions about their job. The movie gets finished, it is a great success, and Bergmann gets a contract from Hollywood.

But this story that Mr. Isherwood tells is merely the pebble in the lake from which his novel ripples out in ever-widening circles of implication. In what we might call its first circle *Prater Violet* is a narrative of social observation and of light incisive humor about modern personalities. Then it is a study in sensitivities: it confronts the sensitive poet with the sensitivities of the movie craft, the sensitive foreigner with British insularity. In a next circle it is a study in dedication, a wise insight into the quality of devotion which any job must exact, even the job of making a shoddy movie, if it is to have meaning for the person doing it. In a still further circle, it is a study in the relation of the individual to society, particularly in the relation of the politically conscious man, who is still not a political man, to political action—and it is here, of course, that *Prater Violet* will be most suspect to the liberal reader accustomed to the raising of banners of public allegiance because Mr. Isherwood refers all conduct back to its private sources. Finally, it is a novel about man's relationship to himself: a subtle bold assertion that life has no need of justification by our usual modern moral values, that human affection is enough to support it.

The word "human" is important. We have been told that Mr. Isherwood has joined the Aldous Huxley–Gerald Heard group of California mystics, and that for some years he has been living a monastic life in this country, working on a translation of the

Bhagavad-Gita. Were we not acquainted with these biographical facts, we would not guess them from *Prater Violet,* which is a thoroughly worldly book, unless perhaps from its informing emotional tone which struck me as remarkably innocent of the contemporary social and personal guilts. But unlike Mr. Huxley in his recent novels, Mr. Isherwood takes his quiet stand on principles which are accessible to the least mystical of us: they are nowhere made to draw their strength from beyond the naturalistic universe and, even more important, they have no root in negation—much of our pleasure in the book is a response to the gusto with which Mr. Isherwood's characters inhabit this faulty world of ours. For instance, to compare Mr. Isherwood's Bergmann, with his poetry-making, his curiosities, his wonderful re-enactments of the Reichstag-fire trials, to the analogous father-people in Huxley's recent books is to discover that the author of *Prater Violet* is not at all concerned, as Mr. Huxley is, to make the father-person a saint. Bergmann is not an emasculated savior in the protection of whose love a merely mortal young man plays out his small sexual game. He is allowed his full humanity and manhood; and as a consequence Mr. Isherwood's novel has a dignity and an intimation of tragedy which are always finally missing from Huxley. If, that is, it is out of his knowledge of God that Mr. Isherwood has come to, or confirmed, his knowledge of man, it is still man to whom his novel, in the end, gives godhood.

And indeed I suspect that it is to what I would call his worldliness that Mr. Isherwood owes even the quickness and warmth of his prose. It is one of our fashions these days to write "simply." Mr. Steinbeck does it, Mr. Hersey does it, Katherine Anne Porter does it. In Steinbeck or Hersey simplicity is a validation of social virtue; and while I do not question the good-will of these writers I question whatever underlies their good-will which produces a prose so heavy with condescension to the people it is used to describe. On the other hand, the simplicity of Miss Porter's prose, however skilled and tasteful, is that of the over-conscious artist; Miss Porter does not condescend to her subject but she asserts her superiority to it. The simplicity of Mr. Isherwood's style is a reflection neither of condescension nor assertion, it is the style of a free and generous intelligence most happily balanced between self-tolerance and tolerance of others.

It would be a pleasant comment on our present literary culture if one could be certain *Prater Violet* would get the reading it deserves. Properly, there should be several books as good as this each season and the publishers of this one, just by the way, should not feel impelled to veer between advertising it as a "satirical" novel and announcing it on its dust jacket in terms of "fascist terror," "opportunism and appeasement," and Europe's "bath of blood." But fearful that it will not reach its audience through the usual channels—and in fact one influential critic has already reported his doubt that it was worth writing—I for once urge a novel on the readers of this column. More than any book of the last three years, *Prater Violet,* small as it is, provides the kind of satisfaction which some few of us still ask from current fiction but which current fiction persistently refuses us.

January 5, 1946

When it was predicted that the war would give a new impetus to religion, it could also have been predicted that of all religions the Catholic would be bound to be most compelling, especially to writers and other intellectuals who like their emotions of faith to be as well-organized and traditional as possible. But by any traditional standard it has surely been an odd kind of celebration that the Catholic church has been recently experiencing. For example, there was the movie *Going My Way* which gave us a church whose charms existed without benefit of sacrament. And now there is Evelyn Waugh's *Brideshead Revisited* (Little, Brown, $2.50), a novel whose appeal to faith rests on the most familiar cynicisms of non-faith.

140

Brideshead Revisited is a more incoherent book than a summary suggests. This is the story Mr. Waugh tells: During the war a company of soldiers, including a Captain Ryder, the narrator, is billeted in an English country place called Brideshead, the estate of the Marchmain family. Ryder had known the Marchmains intimately, and he recalls his long difficult relationship with the family: his love for Sebastian, the younger son, when they were together at Oxford; his first meeting with Sebastian's gallant sister, Julia; his early sympathy with Lady Marchmain and his later disaffection from her as he discovers the pious tyranny she exerts over her family; then the long years in which Sebastian falls steadily into drunkenness, in which Julia makes a miserable marriage, and in which Ryder himself marries unhappily; finally, his reunion and love affair with Julia which is terminated by Julia's sudden return to the church in which she was born and her recognition that her life has been a sinful one. The book ends with the strong indication that Ryder, agnostic during the extended period of the narrative, is himself now a convert to the faith of the Marchmains. Since there is nothing else to explain Ryder's religious regeneration, one assumes that it is a consequence of his experience with this family.

But why an experience of the Marchmain family should turn one to, instead of away from, religion is the most immediate of the many questions raised by Mr. Waugh's new novel. For the main emphasis in Mr. Waugh's portrait of this Catholic household is its sharp condemnation of Lady Marchmain for a piety which has wrecked her husband and children. It is Lady Marchmain's unfeeling self-righteousness that is shown to have driven her husband into social ostracism on the Continent, her son Sebastian into drunkenness, her daughter Julia to despair, and even her older son, Bridey, to oafishness and her younger daughter, Cordelia, to a spinster's life of good works. Except perhaps in the case of Cordelia and in the case of Sebastian's beloved Catholic Nanny, *Brideshead Revisited* has scarcely a good word to say for any conventional professors of the Catholic faith. When they are not wicked like Lady Marchmain, they are silly like Bridey and Bridey's wife. All our sympathies are enlisted for the upper-class bohemians and sinners of the novel, for Sebastian and Julia and old Lord Marchmain. Mr. Waugh's Catholicism, that is, looks to be a religion for well-placed reprobates, which may not constitute an absolute heterodoxy— I dare say that Mr. Waugh's conviction that Sebastian is a holy man within his drunkenness represents an orthodox view of one possible road to salvation—but which surely constitutes a curious bias.

The disproportion between Mr. Waugh's affectation of non-belief and his protestation of belief is the chief interest of *Brideshead Revisited*. Although Mr. Waugh employs all the old sophisticated arguments against his church, he has nothing except the sudden will-to-faith and the inevitability of death— Julia's return to the fold coincides with that of her father on his deathbed—to offer in its support. When, for example, Julia renounces her love because it is the sinful continuation of a life of sin, nothing in her action assures us that it is anything more than either masochistic or superstitious; religiously, it is no more meaningful than Iris March's running herself into a tree in Arlen's *The Green Hat*. By masquerading or burying its religious convictions in cynicism *Brideshead Revisited* makes so much better a case against conviction than for it that even to grant that its author's attitude is merely a device of proselytization requires the help of the biographical record, the knowledge that Mr. Waugh was himself converted to Catholicism some years ago. Not that this form of religious dissembling is without precedent: Aldous Huxley, for one, is a practiced hand at it. But I find it none the less suspect for being an established method of disputation.

I have never belonged to the growing group of American admirers of Mr. Waugh, even as a satirist. I have not read all of his books, only *Decline and Fall* and *Put Out More Flags,* and both of these, perhaps because I am not very sensible of the virtues threatened by the objects of Mr. Waugh's satire and because I cannot share Mr. Waugh's sorrow for the fate of the prodigal sons of England's stately homes, bored rather than enlightened me. And even my small sampling of Mr. Waugh's previous work prepared me for his religious solution to be at best a counsel of despair, and at worst what it has turned out to be, an effort to put God on the side of the dying upper classes. For it is the other noteworthy point about Mr. Waugh's Catholicism, in addition to the uneasiness with which it lives in his sophisticated world, that it is the property of a small, embattled, and highly-privileged class. The Marchmains of *Brideshead Revisited* are wonderfully rich as well as beautiful: Brideshead itself is a kind of architectural object lesson in the conspicuous consumption of the best that England has had to offer for several centuries. Between this Catholic aristocracy and any other English aristocracy Mr. Waugh makes no distinction except that of religion; yet whatever the religion of its owner, Brideshead could not have been built on very solid ground or there would perhaps not have had to be a Second World War in which it degenerated into a billet, and one wonders why Mr. Waugh should hope that faith will be able to restore a class that faith has not succeeded in holding together. By ignoring the political and economic realities that underlie the dissolution of the Marchmains and blaming their tragedy solely on Lady Marchmain's piety, Mr. Waugh tempts us to indict all the evils of life in the name of piety, an amusing position to have worked himself into.

January 26, 1946

Anaïs Nin has never been published commercially. She has printed her work herself and distributed it through private channels. Nevertheless, her reputation has spread until she has become, in a small way, a sort of legendary literary figure. Rebecca West is reported to have called her a genius. Henry Miller has made the prophecy that the diary of some sixty-five volumes on which she is engaged will rank with the great monuments of self-revelation, with Augustine, Rousseau, Petronius. One hears of a new literary method based on psychoanalysis. It was therefore with considerable curiosity that I took up my first sample of Miss Nin's writing, a volume called *This Hunger* . . . (Gemor Press, $3.00) which came out recently and which can be obtained from the Gotham Book Mart in New York City. The volume contains three stories, connected by the fact that each of them is about a gravely maladjusted woman hungering for affection. The first, Hejda, is about an Oriental girl who emerges from her veils to become something of an exhibitionist. The second, Stella, is about a movie star unable to love because of her excessive need to be reassured that she is loved. The third and most complicated, bearing the names of two women, Lillian and Djuna, is mostly about Lillian, a woman of conspicuous energy, who is confused—so I seem to make out—between her need to protect and her need to be protected.

I refer to the three pieces as stories. Actually, though they borrow the manner of narrative, they are much more like case histories than short fictions. Miss Nin's characters have many of the conventional appurtenances of fictional life: they have been born, presumably they live and will die; they look a certain way; they have friends, money, sexual relationships, even children. But they exist for their author as the sum of their clinically significant responses and we are made aware only of such of their activities, physical surroundings, and encounters as Miss Nin conceives to be relevant to their mental health. Every writer establishes a role for himself in his books: Miss Nin's is that of psychoanalyst to her typical women. She has a single interest in her characters (I almost said patients) and that is in the formation and expression of their symptoms; what goes on in the rest of their lives she rigorously ignores. For instance, we are told of Hejda that, having been born in the Orient, her face was veiled through her early years, but we are not told the name of the country of her birth. And in connection with Lillian, Miss Nin

144

suddenly refers to a husband and children but apparently neither husband nor children had any effect on Lillian's emotional development and therefore Miss Nin doesn't consider it pertinent to tell us anything about them.

So much abstraction of her characters from the context of their lives, combined with such a quantity of specific detail when it suits Miss Nin's strange ends, gives a certain surrealist quality to her stories. Yet her approach is not properly described as surrealist since in the instance of each of the women Miss Nin is presenting a case. But while the method of *This Hunger* . . . is that of clinical history, there are two important differences: the first, that Miss Nin relies as she does not alone on clinical observations and conclusions but on literary skill, and second, that whereas the purpose of a case history is to add to our clinical knowledge and any wider significance which may appear is present only by happy accident, Miss Nin's purpose is to make a literary comment upon life.

Yet I am forced to regret that to my view *This Hunger* . . . is both less good reading and less life-enhancing than many simon-pure case studies. This is not because I object—though I do—to the dominant poetical tone of Miss Nin's prose. Nor is it because I reject—though I do—the major implication of Miss Nin's stories, that women are done in more than men are and largely *by* men, and that since the sufferings of men occasion suffering in women they should be the objects of our bitter resentment even while the sufferings of women rouse our deepest sympathies. *This Hunger* . . . is inferior to good psychoanalytical case records for the simple reason that its psychoanalysis is less science than pretension.

Let me make myself drearily plain: it is not my belief that in order to write fiction that is psychologically sound one requires technical psychiatric knowledge. Quite the contrary: we have only to compare the novelist's insight into human motivation before Freud and after him to see how steady has been the deterioration in psychological understanding as the post-Freudian novelists have tried to incorporate the findings of

145

psychiatry into their art. But inasmuch as Miss Nin bases her aesthetic on the value of her clinical insights, it is natural that we should expect them to be at least as reliable and revealing as those that make up the stock-in-trade of the analytical practitioner. If Miss Nin were writing traditional short stories she would employ such traditional fictional means as dramatic conflict, the development of circumstances, etc., to extend our experience of life. But Miss Nin has discarded these means and instead she depends on science to give poetic intensification to the life we know. Her science must therefore be of a kind to set up good poetic vibrations, which is to say that it must be good science.

What I mean when I suggest a correspondence between good science and good poetic overtones is perhaps illustrated by a sentence from *The Development of Modern Physics,* by Einstein and Infeld. Expounding the rudiments of relativity, these authors write: "A straight line is the simplest and most trivial example of a curve." The statement is a simple scientific one yet in the perfection of its simplicity and scientific accuracy it becomes, as well, a very beautiful poetic statement. Similarly, a good case history that stays with scientific truth can turn out to be an arresting poetic statement about life. But Miss Nin's case histories substitute a conscious poeticizing of their material for the poetry inherent in the literal material itself; and they make their observations on a drawing-room level of the psychoanalytical science. As a result they are neither good poetry nor good practice. I have space for only a single example, Miss Nin's treatment of Hejda's youthful sadism. On the first page of her first case Miss Nin reports: "Hejda was then a little primitive, whose greatest pleasure consisted in inserting her finger inside pregnant hens and breaking the eggs, or filling frogs with gasoline and setting a lighted match to them." This rather sensational activity is never traced to its psychic causes nor is it connected with later manifestations of Hejda's character, though Miss Nin remarks upon a certain carnivorousness in the young woman's disposition and reports another cruelty which she perpetrates upon a school friend. Then, on the last page of

Hejda's history, when she has reached the stage where "when everything fails she resorts to lifting her dress and arranging her garters," Miss Nin adds: "She is back . . . to the native original Hejda. . . . The frogs leap away in fear of her again."

Such diagnostic procedure may of course reveal no more than Miss Nin's ignorance of the profession she practices. I am tempted, however, to borrow her own deterministic bias and to diagnose this kind and degree of psychoanalytical waywardness as wilful—after all, more information was available to Miss Nin if she wanted it. It would seem that Miss Nin looks to psychoanalysis only for what serves the sexual chauvinism, self-pity, and self-enhancement of the modern female writer of sensibility.

Every so often Miss Nin's writing descends from the feminine heights and indulges in straight commonsensical observation of human beings and even in undecorated prose. Then we recognize that somewhere in her Miss Nin has perhaps the powers that have always been necessary for good science, good fiction, good poetry. But such deviations are only occasional, so I wonder why a book like *This Hunger* . . . hasn't had commercial publication in these days when nothing sells like the sick psyche.

March 9, 1946

If literature ruled we can be fairly certain that there would be no anti-Negroism or anti-Semitism in this country. The American novelist's pen is firm, if not sharp, in defense of the minorities; I can recall only one novel of the last few years which formulated a reactionary position toward oppressed racial groups, and remarkably few instances where the instinct of intolerance was even accidentally revealed. But of patronage and condescension, of over-simplification and muddle-headedness and self-deception, there is a sufficient abundance. No doubt the conscious process of reform must always be accompanied by these unattractive manifestations of missionary zeal.

In recent weeks there have been two new novels on the Negro

problem, Fannie Cook's *Mrs. Palmer's Honey* (Doubleday, $2.50), winner of the George Washington Carver Award, and Ann Petry's *The Street* (Houghton Mifflin, $2.50), a Houghton Mifflin Literary Fellowship novel. I should say at once that neither of them challenges the prestige of Lillian Smith's *Strange Fruit*; indeed, neither is particularly rewarding as a work of fiction. But there is much provocation as well as irony in the fact that the far more cerebral of the two, *Mrs. Palmer's Honey,* which undertakes to name the economic and political sources and cures of anti-Negroism, turns out to be far thinner in its "message" than *The Street,* which undertakes no more than to explain how its author, herself colored, feels about her situation.

Mrs. Cook has unquestionably thought hard and long to reach her conclusion that as labor goes, so goes the fate of the Negro. Her novel is well-instructed in local affairs—housing, schools, community activities—and in the larger political affairs of the nation, and Mrs. Cook is not lacking in the courage to proclaim her political preferences: a considerable section of *Mrs. Palmer's Honey* concerns the last Presidential campaign— she mobilizes her good Negroes to rally votes for Roosevelt and pleads without reservation the case for P.A.C. Indeed, it is specifically in the C.I.O. that she puts all her hopes for the solution of the Negro problem. But even while she recognizes such social and economic contradictions as segregation within the army and trade unions, she would seem to be unwilling to recognize any contradiction in Negroes themselves. If her characters can be said to be motivated at all, it is only by positive or negative social impulses; once a path of action has been chosen, there is no modification of feeling, no conflict of desires. Her heroine, Honey, is in fact a parody of virtuousness, an Elsie Dinsmore of the kitchen, home, and trade union.

Yet to find more human verisimilitude in Mrs. Petry's Lutie than in Mrs. Cook's Honey is not to replace the one with the other as a social ideal. Lutie's is the story of a young colored woman who, having lost her husband when the depression forced her to "live in" in domestic service, tries to make a decent life for herself and her small son in Harlem. Lutie is very pretty and energetic and she has had a high-school education. The degradation she suffers despite such advantages is symbolized by the dreadful apartment in which she must live, just as the whole of the Negro degradation is symbolized by the dirt and wretchedness of Harlem's 116th Street.

In her period of domestic service Lutie works in a white household in Connecticut. Her employers are a miserable family: Mr. and Mrs. Chandler are unhappily married, Mr. Chandler drinks, Mr. Chandler's brother shoots himself before their eyes, the Chandler baby is a sad little youngster. But the Chandlers not only have a lot of money, they are on the way to having much more. Lutie has seen what a pleasant surface money can put on suffering; her sole complaint against being colored is that it denies her the opportunity to live with the cleanliness and financial ease of Mrs. Chandler. No matter how hard she works, no matter what her abilities, she is unable to rise above the Harlem ghetto.

By quite opposite routes, that is, both novels arrive at the economic core of the Negro problem. But whereas to Mrs. Cook equal economic opportunity is predicated on both Negro and white proletarian consciousness, to Mrs. Petry equality of opportunity means a free capitalist economy in which Negroes no less than whites can get as much as they desire and are capable of getting.

I say of Mrs. Cook's very thoughtful book that in the long run it is thin compared to Mrs. Petry's *The Street*. What I mean is that *Mrs. Palmer's Honey* fails to take into account the fact that class feelings are as firmly ingrained in the colored population of his country as in the white, and that there is nothing inherently virtuous, even politically virtuous, about being a member of a mistreated minority. Mrs. Cook's idealism on the score of class solidarity does her credit. But in the light of Mrs. Petry's frankly middle-class document, it asks to be corrected by a confrontation with our realities of class. And as a corollary, *Mrs. Palmer's Honey* calls attention to a common important error in much of our contemporary political thinking, that of assuming that it is in the degree that people are virtuous that they deserve just treatment. Basic to much of our writing on minority problems, especially in fiction, there seems to be the idea that we must prove that members of minority groups—whether Jews, Negroes, Italians, or whatever—are more than good, better than the rest of us, before we demand that they be treated like everybody else. Must a white Protestant resident of Westchester be certified for character before he enjoys his full rights as a citizen? As I read *The Street,* I couldn't help wondering whether the author of *Mrs. Palmer's Honey* would be as exercised over the inability of a girl like Lutie to achieve her house in Connecticut and her mink coat, if that is what she wants, as over the restrictions in the path of a girl like Honey, whose ambitions are so much nobler. Properly, even politically, she of course should be.

March 30, 1946

It is now seventeen years since the publication of Edmund Wilson's earlier work of fiction, *I Thought of Daisy.* Seventeen years are seventeen years in whatever social or political situation, and if one's sense of time is stirred by the appearance of Mr. Wilson's present collection of connected stories, *Memoirs of Hecate County* (Doubleday, $2.50), it may be because of the emotions that naturally attend the contemplation of any small completed arc of experience. But in addition there is our awareness of the special nature of these years, an awareness sharpened by Mr. Wilson's own intense response to them. Of all critics, Edmund Wilson is perhaps most torturedly alert to the social-moral disintegration of the last two decades and to the effect of awful political events upon our intellectual life. He is preeminently the critic of our contemporary despair, to whom

150

present-day culture presents itself as the record of a hopelessly dissolving society. Distinguished for his deep roots in traditional values, he draws but bitter nourishment from them. He is an instance in which knowledge ranging far into the past provides none of the solace of a long-range point of view. On the contrary, his feeling about the past seems increasingly to exacerbate his feeling about the present, until—in turn—his feeling about the present sends him back to reinvestigate the past for confirmation that, even in a better day, disease—within the individual as in the surrounding world—was the expectable state of sentient man.

It is so highly subjective an attitude, however accurate may be the perception of the objective circumstances on which it is based, and in his criticism Mr. Wilson projects it so handsomely, that it is both futile and impertinent to argue with it other than to record one's own conviction that no matter how bad the dominant social tendencies of our time, the creative will of the individual is not always at their mercy. But the fact that it is subjective does not mean that it is peculiar to Mr. Wilson alone or that it does not have its clear source in recent intellectual history. For every destructive social event there are the temperaments prepared to receive its full painful impact, and a considerable section of our best-trained literary opinion operates on a similar sad recoil from the broken promises of Marxism.

Even more directly than his recent critical writing, Mr. Wilson's present volume of stories responds to the contemporary social and cultural situation of this country. Consciously or unconsciously *Memoirs of Hecate County* is a sequel to *I Thought of Daisy*: the earlier book was Mr. Wilson's record of American artistic and intellectual life in the Twenties; the present book is his record of American artistic and intellectual life in the Thirties and Forties. Mr. Wilson is still as fine a social reporter as before, with a Proustian eye for social deportment. The cultural alterations he notes from these intervening years are numerous and significant: taken together, the two books make an enormously valuable document of social change. Now,

151

instead of Greenwich Village, the setting of bohemia is the expensive suburbs and the East Sixties. Now, instead of the romantic lure of the theater, there is the commercial lure of Hollywood and the radio. Through Mr. Wilson's keen observation we see, as the years pass, a small private income metamorphose from security into inconsequentiality. We measure an appreciable increase in alcoholic consumption. We watch the abortive effort of the intellectual to break down his intellectual isolation and come to terms with economic and political realities. We see the transformation of important, if frenetic, sexual relationships into the cold phenomena of the psychiatric textbook. Most significant of all, we study the alteration in the author's own relation to his world, his loss of a sense of coherent connection with the people among whom he lives. For while it is questionable whether there was more integrity in the artistic life of the Twenties than today, certainly there was more cohesion—for instance, in *I Thought of Daisy* it was still possible, if one were not oneself a member of the bohemian élite, to be made to feel an outsider at a Village party but in *Memoirs of Hecate County* the gates of the pseudo-Elizabethan suburban houses can be crashed by anyone with the right pretensions. It is only the narrator who, in the degree that he remembers a day of greater dedication, himself feels at times an outsider.

And yet there is a curious contradiction in the new stories between the narrator's lack of sympathy with his social milieu and the nature of his participation in it. Mr. Wilson's protagonist is a sociological critic of art, a person of taste and learning. Yet, though he might associate with anyone he pleased, he is apparently compelled to select this riffraffish company for no better reason than that it is the most readily available to him. That is, Mr. Wilson implies an absence of free will even in our choice of friends. But even if it were true that we are such willless victims of the environment in which we find ourselves, there would still be no need for his narrator to act as he does *within* this dreary society. The jacket of *Memoirs of Hecate County* describes the book as the "adventures of an egotist among the bedeviled," and one must be egotist indeed to have so little heart for the stragglers and swaggerers among whom one has thrown in one's lot—why should a group of poor devils be seen as such a group of incarnate Devils? There is a very rigid moralism in Mr. Wilson's book. The criterion by which his spokesman makes his discriminations between good and evil is so close to a religious one that we are tempted to accuse him of the very Manichean heresy—the belief that "the devil is contending on equal terms with God and that the fate of the world is in doubt"—which he himself protests in one of the stories.

Mr. Wilson's unrelenting heart is particularly distressing in his central and longest story, "The Princess with the Golden Hair," which is already attaining a certain subterranean fame for its supposed pornographic interest. I myself find Mr. Wilson's detailed sexual passages disturbing not because they are daring but because of the breach they make between sensation and emotion. As in *I Thought of Daisy,* two girls divide the attention of the narrator of "The Princess with the Golden Hair," a remote figure of fantasy and a real human figure. And just as in *I Thought of Daisy* his encounter with the warm proletarian Daisy has the purpose of breaking down the "dreadful isolation of the artist" which has been reinforced by the goddess-like Rita, so in *Memoirs of Hecate County* the narrator's encounter with the dance-hall hostess, Anna, serves as a health-giving counter to the worship of the fairy-tale Imogen. But the new story carries this opposition of reality and idealism a dangerous step farther than it was carried in the early novel. Now it is not sufficient to show that compared to the invigorating nature of reality, romantic idealism is poor stuff to feed on; idealism (Imogen) must be shown to be morbidly diseased. But so, too, must reality (Anna) be shown to be diseased: she gives the narrator gonorrhea. There is, then, no one in either the mythological upper world or the proletarian under world to break down the artist's isolation. He is doomed by his circumstances as given.

But the point is that Mr. Wilson's protagonist does nothing to improve these circumstances. His sexual relationships with Imogen and Anna are in the nature of laboratory tests of society, and laboratory tests are cold things compared to love. If the hero of *Memoirs of Hecate County* had loved Anna, he would have got her to a doctor as quickly as he got himself; if he had loved Imogen, he would have made a move to see that she got help for her neurotic disorder instead of grimly shutting her out of his life with the grim shutting of the textbook in which he discovered what ailed her. There are, after all, ways in which we can still alter, or at least will to alter, unhappy fact.

Clearly, I do not mean this to say that it is the job of the intellectual to go about doing good in a bad world. But we do, I think, have the right to ask that he maintain, amid disorder, some principle of private order from which a principle of general order could be adduced—that he keep, for one thing, a sound integration between head and heart, which of course is another way of asking that he distinguish between sensation and emotion. For if he allows himself to be disordered by his disordered society, all he will generalize is mess, whereas if he maintains personal order within a disintegrated society, he will at the least have a tragic—which is to say, a meaningful—experience of pain. And that is everlastingly the intellectual's job: to be meaningful, despite and above his social situation.

April 6, 1946

Adolescence is the theme of two enormously talented short novels, Carson McCullers's *The Member of the Wedding* (Houghton Mifflin, $2.50) and Denton Welch's *In Youth Is Pleasure* (L. B. Fischer, $2.50). Miss McCullers's book is about a twelve-year-old girl in Georgia; Mr. Welch's is about a fifteen-year-old boy in England. Both children are manifestly their authors' not very distant selves, and both books mirror this anguished season of our growth against the most anguishing

154

season of a young person's year, summer, when the cessation of school throws a child so completely upon his own incoherent resources and when the very physical world would seem to burn with an intensity of hopelessness. If only for their ability to re-create a child's experience of summer, both novels are remarkable. Miss McCullers and Mr. Welch have powers of observation and recollection quite beyond the ordinary, and an unusual gift for translating remembered physical or visual sensation into language.

Miss McCullers, especially, communicates almost more of a child's emotions of boredom and emptiness, of the stoppage of time and of the draining of meaning from a world in which the air is yet heavy with unformed meanings, than the reader can receive with equanimity. Indeed, it is with a certain relief, as at the lifting of the atmosphere after rain, that one turns from the Addams's kitchen in Georgia—from Frankie Addams's unmoving hours in the company of the colored maid, Berenice, and her six-year-old cousin—to the English countryside of Mr. Welch's Orvil Pym. Then one realizes that the fresher air of *In Youth Is Pleasure* is perhaps less a matter of the difference in climate of the two countries, America and England, or of a difference in the temperaments of the two writers, than of the difference in age between their youthful protagonists. Orvil has lived three years longer than Frankie and in this interval between twelve and fifteen his impulses, madly confused as they may still be, have become at least less diffuse. He collects china, writes poems, has an interest in architecture. He recognizes his sexual desires and explores the possible avenues of their gratification. At the end of *The Member of the Wedding* we discover that Frankie, too, has begun slowly to move down the road Orvil has already covered. She has accommodated herself to the idea that she cannot be a part of her brother's marriage. Now thirteen, she is "just mad about Michelangelo" and about her new girl-friend, and one suspects that if the kitchen knife still holds charms for her, she will at least not throw it around so carelessly.

But if both novels share uncommon gifts of perception and evocation, they also share their failure as complete literary works. The nature of the failure is suggested by the temptation, even the necessity, for the reviewer to discuss them as much in clinical as literary terms. Anyone writing about current fiction is of course constantly urged in this direction and not merely because of the clinical character of our greatly-favored present-day subject matter but because of the relation in which the authors stand to it.

Both Miss McCullers and Mr. Welch, Mr. Welch even more than Miss McCullers, are over-identified with the child protagonists of their stories. What I mean by this is exemplified in a comparison between the books they have written and such widely differing stories of childhood as, say, *Huckleberry Finn, Swann's Way,* and Elizabeth Bowen's *The Death of the Heart.* Granted that with each passing year we are permitted more freedom of self-revelation and that even since the publication of *The Death of the Heart* the boundaries of literary reticence have considerably widened, what we note in Miss McCullers's book or Mr. Welch's is not merely a greater frankness than in these earlier works but a significant new emotional-intellectual attitude. In Miss Bowen's novel as in Proust's or Mark Twain's, it is through the mind and emotions of an adult that the recollection of childhood has had to be filtered. In Miss McCullers's novel or Mr. Welch's, a major aesthetic point is made of the absence of this interference. Today the experience of childhood rolls from the writer's pen with an ease and lack of inhibition that is bound to persuade us that in recollection it has met none of the resistances that in actuality attend the progress from youth to maturity.

This lack of inhibition is distinctly more pronounced in *In Youth Is Pleasure* than in *The Member of the Wedding.* It is as if Orvil's feelings have translated themselves to paper quite as they presented themselves in adolescent reality. But surely a fifteen-year-old boy would hesitate to describe himself so forthrightly even in a private diary; the moment he would set about

156

committing his feelings to paper he would wish to be superior to them. And behind this impulse to falsify experience, to give it, if you will, a meaning more acceptable to maturity, would lie the healthy impulse to be himself mature. Mr. Welch's too great pleasure in youth is, in fact, underscored by the conclusion of his novel, where Orvil—unlike Frankie, who by the end of her story makes a definite advance in growth—rather retrogresses even from the age of fifteen: *In Youth Is Pleasure* ends with its young hero screaming happily like a baby.

To say that both Miss McCullers and Mr. Welch are too close to the adolescent states of mind of their central characters is not, however, to imply that they do not make choices or eliminations among remembered facts. Both writers are far too sensitive to literary style to be literalists; and style is in itself of course a form of maturity. But just as so many of our present-day novelists who deal with psychopathological subjects betray their overvaluation of the psychopathological by putting too little distance between themselves and their sick subjects, just so both Miss McCullers and Mr. Welch betray the exaggerated valuation they put upon the condition of childhood by refusing to exercise mature judgment upon their child subjects.

I am struck by one thing further about Miss McCullers's and Mr. Welch's novels, the degree to which each of them deals with a special rather than a universal child case. In even the small measure that Miss McCullers is more willing than Mr. Welch to allow her protagonist to advance in growth, she makes more of a generalized statement about childhood. Yet to compare either of these pictures of a child to Miss Bowen's or Proust's or Mark Twain's is to recognize how particularized both of them are. Despite all the truths about boyhood that a Proust or a Mark Twain may omit but which Mr. Welch records, there is infinitely more universalized "boy" in the young Proust or in Huck Finn than in Orvil Pym, and similarly there is much more universalized "girl" in the reticent Miss Bowen's little heroine than in Miss McCullers's more freely described Frankie. Here, I suppose, is one of the nice paradoxes of art, that it depends for so much of its truth upon omission or even falsehood, and not alone the falsehood of style but also the falsehood of bringing intellect and ideal to bear upon fact.

April 20, 1946

The English magazine *Horizon* was established in December, 1939. Therefore although some of the stories reprinted by Cyril Connolly, the magazine's editor, in the volume *Horizon Stories* (Vanguard, $2.50) may have been written before the war actually began, the volume as a whole can fairly be regarded as a product of the English war years. From this point of view its almost total avoidance of the war is startling. There are twenty stories in Mr. Connolly's collection, but only one—J. Maclaren-Ross's "I Had to Go Sick," a superficially humorous, hiddenly bitter account of a soldier's entanglement in medical red tape—deals with life in the armed services. And only one other—Elizabeth Bowen's "In the Square," a sketch of the reunion of two friends in the war-unsettled home of one of them—deals with civilian life in wartime. Rollo Woolley's "The Pupil" does take off from an airfield, and Fred Urquhart's "Man About the House" mentions in passing that its unpleasant central character will soon have to register for the draft. For the rest, it is as if the war had never been.

The story of Elizabeth Bowen's that Mr. Connolly reprints also appears in Miss Bowen's volume of stories, *Ivy Gripped the Steps* (Knopf, $2.50). In a very interesting preface Miss Bowen comments on her use, in the place of immediate war themes, of what she calls the "hallucinatory" materials of wartime life. "The hallucinations in the stories are not a peril," Miss Bowen writes. "Nor are the stories studies of mental peril. The hallucinations are an unconscious, instinctive, saving resort on the part of the characters. Life, mechanized by the controls of war time, and emotionally torn and impoverished by changes, had to complete itself in some other way. It is a fact that in Britain . . . people had strange, deep, intense dreams." This thread of dream runs through all Miss Bowen's stories, no doubt accounting for their fragmentariness, but binding them together and making them unmistakably relevant to the background of disruption against which they were conceived. However remote from the reality of war the manifest content of much of Miss Bowen's volume may be, it deeply connects with the experience of its time. Even something as subtle as her too acute alertness to sound—and there is scarcely a story in which the striking of a clock, the ringing of a telephone, or the shutting of a door doesn't have an extreme meaning—reflects the sensory over-alertness that is characteristic of fear.

The remoteness from wartime reality of the *Horizon* stories doesn't have this import: the war doesn't exist even as something to be turned away from by fantasy. The volume opens with a piece called "When I Was Thirteen," another slice of the autobiography of the talented disingenuous Denton Welch, and closes with the nice orderly ironies of Philip Toynbee's "Interment of a Literary Man." In between we have been given a fashionably nasty bit of amoralism, "I Live on My Wits" by Alfred Perlés; an unfashionably moralistic tale of a fallen woman, "The Wages of Love" by Rhys Davies; a story of sadistic childhood, "The Scissors," translated from the Spanish of Arturo Barea; a neo-Nicolsonian divertissement called "The Third Secretary's Story" by Tom Hopkinson; an unreadable evocation of the past, "Ivanhoe" by Logan Pearsall Smith; "Happy All Alone," by Roland Lushington, which is an inspiration from *The Magic Mountain* tailored to the dimensions of a *Collier's* short-short; "The Suitcase Hunt" by John Bryan, which could expand into one of those volumes of eccentric family reminiscence now so much in vogue in our own country; a chic anecdote, "Crossing the Atlantic," by Diana Gardner, about a man whose solo sail across the ocean is crashed by a newspaper girl (I had almost said "gal"). Even the single symbolic story in the volume, "The Long Sheet," by William Sansom, exudes an air of prefabrication, and even the stories which deal with the uneasiness of faith—"The Saint" by V. S. Pritchett, and "Prothalamion" by Edward Sheehy—are considerably too easy for our contemporary problems of faith. As to the expectable studies in psychopathology—the itself quite mad "Room Wanted" by G. F. Green, or Antonia White's well-worked "The Moment of Truth," or Anna Kavan's touching "I Am Lazarus" —they speak of a mental derangement which is not of the province of foxholes or air raids.

I suppose the volume's low level of literary significance, as opposed to its high level of literacy and craft, is not unrelated to its refusal of contemporary engagement. Miss Bowen's volume, too, is something of a literary disappointment; only two of her stories, "Sunday Afternoon" and the title story, are brought off with the flourish an admirer has come to look for in her work. But at least when we put down *Ivy Gripped the Steps* we know what it is in the author's troubled mood which has stirred us, whereas our final response to Mr. Connolly's collection is confusion as to what his writers thought or felt they were doing. "The leading literary magazine in Great Britain [*Horizon*] has survived the London blitz and philistinism in literature with equal gallantry," say the publishers of *Horizon Stories*. One must wonder what philistinism means in this context. Curiously enough, if by philistinism we mean either an antagonism to change, or a smug antagonism to the truth of art, this is perhaps the word that most closely describes the pervasive tone of the volume itself.

For after all, there is a philistinism of the educated spirit as there is of the mass or uneducated spirit, and none the less to be remarked because it may operate to preserve traditional values at a time when they are gravely threatened, also none the less to be battled against because it may itself be doing gallant battle— so, too, does conservatism often do gallant battle. The discrimination between philistinism and the sound effort to preserve traditional values rests on the nature of the traditional values that are being preserved, and so far as I can see there is very

160

little to choose between the values of *Horizon Stories* and those against which it stands. Suppose that by avoiding the war these stories avoid the taint of chauvinism that might possibly result from a sympathetic identification with the general temper of the time: what have they introduced in its stead? Certainly nothing that is a corrective to the excesses of national pride but only a kind of nullity of both intellect and feeling, a blind retreat of the mind and spirit rather than a "saving resort."

There is a sentence in one of Miss Bowen's "non-war" stories about a man in uniform. "His uniform fitted and suited him just a degree too well, and gave him the air of being on excellent terms with war." This is the method by which Miss Bowen feels and expresses the "high-voltage current of the general" as it passes through the particular, so excellent a method that we do not miss her failure to carry her character into a war activity or to specify another military fact about him. One could wish the writers of the *Horizon* stories had permitted themselves a similar participation in the situation of these years, for their hearts speak no more poetically and their minds are no more fruitful for their having so entirely refused the war experience. Quite the contrary, in fact.

April 27, 1946

A wonderful contemporary subject which, so far as I know, has never been explored with either true seriousness or true humor in our fiction is American revolutionary politics. This is not to say that there have not been novels in which the radical movement has played a part. But it has been a hero's part. The portraits have been idealized to the point where if the truth appears at all, it is plainly without the author's knowledge or approval. As a catalyst of important emotions or as the arena of moral conflicts or even as a source of high comedy, the American revolutionary movement would seem to have been avoided by our novelists, and one can understand why. After all, anyone who has been sufficiently close to either the American Communist Party or the dissident Communist movement to know its tragic and comic possibilities has no doubt been too closely involved to want to use it as a fictional theme. Then, too, in dealing with radical politics, there is always the danger that one's revelations will be appreciated by the wrong people or for the wrong reasons.

Now Eleanor Clark has dared somewhat to break through this inhibition. *The Bitter Box* (Doubleday, $2.50) is a serious, funny, and truthful picture of Communist doings in this country, and therefore a work of courage. But one could wish it had carried its daring to the point of actually naming its parties, newspapers, and magazines instead of clouding them in anonymity or pseudonymity. Miss Clark's novel is also—I should say at once—a work of unquestionable moral-political taste. If the "class enemy"—or does this concept perhaps no longer obtain among the people who first taught us our scrupling?—can take any comfort from Miss Clark's frank admission that the Party doesn't always honor its financial obligations or that every switch in tactics finds a couple of thousand comrades dangerously thrown off balance or even that a not too thoughtful generosity in the direction of the proletariat is often matched by a not too thoughtful sexual generosity, then the Communists have only themselves to blame. Miss Clark has good fun at the Party's expense but she never stretches the truth to make a joke; there is no malice in her comedy. In fact, she manages without a touch of piousness to convey her own sorrow that the radical situation is as she reports it.

But while the best sections of *The Bitter Box* are its sections of Communist satire, the book as a whole cannot be fairly described as satire. For satire is the approach most open to the naturalistic novelist, and Miss Clark's story, like the little bank clerk, Mr. Temple, who is its central character, lives most of its life under wraps. Despite its precision of naturalistic detail—and what an eye Miss Clark has for the split seams and minds

162

of the comrades!—*The Bitter Box* is predominantly abstract, shadowy with the suggestion not only of unnamed political forces but also of unnamed literary purposes. One necessarily stands with its author at a significant remove from its material, the remove of a semi-symbolical method.

Mr. Temple is himself an adding-machine person, one of those automatons of efficiency and fear who are so frequently isolated as the typical product of our civilization. *The Bitter Box* opens on a fine spring day with Mr. Temple, a trapped man, walking out of his bank cage. Moved by a series of fortuitous influences, the bank clerk becomes a revolutionary. He steals for the Party, he is ready to kill for the Party, he is betrayed by the Party, he has his eyes opened by the Party. The novel ends on a bleak winter day when, having learned something of both the "Cordiall and Corrosive" in "the bitter box" of life, Mr. Temple is free to be trapped by normal circumstance: to be out of a job, to be hungry, cold and ill-clad, to be confusedly in love. The biography is a touching one but the motivation of Mr. Temple is so haphazard and his history developed with so little regard for the logic of character, that it is as if he had been designed to accompany a story rather than to have a story grow out of him. He is not a created person but a poetic device, like meter. Because its central character fails to explode for us, the whole book carries its charge, even its satiric charge, largely unexploded.

In basic conception *The Bitter Box* strongly reminds me of Henry James's revolutionary novel, *The Princess Casamassima*. In both books there is a small hero who lives outside the world of adventure and love and big hopes. In both, this world of possibility is entered by way of the radical movement. And in both, the life of promise is no sooner apprehended by the hero than it is denied him. Miss Clark's novel, like James's, is a tragedy of growth. But what particularly strikes me in comparing the two books—and the comparison is made neither to be pressed nor to be invidious: for all its humor Miss Clark's story is deeply grave and for all its refusal to announce its passions it is deeply passionate—is the limitlessness of meaning achieved by the naturalistic novel as opposed to the bounds put upon imaginative intention by the abstract or semi-abstract novel. As I understand the purpose of symbolic fiction, it is to add dimension to naturalistic story-telling. But actually it seems to me to produce a contrary effect: instead of widening, it narrows the possibilities of the novel; instead of giving it new significance, it diminishes a novel's range of reference. Comparing the method of *The Bitter Box* with the method of *The Princess Casamassima* is for me like comparing the blank whiteness on a canvas of Mondrian's to the white of a tablecloth painted by Chardin. There is still so much white in tablecloths that has never been painted that Mondrian's dead-white spaces seem more a retreat than an advance from Chardin. In Miss Clark's abstraction of Mr. Temple, too, more has been taken away from Henry James's Hyacinth than added to him. There is still very much to be written out of the traditional powers of observation and insight which Miss Clark has at her command but which she has apparently ceased to trust or respect.

May 11, 1946

I find it difficult to determine how much of my distaste for Eudora Welty's new book, *Delta Wedding* (Harcourt, Brace, $2.75), is dislike of its literary manner and how much is resistance to the culture out of which it grows and which it describes so fondly. But actually I believe that Miss Welty's style and her cultural attitude are not separable. I cannot conceive of a Northern or Western or even a European or Australian or African scene that could provoke an exacerbation of poeticism to equal Miss Welty's in this novel. Compared to Miss Welty's sensibility, the sensibility of a Katherine Mansfield, a Sylvia Townsend Warner, a Christina Stead, or an Edita Morris—to name some of the writers, all of them women, notable in our time for the delicacy of their intensities—presents itself as a crude, corporeal thing indeed. Dolls' houses, birds, moonlight, snow, the minutiae of vulnerable young life and the sudden revelations of nature may have their distressingly persistent way of agitating the modern female literary psyche in whatever climate or social context but it seems to me that only on a Southern plantation could the chance remark of a gardener to the effect that he wished there "wouldn't be a rose in the world" set the lady of the house to "trembling . . . as at some impudence."

It is out of tremulousnesses like this, as a matter of fact, that the whole of Miss Welty's novel is built. Dramatically speaking, nothing happens in *Delta Wedding*. Miss Welty tells us of seven days in the life of the Fairchild family of Mississippi: it is the week in which Dabney, the seventeen-year-old daughter of the house, is being married to her father's overseer. Relatives pay calls and are called upon, meals are eaten, gifts arrive, people dance, servants rally in the established plantation fashion. Domestic bustle and a spattering of family reminiscences are all the narrative structure Miss Welty needs to house her treasures of perception.

And yet one must suppose that for all its tenuousness *Delta Wedding* says just what it meant to say. Among evocative novelists Miss Welty is extraordinarily gifted so that if I finish her book much confused as to Miss Welty's judgment upon certain aspects of Delta life, I have no reason to feel that this is because Miss Welty lacks the ability to communicate anything she wants to. For instance, in common with most of our talented Southern writers, Miss Welty acknowledges blemishes on the surface of the society she so much adores: she specifies snobbery, xenophobia, "mindlessness"—the kindly euphemism, we gather, for idiocy or insanity—and other distractions and sorrows that we have so often been told are part of the price the South pays for its heritage of pride. Yet this much honest revelation is not to be taken as an adverse criticism of the Fairchild way of life. On the contrary, it constitutes a test of Miss Welty's love for it, a love so strong that it can not only admit these failings but cherish them. For just as the Fairchild women have always loved the large indolences which they see as the other side of the coin of the large generosities of their men, so Miss Welty loves the Fairchild meannesses and arrogances and weaknesses as the inevitable other side of the coin of their aristocratic grace and charm. Her honest observations are left in rosy poetic solution exactly because she does not wish to precipitate them as moral judgment.

Now obviously in asking for moral judgment I am asking only for moral discrimination and not for what usually substitutes for it, moralizing hostility. Even more than other forms of life, art flourishes in affection. And certainly the careless abundance of Fairchild life, the quantity of children, of visitors, fondness, hams, beaten biscuit, iced lemonade, coconut layer cake and even indulgence of a daughter's wilfulness in selecting a socially undesirable husband, is something to be cherished; I have no wish to replace it with the brittle and meager domestic ideal of much of our "progressive" Northern literature. But *Delta Wedding* pervasively implies that the parochialism and snobbery of the Fairchild clan is a condition of its charm and that the Fairchild grace necessarily has its source in a life of embattled pride. This is a value system to which I deeply oppose myself.

In writing about Miss Welty's last book, *The Wide Net,* I spoke of the narcissistic dream quality of the stories in that volume. Now one begins to see the connection between Miss Welty's style as it has developed and her developing relation to traditional Southern culture. In the best of her stories, her earliest ones, Miss Welty gave us what was really a new view of the South, indeed a new kind of realism about it, and for this she employed a prose that, though not at all pedestrian, walked on its feet. It didn't dance. But as time has passed she has been steadily turning away from the lower-middle-class milieu of, say, "The Petrified Man," to that part of the Southern scene which is most accessible to mythologizing and celebrative

166

legend and, in general, to the narcissistic Southern fantasy, and for this her prose has more and more risen on tiptoe. As a result, one of our most promising young writers gives signs of becoming, instead of the trenchant commentator we hoped she would be, just another ingenious dreamer on the Southern past.

May 18, 1946

From its start as a Jewish genre novel—and its first chapter is perhaps the most charming bit of Jewish genre I have ever read—Isaac Rosenfeld's *Passage from Home* (Dial Press, $2.50) develops into a novel of profound universal meanings. The development is a startling one and points to what is not the least of the many extraordinary virtues of Mr. Rosenfeld's book, its ability to use its Jewish background as a natural rather than a forced human environment. I am not acquainted with Yiddish literature; it may be that there are Yiddish writers who avoid the well-established emotions of Jewish separateness—the emotions of specialness, embattledness, social overdeterminism, self-pity and self-punishment. But among novels of Jewish-American life Mr. Rosenfeld's is, to my knowledge, the sole instance in which the fact of being Jewish is handled as simply another facet of the already sufficiently complicated business of being a human being. In most Jewish fiction the characters are allowed only that kind of personal drama which reflects their drama as a people; the problems or conflicts of love, age, status, worldly ambition and the acquisition of knowledge are all of them assimilated to the parent problem of the relation of a subordinate social group to the dominant culture. It is out of the power to endure that the Jewish novel most commonly draws its sustenance. Unable to believe that his environment really belongs to him, the Jewish novelist cannot envision a valid personal drama of development within it. At best he writes a fiction of dignified resistance or acceptance, at worst a fiction of fierce personal aggression and of the individual effort to rise above the restrictions of Jewish birth. Dealing with the Jewish subject, he never writes a heroic fiction of growth.

But Mr. Rosenfeld's novel has a hero or at least the makings of one: its principal character is a fourteen-year-old boy, Bernard, who has the emotional and moral stature to be a beautifully adequate projection of his author. This choice of hero is another indication of the high order of Mr. Rosenfeld's novelistic gift, for just as an underestimation of the personal possibilities of Jews is a betrayal of Jewish fiction at its source, so an underestimation of the wisdom possible in youth and the moral dignity of the young is a betrayal of all of fiction at its source. There has never been a novelist worth his salt who has failed to recognize the grandeur of man in the child. The tendency of current fiction, while dwelling so persistently on child themes, to picture youth as fixed in its most infant aspects is, I think, the mark of its disrespect for the whole human possibility. The accusation that will no doubt be made against Mr. Rosenfeld, that his fourteen-year-old spokesman sees more than any fourteen-year-old can see and learns more than a fourteen-year-old can learn, is the softest of impeachments; a similar criticism is made of Henry James who also tried to flatter us into maturity. What Mr. Rosenfeld might learn from James, however, is certain technical tricks, tricks chiefly of verisimilitude, with which to conceal his method of seduction.

But its high estimation of the young mind and spirit is of course not the only regard in which *Passage from Home* proposes a comparison with James. In its preoccupation with the moral nature of the early educative process, Mr. Rosenfeld's novel recalls Henry James's *What Maisie Knew* and *The Pupil*. Stated crudely, Bernard's story is that of a boy's effort to learn the meaning of love, and the frustration of this effort by the adults who surround him. Always aware of his father's need to assume the part of virtue, Bernard looks to a small group of grown-ups outside the immediate family circle—his ostracized, bohemianly "independent" Aunt Minna; his dashing Gentile cousin-by-marriage, Willy; even his aunt's anarchic friend, Mr.

168

Mason—to teach him some kind of truth to match his own ideal of maturity. The search is an abortive one or, rather, Bernard's education is an education by negatives: the boy discovers not only that these grown-ups do not love but also that they are unable to acknowledge the hatred which, if it were admitted, might permit them to love. On the last page of his history Bernard realizes that "my own hope had been to confess that I did not love him [his father], to admit I had never known what love was or what it meant to love, and by that confession to create it. Now it was too late. Now there would only be life as it came and the excuses one made to himself for accepting it." And we are reminded of E. E. Cummings's wonderful lines:

> Women and men (both little and small)
> cared for anyone not at all
> they sowed their isn't they reaped their same
> sun moon stars rain
>
> children guessed (but only a few
> and down they forgot as up they grew
> autumn winter spring summer)
> that noone loved him more by more

Except that no more than Cummings has himself forgotten down as up he grew—or would he be capable of so much lyrical assertion of life—do we feel that Bernard's process of growth will be downward. Sound as is Mr. Rosenfeld's comment on what has happened to his young hero as an intellectual "resolution" of the book, we have the novel's emotional tone and Mr. Rosenfeld's own relation to his protagonist to dispute the assumption that Bernard's will be a future of "excuses."

And just as Bernard's future is full of the promise of truth and growth, Mr. Rosenfeld's novelistic future offers the same promise. Indeed, I can think of no one now writing fiction in whose development I have greater confidence. A first novel, *Passage from Home* is not without errors and shortcomings. They are of minor consequence compared to its accomplishment, that of taking life at so high a moral pitch.

Nowadays, when one is constantly amazed by the skill with which novelists who have nothing to say get the whole of it down on paper, a novel like Merriam Modell's *The Sound of Years* (Simon and Schuster, $2.75), which has so much more potential content than its author seems able to communicate, comes as something of a shock. Not that Miss Modell's book suffers from obvious technical defects: it is more than competently contrived and written. But Miss Modell, whose stories in the *New Yorker* have always suggested if not fully explored a psychological subtlety which sets them apart from the run of fiction in that magazine, has conceived for her first novel a psychological situation which is apparently beyond her present powers. A book with a brave, bitterly valid basic idea can be read—I am afraid must be read—as a superior kind of comfortable entertainment. Its smooth execution entirely conceals the coarse grain of what I am sure was its original intention.

A few weeks ago, in reviewing Isaac Rosenfeld's *Passage from Home,* I referred to E. E. Cummings's "And down they forgot as up they grew." The quotation is even more apposite to Miss Modell's novel than to Mr. Rosenfeld's. Here is the story of Ellen Cole, who at twenty-one might still have chosen between the line of her own youthful decency and generosity and the line of her unfeeling parents or of whom the fact that the choice has already been determined in favor of the parental direction could be discerned by only the most penetrating eye but who, in maturity, has so accepted the parental way that it is as if the instincts of love and graciousness had never been. At thirty-eight, the potential rebel of seventeen years earlier may still parade the fashionable small flags of emancipation but she has in fact become the very blood and spirit of educated conformity. She is married to a successful, highly ethical lawyer;

she is the mother of a four-year-old exemplification of the best theories of child training; she is the mistress of a home built upon our most advanced and conscientious domestic principles. Ellen might have been dreamed up in a conference between the editors of *Good Housekeeping* and *PM*. Beautifully even-tempered with her family, just friendly enough with servants and elevator boys, just enough against fascism and in favor of ration points, Miss Modell's heroine is the archetype of modern progressive young womanhood. She meshes perfectly with the wheels of our present-day practical idealism—until she must meet the kind of emotional test with which it is the proper task of the novelist to confront such a nicely packaged product. The test of Ellen Cole is the sudden appearance in her life of Brigitta, the seventeen-year-old child of her youthful indiscretion, who has been raised by acquaintances abroad. It is in Ellen's behavior to Brigitta that we discover the depths of self-interest and the atrophy of heart that can lie behind a front of so much seeming decency.

But although this, I feel sure, is the story Miss Modell meant to explore for its psychological and social truth—and she may even have intended a good deal of satire of manners in her devastatingly accurate picture of Ellen Cole's way of life—what she has actually got down on paper is no more than a middling-thick "problem" novel: "What would you have done in Ellen's place?" as one reviewer inquires.

The discrepancy may be accounted for in several ways. Superficially it may be the result of a mistake in formulating Ellen's character. If Ellen is to be regarded either as the embodiment of the moral and emotional degeneration to which all people are prone as they advance in years or as a representative of a section of society whose gifts of self-deception are particularly well-developed and peculiarly dangerous, her conduct must be held strictly within the sphere of the normal. But it is not normal for a woman to desert her child at birth as Ellen did, and it is distinctly pathological for her to forget the child's existence for seventeen years. Ellen's coldness to Brigitta when the girl reappears has only a personal, clinical logic; it has no wider significance.

On a somewhat deeper level, the failure of Miss Modell's book can be ascribed to the imbalance between the quality of her perceptions and the quality of her literary standards. I have the impression that the author of *The Sound of Years* has seen and felt a lot better than she has read, and that she lacks, not the courage of her knowledge of people, but a literary model which would teach her how to be as courageous as so much insight requires. This lack reveals itself in a style which creates no overtones of the author's own comment on her narrative but many overtones of *New Yorker* chic.

Finally, the inadequacy of Miss Modell's performance may be understood as the responsibility of the culture that produced it. There is marked cultural meaning in Miss Modell's relation to her heroine. I mention the error of making Ellen so pathologically cold: is this merely an accident of conception? Is it not the single means available to Miss Modell to separate herself from a central character with whom at all other points her culture presses her to be sympathetic? Ours is a society that imputes an unquestionable virtue to Ellen's kind of woman. It constantly tells us that anyone so social-minded, so domestically dutiful, so slim, so tastefully dressed, so literate, so unfrigid (in her head), so colloquial, so able to mock herself, is the best possible modern female being. Miss Modell knows better, but where does our society give her an ideal to set against the Ellen ideal? What language does it teach her for attacking the plausible idiom of Ellen Coles? To undertake to destroy the Ellen-image of modern woman would constitute a revolutionary cultural act, by extension even a revolutionary political act. Although Miss Modell is enough of an artist to have conceived such a purpose, she is not enough of an artist to have executed it.

I have been judging *The Sound of Years* by what it promises but falls short of achieving; to do less would be a grave injustice to a writer of Miss Modell's potentiality. This is not to say that

172

the novel, even as it stands, is not in many ways unusually pleasing. The description of the child Brigitta is entirely delightful. The handling of the book's subsidiary characters is deft and satisfying. And almost all of Miss Modell's reporting of manners is evidence of more than a sharp eye; it is proof of a mind able to penetrate well beneath the surface of deportment.

June 22, 1946

Somewhere along in the middle of *The Hucksters* by Frederic Wakeman (Rinehart, $2.50) there is a scene in which Kay Dorrance, in love with Vic Norman, the novel's hero, tries to persuade him to give up his successful distasteful radio career and write a book. "I told you I am not an artist," Vic protests. "I don't feel like an artist. I don't have any position about life that is even slightly artistic." Since Mr. Wakeman has up to now clearly been speaking through this hero, it is ungenerous to suspect him of playing a double game when he has Vic assess his artistic potentialities this cruelly. Actually we have no reason to accuse Mr. Wakeman of supposing that *The Hucksters* is even slightly artistic. The responsibility for raising his book to the status of a best-seller and submitting it to literary examination rests elsewhere than with the author himself, chiefly with the Book of the Month Club which has bestowed on it the literary accolade of making it its June selection.

But negligible as *The Hucksters* may be as literature, it is anything but negligible as sociology. An exposé of radio advertising, it tells us little about the role of commercialism in radio that we could not ourselves comprehend simply by listening to the commercial programs on the air; but what it does tell us which we might not guess is how big the stakes are and how they are won or lost, the quality of the personal emotions it creates and feeds on, the values by which a Vic Norman publicly lives and privately dies. Both knowingly and unknowingly Mr. Wakeman has compiled a Baedeker to the spirit of modern corruption.

By modern I mean the year 1944, which is the period of Mr. Wakeman's story. We make a great mistake if we assume that any social disorder is ever static. A comparison of Mr. Wakeman's report on the radio business with, say, Kaufman and Hart's report on the movie business in 1930, the date of *Once in a Lifetime,* shows a distinct increase both in objective horror and subjective fear. There is a passion of contempt in *The Hucksters* which I cannot remember in the Kaufman and Hart play: it makes Mr. Wakeman's book much closer to evangelism than to farce—and I am certain this describes something far more significant than a mere temperamental difference between the author of *The Hucksters* and the authors of *Once in a Lifetime.* A great deal of troubled water has flowed under the bridge since the days when to be tempted by Hollywood was only the good clean fun of being tempted to sell your sanity along with your talents. The sell-out of 1930 was an innocent pastime compared to the sell-out of 1944, when we have had fourteen years in which to learn that if we barter our wits, our souls are likely to be included in the package. Vic Norman himself has an insight of which his predecessors in the entertainment field would have been incapable. He has perceived that the pressures in our individual lives are not unrelated to the pressures in the world. He begins to glimpse the connection between his terror and degradation and the terror and degradation that are undermining whole nations. His desperate need to find an "out" from the tyranny of the Beautee Soap account reproduces, in however paltry terms, the need of large sections of mankind to find freedom: hence the piety and anger that play around Mr. Wakeman's satire.

This is perhaps to take *The Hucksters* on higher ground than it consciously claims. It is to take it, I suppose, on the level of art, and both art and a happy family life are conditions of existence which Mr. Wakeman's hero can scarcely hope for; they are beyond his income—when Vic earns $25,000 a year, plus bonuses, he can afford antique furniture but he can only dream of owning his heart's desire, an El Greco. Similarly, with $25,000 a year Vic can afford an affair with Kay Dorrance, but he cannot afford marriage and the support of her and her two children. Indeed, the very merit of Kay lies in her unavailability to a mere $25,000 hireling, for Kay is not only extremely well-born and as beautiful as Ingrid Bergman but already the wife, albeit unsatisfied, of a man of great wealth and distinction and the mother of a pair of children on whose questionable charms Vic puts a high financial as well as human price. The economic-moral principle on which Vic operates is plain enough: unless you are fortunate enough to inherit the gifts of the truly good life you must either sell your soul to acquire them or be denied them forever. Thus is economic reality at odds with idealism.

But in Mr. Wakeman's book idealism is circumscribed by more than economic necessity. One begins to sense an equation between economic reality and Original Sin. The mere act of earning a living is a falling from grace; therefore for most people salvation is not of this life. I do not mean that Mr. Wakeman actually uses the language of religion but certainly he lays a sturdy psychological foundation for it. Throughout *The Hucksters* we are aware of its buried assumption that everything that is attainable is worthless and that only that which is inaccessible is good and desirable. The values of Vic Norman's "real" life are such things as good food and liquor, "sleepable-with" women, $35 neckties, "21," the Century and the Super Chief, and he opposes to them a series of virtually Platonic ideals: the ideal of democracy, a self-lacerating ideal of service to one's country, an ideal of "constructive" work (engineering, for example), an absolute of pure love and perfect sex. To study Mr. Wakeman's systems of reality and idealism is to shudder for a civilization that proposes such widely separated alternatives, and we recall the not dissimilar oppositions that foretold Aldous Huxley's religious conversion.

Naturally there is also a strong subjective factor in Vic's revulsion from his life. It is not only because expensive neckties, fast trains, glamour girls, all the rewards of success, are mean in themselves that Mr. Wakeman's hero comes to scorn them. It is also because they are *his* that they lose their magic. The achievement is no better than the achiever, and who, better than the achiever himself, knows the integrity he has sacrificed to be a success? Whatever he touches must be defiled since he himself is pitch. But how remain undefiled in a world of pitch? In this fashion spins the familiar coin of sentimental cynicism: the one side self-hatred, the other self-pity. It is the recognizable coin of the half-realm—the realm of half-thinking and half-feeling—of the parasitical professions.

But the point is, of course, that there have always, at all times and in all places, been parasitical professions. The advertising-radio man of today was the adventurer-mountebank of yesterday. Back of every Vic Norman stretches a long line of people who have lived by their wits, making a good if not always peaceful thing of the gullibility of the public. The phenomenon is not new to society but what is new is the seriousness with which we and Vic himself now take it, a seriousness for which, obviously, there is sound reason. For if we can no longer laugh at a Vic Norman it is because there are too many of him and he has too much power. We could make a comic or romantic or picaresque novel out of a river-boat gambler because the river-boat gambler was not forming our society; he was a special instance, at odds with the dominant forces of his culture. But a Vic Norman is neither a special case nor at odds with the dominant influences of his day. He *is* a dominant feature of his day. Already he controls important avenues of communication and education, and at the drop of a hat he can control government and our actual physical as well as spiritual fates. (Vic himself was in the OWI, Mr. Wakeman tells us.) To read a book like *The Hucksters,* then, as mere amusement—indeed, as anything less than a frightening document of our times—is to fool ourselves that when we are given the radio spectacle, we are given a show for which only the producers pay. Soon enough we shall have to reckon the cost to ourselves.

Having been told that William Saroyan's *The Adventures of Wesley Jackson* (Harcourt, Brace, $2.75) was the first anti-war novel of World War II, I ignored the warning of nausea induced by its opening sentence—"My name is Wesley Jackson, I'm nineteen years old, and my favorite song is 'Valencia' "—and followed it through the whole of its maundering maudlin length. It is a form of punishment distinctly not recommended to friends of this column. Even the most masochistic reader should be content with a lightning tour of Mr. Saroyan's chapter headings—Wesley Makes an Astrological Bargain, Sees a Star, and Learns a Secret; Wesley Escapes a Life of Lying and Dreams a Terrible Dream; Wesley Witnesses a Strange Sight, Receives a Number of Letters Addressed to the People of the World, and Is Visited by His Father; Wesley Is Banished to Ohio and Has a Farewell Drink with the Modern Woman; Wesley Tries to Tell Joe Foxhall What He's Gotten Hep to, and Pop Tries to Tell Wesley Something He Can't Remember; Wesley Goes A.W.O.L. Looking for Pop and Finds a Woman Singing "Valencia" in the Snow; Wesley and Jill Cleave Together for a Son if It Is the Will of God. There are seventy-six of them.

That Mr. Saroyan's novel adds up to some kind of anti-war position there is no question. Neither Wesley Jackson nor any-one else his author trusts wished to be drafted; no one Mr. Saroyan respects has any conviction of what he is fighting for or finds either joy or intelligence in army life. And conceivably it took a certain courage for Mr. Saroyan to announce his strong sentiments against war so soon after the termination of hostili-ties. As to his specific indictments of army organization, temper, and procedure, while of course no civilian is equipped to sup-port or refute them, the most non-military reader must recog-nize the thread of illogic that runs through them. One notes, for instance, that whereas the unwillingness to go overseas and be killed is presented as proof of the virtue of Wesley and his friends, the same distaste for danger and death is proof among the officers only of their cowardice. One observes that when the higher-ups have recourse to "influence" Mr. Saroyan offers this as evidence of their venality, but when the Wesleys of the army use influence Mr. Saroyan offers it as evidence of the brotherhood of man. One need be little a moral absolutist to hold judgment in reserve before such an easy (and quite unconscious) relativism.

The brotherhood of man has always been Mr. Saroyan's Atlantic, Pacific, and Indian Ocean Charter. What is freshly interesting about *The Adventures of Wesley Jackson* is the further insight it gives us into the kind of man with whom Mr. Saroyan feels his strong brotherly connection, and its data on the structure of the society he opts for. The people with whom he would make fellowship are vagrants, half-criminals, the insane, prostitutes, drunkards—all the rootless elements of the population who, since they do not fit comfortably into our present system, Mr. Saroyan believes to have some special knowledge of happiness. His social ideal has nothing in common with the socialist ideal. He has no bias in favor of the proletariat; indeed, his society gives a particularly warm welcome to millionaires, provided they are sufficiently eccentric. His Utopia, like John Steinbeck's, is a state of irresponsibility. And in relation to his society of irresponsibles, the Writer—the capitals are Mr. Saroyan's own—has two functions: he is its promotion manager and he also writes its popular songs.

Expectably, the songs are songs of love. Mr. Saroyan sings in praise of the love of man for man, of man for woman, of parents for children (especially of fathers for their unborn sons), of children for parents. He sings of our love of God, of our love of our friends who are called our enemies, of everything, in fact, except our love of our enemies who are called our friends: these he hates with un-Christian fervor. For the aggression of war Mr. Saroyan offers the substitute of the aggression of love. Obviously he doesn't himself recognize his pious emotions as even a weapon of self-defense let alone a counter-attack. But I can scarcely imagine the reader who at the end of 285 pages of Mr. Saroyan's suffocating affection would not sooner face a machine-gun than be loved to death by Wesley Jackson.

There is perhaps one further point worth calling attention to in Mr. Saroyan's book, the curious anatomy of its sexual emotions. The naughty imaginings of a little boy—all a matter of tearing off women's clothes (chiefly older women than Wesley), of "sporting around" to the tunes of Brahms and Tschaikowsky, and of getting for nothing what other men pay for—combine with ambitions of such purity and exaltation that they can be rendered only in the Biblical language of cleaving and begetting. Although Wesley Jackson occupies his army leaves very efficiently and entirely gratis between the Modern Woman and the madam of an expensive house, these amorous adventures are shown to be merely affectionate interludes in the serious business of searching for a girl-wife. Eventually he finds "darling Jill" and marries her: he holds her in his arms until morning and "it was the same many nights." And when Jill is finally allowed "to take unto herself his heart's delight in her . . . to see if their smiling together might be, by the grace of God, themselves together in their own son," Wesley records the happy consummation in the family Bible.

After the viscous experience of Mr. Saroyan, almost anything, even Somerset Maugham's *Then and Now* (Doubleday, $2.50), would come as a breath of free air. In its own fashion, however, Mr. Maugham's new book too is something to cause the spirits to fail. A re-creation of Machiavelli's life in the years that preceded the writing of *The Prince* and *Mandragola, Then and Now* alternates between a textbook dryness of historical pedagogy and an embarrassingly primitive effort to liven things up. "He had not spared his wit and wisdom to teach him the ways of the world, how to make friends and influence people. And this was his reward, to have his girl snatched away from him under his very nose." Such is the idiom in which Mr. Maugham acquaints us with the working of Machiavelli's mind! Perhaps not every page of *Then and Now* is the equal of this in vulgarity but few of them fail to proclaim, by their deadness or coyness, its lamentable inadequacy to the historical subject it purports to fictionalize. The single section of *Then and Now* which at all reveals the practiced hand of the craftsman for which its author is renowned is the passage in which Machiavelli starts giving a literary form to an adventure he has just passed through; Mr. Maugham's version of the transmutation of actual events into drama is engaging. But even this isolate instance of pleasure in watching fact being alchemized into fiction is shadowed by the realization of how little *Then and Now* itself commands this sorcerer's art.

July 6, 1946

Apparently the vogue for extravagant family reminiscence has hit our English cousins too. Although the main burden of Nancy Mitford's popular *The Pursuit of Love* (Random House, $2.50) is romantic, at least its first half can be read as an English *Life with Father.*

The tyrannical patriarch of *The Pursuit of Love* is Uncle Matthew (also known as "Fa," also Lord Alconleigh), a great patriot and xenophobe—he particularly hates Germans—a believer in horses and home cooking, and a gentleman of such rages that he grinds down several pairs of dentures a year. According to Miss Mitford, the whimsical graces of English upper-class children flourish mightily in such rocky soil. Valiant little riders and hunters, the Radlett youngsters are also given to a morbid sensibility about pet mice, to cute spontaneous verse-making, to dreams of love in an attic linen closet. The only warm spot in the great country house, this closet is called the Hon Cupboard. It is the place where the children play their favorite game of parceling the world into Hons and non-Hons. Hons are the offspring of Lords; a non-Hon is anyone the children dislike. Honorary membership in the Hons is bestowed upon a favorite stable boy, and we are little surprised when, in later years, the Spanish Loyalists can also be referred to as "terrific Hons." But some time before this natural widening of the Alconleigh horizon, Miss Mitford's conscious humor has begun to thin; from childhood reminiscence her novel has progressed to the emotional history of Linda, most beautiful and delicate-minded of Uncle Matthew's daughters, who after two unsatisfactory marriages, to a banker and a Communist, finds true love with a French duke who picks her up in the Gare du Nord. Miss Mitford has quite a few good things to say for French nobility—as lovers, as keepers of women (teaching Linda how to dress properly, the Duke throws her nasty English mink into the wastepaper basket), as doers of their Free French duty. Such fun as you will find in the so-to-speak adult sections of *The Pursuit of Love* is largely unintentional.

Notice should be called to one episode in Miss Mitford's novel which is so genuinely witty that one would expect more than one gets from its author—the meeting between Uncle Matthew and his new brother-in-law, a mild-spoken, rather wan literary man, as learned as he is hypochondriacal. The family has been fearful about introducing this new relation, convinced that Uncle Matthew will despise him with all the vigor of his own non-intellectuality. On the contrary, Uncle Matthew conceives a deep respect and affection for the newcomer based on the latter's refusal to discover the least value in any of the Alconleigh household treasures. A much-cherished bronze is pronounced Japanese and not Chinese, therefore worthless; a collection of minerals, legendarily "good enough for a museum," is diagnosed as diseased and not worth keeping. "I never saw such a fella," says Uncle Matthew in delight before a scholarship of such destructive proportions.

July 13, 1946

Helen Howe's new novel, *We Happy Few* (Simon and Schuster, $2.75), is about a Boston girl who learns to be an American woman. Bred in the isolate culture of Boston and its environs, Dorothea Natwick is priggish and self-absorbed, oversensible of the social and intellectual values which are her birthright, a flagrantly inconspicuous consumer of very expensive advantages. The process of her education is the process of opening out horizons beyond herself and her immediate world until her spirit includes all the multitudes that are democratic America.

The chief point, that is, of Miss Howe's novel is the equation it makes between parochialism and infantilism, between maturity and the ability to encompass the multitudinousness of life beyond the borders of one's own parish. But curiously enough, it is in the first half of her book, when Miss Howe is concentrating on the embattled culture of her small section of New England, before she introduces her heroine to the enlarging experience of the great West, that she manages not only to be most entertaining but also to suggest the most mature and universal meanings. It is in the early portions of *We Happy Few,* laid in Constable where Dorothea's father is master of a boys' school and where her mother has such a happy field for her eccentricities of pride, or in Cambridge, where Dorothea, as the wife of a Harvard instructor, continues the Natwick tradition, that Miss Howe, for all that she is dealing with such highly special individuals, yet tells us most about our least special selves. This is of course the genius of satire, that, with the exaggeration of humor, it extends the particular into general truth. But in the second half of her novel Miss Howe deserts Boston to have Dorothea discover the range and humanity of America. The selflessness that neither marriage, motherhood, adultery, war

182

work nor death has been able to teach Dorothea, an experience of ordinary Americanism does teach her—the lesson of democracy finally cuts Dorothea down to size. The only flaw is that democracy itself gets cut down to size along with Dorothea: *We Happy Few* ends with the wide American panorama presenting itself as little more than a series of small-spirited, harassed, and unhappy people who in their untutored fashion are just as egotistical as Miss Howe's well-educated heroine. The commonality of man, therapy for a poorly balanced emotional nature, shows itself to be largely a matter of helping make sandwiches with the other ladies or holding a neighbor's crying child. Miss Howe's novel falls apart in the middle and the break, it seems to me, is the result of a fault not so much of narrative structure as of basic idea.

The idea is a popular one. Miss Howe is scarcely alone among current novelists in regarding democracy—or the proletariat, or the fight against fascism, or a sweeping view of the multitudinousness of American life—as if it were medicine for the sick soul of the modern individual. One recalls the novel of a few years ago in which a young woman was cured of neurosis by giving visas to refugees, or a more recent fictional instance where the heroine was saved from nervous collapse by joining the movement for cooperatives. As a matter of fact, if I were asked to name, on the evidence of contemporary fiction, the chief trend in our progressive literary culture I would no doubt point to this mechanical notion that the individual finds himself by losing himself in some larger social manifestation.

That, despite her belief in this kind of social therapy, Miss Howe herself undermines it by giving us so dreary a picture of indiscriminate American life speaks well, I think, for her deeper novelistic impulses—I say this without irony. It is as if the eye and ear that are able to catch the subtle nuances of the first sections of *We Happy Few* seem almost inevitably to betray Miss Howe's formulations of conscience. While Miss Howe's program calls for Dorothea's regeneration through acceptance of some vast body of corporate virtue called the United States of Democracy, her literary senses feel out all the petty snobberies and prides that are bound to inform a nation of human beings. One can only hope that in future Miss Howe will trust her senses, and that her literary career will proceed not by good works but by her gifts of grace.

August 24, 1946

Robert Penn Warren's *All The King's Men* (Harcourt, Brace, $3.00) is not the first novel to draw its inspiration from the career of Huey Long. Some years ago there was John Dos Passos's *Number One,* which I have not read, and a few seasons ago there was Hamilton Basso's *Sun in Capricorn,* which, as I remember it, dealt rather freely with the actual life of the Louisiana Kingfish. Mr. Warren would seem to stay closer to his original: he gives us a complete biography, from the days when his Willie Stark was an earnest, urgent, back-country farm boy to his early years in law practice and his first venture into politics, through his flashing rise to political power and the governorship, to—finally—his assassination. I say "would seem" because, acquainted with only the broadest outlines of Long's life, I have no way of knowing how much of Mr. Warren's detail is a matter of record and how much supplied by the novelist's imagination. But Mr. Warren offers his story as fiction and the question of factual accuracy need therefore not be raised.

And a very remarkable piece of novel-writing *All the King's Men* is. For sheer virtuosity, for the sustained drive of its prose, for the speed and evenness of its pacing, for its precision of language and its genius of colloquialism, I doubt that it can be matched in American fiction. Mr. Warren's method is that of great photography; one thinks of the camera of Walker Evans inching over mile after mile of the South, piling up its record of personal portraits and place portraits and portraits of things, catching fact after fact of the Southern heat and mystery, indolence and venality and despair.

Nor is its imposing documentary power the only recommendation of *All the King's Men*. There is also its largeness of intention. Mr. Warren's study of a political leader investigates the moral relativism inherent in the historical process: it might be described as a fictional demonstration of Hegel's philosophy of history. With Hegel, Mr. Warren appears to be saying that "spirit" is born out of the ruck of living and the clash of self-seeking wills. He is questioning the absolutes of good and evil which are so much the assumption of present-day political morality.

But all relativistic positions are peculiarly liable to misinterpretation, and especially the Hegelian relativism must be read very purely in order not to be translated into a justification of means by their end, or not to be understood as the belief that good most frequently has its source in evil. And it is in fact difficult *not* to infer from *All the King's Men* that Willie Stark's absolute power is validated by such public benefactions as the fine hospital he builds, and that we should welcome the Willie Stark type of political unpleasantness as a step in political progress.

In part, the temptation to this reading of Mr. Warren's novel is perhaps an inevitable result of translating a man of history into a man of fiction. Concerned with the world historical figure, Hegel was concerned only with his historical, not with his ethical aspect, but fiction always deals primarily with individuals and only by implication with philosophical abstractions, and when Mr. Warren personifies his abstractions, as the novelist must, he in effect alters what is a way of viewing history into a system of personal morality from which in turn we evolve a system of political morality. Thus Willie Stark is not a stage in the evolutionary development of the idea of force. First he is a person on whom his author exercises ethical judgment. And if only because he is the hero of the novel, we assume this judgment to be largely admiring or approving. The result is that a demagogue's dull ambivalence, compounded half of his obsession with power and half of a soft generosity and idealism, is made to stand for the dialectical struggle of good and evil both in man and in society.

But it is not merely because he is the hero of the novel that we assume that Stark is approved by his author. We also have the word for it of Mr. Warren's narrator. *All the King's Men* is told through the point of view of a young newspaperman-researcher attached to Stark, one of those prefabricated figures out of the city room whom Mr. Warren endows with a wonderful eye but with no equivalent moral vision. "Wise," cynical, tough but touchable, Jack Burden is better educated than his usual counterparts in fiction and the movies, but his values are scarcely more fortifying. He is the kind of man, for instance, who, when he perceives that the only thing alive in the face of an Okie to whom he gives a lift on the road is the twitch near his eye, goes on to evolve from this observation an embarrassing maudlin philosophy, a phantasy of the Great Twitch as a god of doom. More significant, he is the kind of man who feels virtually no emotion about his share in the blackmail of a friend, a blackmail that leads the friend to shoot himself, except the pleasure of recognition that a good—a truth—has come from it. But although Jack Burden is so essentially shabby a person that he vulgarizes any thought he entertains or acts upon, it is to him that Mr. Warren entrusts an idea of history that requires the nicest discrimination. It is Burden's morally ambiguous evaluation of Stark that we are obliged to accept as Mr. Warren's.

And if the poor quality of Burden's moral awareness is responsible for most of the ethical and political confusion of *All the King's Men,* so must it in some measure account, I think, for the failure of Mr. Warren's novel to achieve the stature commensurate with its author's remarkable talent. Perceived as it is through the commonplace mind of Mr. Warren's narrator, it is the inner human mystery that Mr. Warren misses as he pursues, with all his own marvelous resources of language, the mystery of the historical process.

In so far as Nelson Gidding's *End over End* (Viking, $2.50) stays with its main job of telling us about an American flier shot down and captured by the Germans in Italy and kept in solitary confinement in the hope that he will give his captors useful military information, it tells an interesting story. Like his hero, Dale Stribling, Mr. Gidding was himself a flier and a prisoner of war; his account of Stribling's prison experience has this ring of authenticity. But although a similar autobiographical accuracy no doubt operates through the rest of Mr. Gidding's novel, it doesn't give it similar substance. Unlike the prison scenes, the flashbacks to Stribling's life before the war are without dramatic weight. Indeed, in their closeness to their source in Mr. Gidding's own experience they seem only egotistical: an inflation, by means of pretentious prose, of lamentably thin material. Thus we learn that the captive flier was once a child, that he had a mother and father, that his mother and father were divorced, that he belonged to a serious literary group at preparatory school, that he thought as his whole generation thought about the possibility of another war, that he was a helluva guy for a girl to love, that he loved a girl named Barbara, that Barbara was pleased that he smoked cigars—in short, that nothing very interesting ever happened to him before he was shot down by the Germans or, rather, that many things happened to him which were important to himself but which he can make of small consequence to the reader. In common with so many young novelists, Mr. Gidding makes the mistake of supposing that the subjective approach to fiction requires merely the ability to see oneself as a fictional subject—I am, therefore I am a novelist.

Also, like many of his contemporaries, Mr. Gidding makes the error of confusing the soft and easy associative process with the hard processes of the imagination. His prose suffers from that

187

most wearisome of clichés, the attempt to appear bold and fresh by making a rude distortion of the familiar: "Home was a seventy-seven layer cake, three miles of white skin above a nylon stocking, a cabin half in the sky and half on the beach, a hot-plate that kept your dreams always warm." Surely it is a sad misuse of the stream-of-consciousness to offer such a poor trickle of associations as a substitute for the activity of mind.

November 9, 1946

Although all of Arthur Koestler's books are tied together by their concern with the large moral-political problems of our time, especially those on the intellectual left, there is an unusually close connection between his last novel, *Arrival and Departure,* and his new novel, *Thieves in the Night* (Macmillan, $2.75). *Arrival and Departure* was about a young man so torn between the desire to act upon his political convictions and the wish to retreat into a life of private satisfactions that he suffered a functional paralysis and had to be psychoanalyzed. In the course of his treatment Mr. Koestler's hero discovered that an important part of his political impulse had a neurotic source but his story ended not with the affirmation of his ability to pursue his political course on an unneurotic basis but with something quite else again, the refusal to be deterred from his political choice by any question of motive. *Arrival and Departure,* in other words, was an up-to-date version of the old reason-versus-religion opposition, with psychoanalysis proxying for reason and with the free radical impulse proxying for religion. Its conclusions could be summed up as follows: that the therapy for indecision is not to seek further clarification but to seek further blindness; that the definition of free will is the freedom to ignore the uncomfortable logic of determinism; that the cure for doubt is not knowledge but, as in the classical theological instance, more faith.

Thieves in the Night takes up where *Arrival and Departure* left off. I do not mean that it has the same setting and characters: Mr. Koestler's new book is set in Palestine, and its central character and author's advocate is a young Englishman living in a Jewish commune. But despite the fact that *Thieves in the Night* is very informative about the complex Jewish national situation, I think that to read it as only a study of this immediate problem is to read it in far too limited a context. *Arrival and Departure* ended with Mr. Koestler's protestation of his faith in the life of action. *Thieves in the Night* is a statement of the articles of this faith: it tells us how Mr. Koestler thinks we ought to act. Its program is applicable not merely to Palestine but everywhere.

The period of Mr. Koestler's story is 1937–39; its hero, a half-Jew, has moved to Palestine after an unpleasant sexual episode with an anti-Semitic Englishwoman. Not wholly Jewish, Joseph is enough of an emotional and intellectual outsider in Palestine to be able to view what goes on around him with an objectivity denied his wholly Jewish comrades. While he takes a full happy share in the life of his commune he becomes increasingly aware that it will require more than dedication to insure its survival. Little by little he becomes convinced, on the sound evidence which is public record, that the British are selling out the Jewish homeland to appease the Arabs, that Palestine is another Czechoslovakia. When the German refugee girl whom he loves is raped and killed by the Arabs, and the deed, instead of being allowed to disappear in the government files, is avenged by the Jewish terrorist organization, Joseph finally formulates what has long been germinating in him, his sympathy with those who favor direct political action. He joins the terrorist underground, the Stern group that has broken off from Haganah, the old moderate Jewish defense organization.

This is *Thieves in the Night* in barest outline: anyone acquainted with Mr. Koestler's work will know with what skill and daring he develops this synopsis, the circumstantiality with which Mr. Koestler's novel suggests the variousness of the

Palestinian scene, and the philosophical ingenuity with which it traces Joseph's intellectual evolution. In a day when all reporters are supposed to be political philosophers, Mr. Koestler is distinguished for his actual grasp of political complexities, his dialectical power, his journalistic flair. Leaving out of accounts its moral point, *Thieves in the Night* is an extraordinary weaving together of the many tangled threads—Jewish, Arab, and British—that make up the Palestinian pattern and a remarkable document of bold social observation.

But unfortunately its moral point must be very much taken into account, and even examined in a larger context than that of the Palestinian situation. Appearing just now, when feelings about the Jewish homeland are running especially high, *Thieves in the Night* is bound to arouse an intense response. This excitation of a particularly Jewish reaction is regrettable. For implicitly and at times even explicitly, Mr. Koestler's novel not only defends the use of terror in Palestine, it also defends the principle of terror. The fact that it weights its case for direct action with the emotions which most of us feel about the immediate Jewish tragedy is almost bound to blind us to what I should have thought would be the main concern of a philosophical novelist: the vital difference between passionately meeting the demands of a particular time and place and the promulgation of a "rational" program of passion.

As I understand it, the present situation in Palestine is so critical that even the most moderate factions have been forced to capitulate to the use of extreme methods of self-defense. The question is, whether this justifies the formulation, at the comfortable distance of literature and political theory, of a philosophy of extreme action. It is surely not the same moral thing to be a Jew confronted by an Arab with a gun in his hand, or an anti-Nazi confronted by a Nazi with a gun in his hand, or a Negro confronted by a white lyncher, and to be a writer with a pen in his hand. We have all of us learned in recent years, if we did not know it before, that there are times in which immediate extreme action is demanded and when to stop to scruple is to be destroyed. This bitter knowledge does not sanction us to forget that moral reflection is still our everlasting duty so long as we have even the illusion of safety. Certainly it is the duty of the novelist not only to remind us of the difference between the emotions of exigency and the emotions of premeditation but also to remind us of the moral consequences of exigent conduct upon the individual who is forced to it. In the sense that *Thieves in the Night* ignores the fact that the morality of conduct is in so many instances dependent upon our distance from whatever it is that activates or de-activates our scruples, it is as much an offense against decency as all the this-is-the-way-to-kill-Nazis novels produced at a several-thousand-miles remove from the Nazi horror. Failing to concern itself with the *tragedy* of necessary violence, it is morally irresponsible.

In *Thieves in the Night,* as always in the novel, it is finally the atmosphere surrounding its principles, rather than the principles themselves, that condition our judgment. The members of Mr. Koestler's underground take a wry amusement in referring to themselves as "Jewish Fascists." (This is of course the name by which they are called by Zionists of other position.) But if the reader experiences sympathetic wryness at this designation, it disappears as the novel goes into its detailed description of the organization of the terrorist movement: its military hierarchies and discipline, its schoolboy oaths, its face-slapping ("That will teach you to hold fast to your gun"), its general smell of Nazi *Blutbruderschaft.* "The Hebrew underground began as purely political movement," Joseph writes in his journal,

and has developed more and more mystic accents. Simeon showed me yesterday some of Yair-Stern's poetry. It has a strange archaic fervor—quite untranslatable:

> My teacher carried his praying-scarf in a velvet bag to the synagogue:
> Even so carry I my sacred gun to the Temple
> That its voice may pray for us.

. . . Though he tries to hide it, Simeon has an almost religious admiration for Yair-Stern. He seems to regard him as a kind of gunman-messiah.

191

Mr. Koestler's Joseph may find it difficult to translate the poetry of terrorism from Hebrew into English. I find it disconcertingly easy to translate it into its essential meaning in any language.

Here, then, in actual practice is the faith that triumphed over reason in *Arrival and Departure*—and a curious form of religious dedication it is. But it is not peculiar to Mr. Koestler; it represents a growing tendency among what we would once have called liberal intellectuals. The assimilation of violence to salvation is not a new idea, but surely only the profound moral confusion of our times could suggest calling a fighter in the cause of freedom a gunman-messiah.

November 23, 1946

For some years now John P. Marquand has occupied a special place among our novelists. Virtually singlehanded he has held the line immediately behind a possible first rank of current writers. Without transcending the high-grade commodity level, he has done a great deal to raise our standards of what a literary commodity can be. Without urging us to regard his novels as "important," he has done more than any writer of our time to close the dangerous gap between important and popular fiction. But now, with his new novel, *B. F.'s Daughter* (Little, Brown, $2.75), one is for the first time aware of Mr. Marquand's own sharp sense of the divisions among the social-intellectual classes, and of himself as spokesman for an embattled majority. There is a new note of defensiveness not only in Mr. Marquand's satire of the long-hairs but also in the main argument of his story. *B. F.'s Daughter* is a study of what constitutes adjustment for a typical modern woman: one could be willing to accept the traditional sexual values for which the book pleads and still be disconcerted by the shoddy terms in which they are cast and the identification Mr. Marquand makes between domestic traditionalism and traditionalism in all spheres of thought. One can scarcely believe that Mr. Marquand means to say what his book so plainly implies—that thinking in any direction to the left of dead center is aberrant, unreliable, or immature; of such a thoroughgoing conservatism one feels that its advocate has really let himself be pushed too far by those to whom he is opposed. As a matter of fact, even technically Mr. Marquand's story betrays its uncertainty: the novel skips around in time in a fashion that is both confusing and useless. And there are pages of empty "bright" talk which are disturbingly reminiscent of that other uneasy champion of unhappy millionaires, Philip Barry.

Although Polly Fulton, the heroine of *B. F.'s Daughter,* is the daughter of a very rich industrialist, she has many of the traits of the contemporary ideal of young womanhood, and pleasant traits they are too—she is intelligent, spirited, humorous, warmhearted, independent, generous, competent, and loyal. But Polly is also, like so many nice modern girls, bewildered by what to do with her life. In natural revolt against her upbringing she marries, not the steady sensible Bob Tasmin of her father's choice, but Tom Brett, an erratic intellectual and New Dealer who she supposes will introduce her to a whole new field for her energies and make her feel useful. But it turns out that she has little outlet for her energies except in domination of her husband. When, upon the outbreak of war, Tom comes into his own on the Washington front, Polly is left high and dry. As to busy successful Tom, he finds his docile secretary much more comforting than a spirited wife, and even Bob, whom Polly meets again, refuses to give up his well-ordered if unexciting marriage for the sake of love for a former sweetheart. At the end of Mr. Marquand's novel Polly is a sad girl although she is at least wiser to the extent of having learned that a woman's sole happiness lies in home, children, and acceptance of the way of life set down for her by a strong-willed man.

With Mr. Marquand's flair for social observation, the story of Polly Fulton is of course never as dull as this summary might suggest: the sections of *B. F.'s Daughter* that describe life among the high military are expectably pointed and amusing, and in general the book has a decent quota of its author's usual good reporting of how things and places look and how the social animal behaves. But dismal indeed is Mr. Marquand's projection of the domesticity that will cure Polly's restlessness—all a matter of playing a good game of bridge and golf, of joining one's husband for nice walks in the country with the dogs, of (no doubt) voting Republican if that is what your husband's boss is voting. There is no question but that the twin virtue to traditional domesticity is political conservatism. Working out his sexual theme against the background of a larger social pattern, Mr. Marquand makes it clear that just as submissiveness to a strong man is the desirable female attitude, so acquiescence in a paternalistic rugged individualism and a regard for gentlemanliness are the desirable social attitudes in her suitable mate. How could the daughter of a great industrialist be expected to submit to a poseur and windbag like Tom Brett? But on the other hand, how could a college professor, a writer, a New Dealer be anything but a poseur and windbag? Mr. Marquand knows which political side the young women of America must be on if they wish to get over their growing pains and come to a healthy, wealthy, and wise maturity.

It is interesting that another recent novel, Elinor Rice's *Mirror, Mirror* (Duell, Sloan, and Pearce, $2.75), which also is about the problem of a modern woman, also weaves together its sexual theme and a political theme. But in Miss Rice's novel the heroine's background is one not of wealth and free enterprise but of poverty and socialist idealism: Mona Biro is the daughter of immigrant worker parents and her revolt consists in breaking with the family idealism and discovering the golden American opportunity. The narcissistic Mona is the very prototype of modern career women; she makes a great success of dress-designing. Just as Polly Fulton carries with her into maturity a father-figure in the person of Bob Tasmin, Miss Rice's heroine carries with her the father-figure of Toby Lang, a left-wing playwright. Even after he marries Mona, Toby still enjoys talk-ing with Mona's old socialist father about things as remote from the fashion world as the Spanish civil war. But neither his radi-cal impulse nor his literary ambition is strong enough to resist the pressure of his wife's large earnings and her willingness to indulge his every luxurious wish even at the cost of his man-hood. There is no principled resolution in *Mirror, Mirror* as there is in *B. F.'s Daughter,* no definition of the positive values a woman should seek in her life, but there is at least this much accord in the two books, that Miss Rice, like Mr. Marquand, assures us that a woman cannot buy happiness in the way that so many men can, and that the female domination of a marriage has within it the seeds of its own destruction.

The relation of Mona and Toby in *Mirror, Mirror* is a much more dynamic thing than the relation of Polly and Tom in *B. F.'s Daughter:* as fictional characters should, these two central figures in Miss Rice's novel take their story into their own hands instead of merely demonstrating various attitudes that their author would explore. In fact, Mr. Marquand's fault of treating people as personifications of ideas—I had almost said, as per-sonifications of political parties—is present only in the early sections of Miss Rice's book, where Mona's reality as a little girl is sacrificed to a kind of schematic representation of bud-ding female self-love. But a more important point of dissimilar-ity is the difference between Miss Rice's approach to the writers, would-be writers, and other assorted "intellectuals" whom Mona and Toby know and that of Mr. Marquand to Polly Fulton's Village friends. Miss Rice's satire is born not of defensiveness but of sympathetic knowledge.

Victoria Lincoln's three stories, *The Wind at My Back* (Rinehart, $2.50), will disappoint readers who enjoyed her successful novel, *February Hill.* It may also disappoint admirers of Miss Lincoln's sketches in the *New Yorker* because the new pieces have a preciousness that one has not usually noticed in her short fiction. Although each of the new stories has a young girl or young woman as its featured character, the volume is less typical of contemporary writing *about* women than of contemporary writing *by* women. Too carefully styled, too delicate in its perceptions, too thin in its narrative materials, *The Wind at My Back* is another instance of the exaggerated sensibility that is such a large part of women's current effort in literature.

November 30, 1946

Isabel Bolton's *Do I Wake or Sleep* (Scribner's, $2.50) is quite the best novel that has come my way in the four years I have been reviewing new fiction for this magazine. Small, anonymous in the welter of current books, it might very well have escaped my notice had Edmund Wilson not called attention to it in the *New Yorker:* the possibility of such an oversight will now become my reviewer's nightmare. Mr. Wilson's high praise prepared me, however, only for a work of exceptional talent. It did not prepare me—nothing but reading the book could—for the extraordinary process of revelation that Miss Bolton's novel turned out to be. Opening as a minor work of poetic sensibility, the kind of writing which Miss Bolton herself goes on to describe as achieved with the nerves rather than with the deeper centers, *Do I Wake or Sleep* gradually deepens to become a work of compelling insight; then the story progresses a bit farther, and the intelligence that one has hitherto noted simply as a restraining force upon poetic excess slowly proclaims its dominion over the novel's whole conception; finally one confronts the real shape and intellectual strength of the book, and recognizes the source of and response to a major fictional experience. I have no idea who Miss Bolton is: the jacket of the novel is provocatively uninformative. Whoever she is, she is the most important new novelist in the English language to appear in years. Whatever her literary apprenticeship, her book—it is a long novelette, really, rather than a novel—is the achievement of a fully matured artist.

And I say this despite the fact that *Do I Wake or Sleep* is not my favorite sort of fiction. It is a very closed book; to borrow a figure from music, its tone is covered. The method of Miss Bolton reminds me of that of Elizabeth Bowen's *The Death of the Heart:* there is the same privacy of approach to its materials, the same scalpel-like precision of observation and expression, the same ability to make the most delicate differentiations between appearances and reality, the same fierce insight into human error held in check by warm human sympathy. But one recalls that even at her best Miss Bowen has always suffered from a certain parochialism of the emotions; her intelligence, marked as it is, has never been able to relate the forces that move the individual with the forces that animate a whole society. Miss Bolton is preeminently concerned, and most successfully, with just this larger intellectual enterprise. Actually her closest affinity is with—I am afraid it must be said—Henry James. Not only in its subtlety and richness of perception but also in the boldness with which it stands up to its responsibilities, *Do I Wake or Sleep* is full in the Jamesian tradition. Even its theme is a present-day statement of a theme dear to James's heart, that of the relation of European and American culture.

There is a strong suggestion of James's Isabel Archer in Miss Bolton's Millicent, through whose eyes *Do I Wake or Sleep* is told. Millicent lacks the charm and beauty of the James *jeune fille américaine* but she shares with the heroine of *Portrait of a Lady* both the American energy of innocence and the American need to find importance in life by an act of dedication. When Miss Bolton's novel opens, Millicent, who had earlier rejected an English suitor on some impulse she has never understood, is about to make the saving gift of her love to Percy, an American novelist. But she is not at all sure that the gift is either advisable or welcome since Percy is also looking for salvation through self-immolation and has just found a new object of devotion in Bridget, a beautiful European refugee. Even more guiltily than Millicent, Percy, being an American too, wants to spend himself for an ideal; his literary sensibility is the other side of the coin of this nervous exacerbation. In the first chapters of *Do I Wake or Sleep* Millicent, Bridget, and Percy are dining together in the French Pavilion at the World's Fair. Over the table, against a background of the General Motors Building, the Futurama, and all the rest of the panoply of American success (the setting is a touch of genius), Bridget tells her friends the story of her life. She has only to reveal the fact that she has left a small daughter behind her in Europe for Percy to seize upon the rescue of this child as the culminating mission of his existence. Driven by her own sympathies and her desire to do anything she can to make Percy happy, Millicent tries to further this pursuit; in the next twenty-four hours, which are the whole period of Miss Bolton's story, she lunches with Bridget and Percy, she goes to the dressmaker with Bridget, she enables Percy to attend a cocktail party to which she and Bridget have been invited. But accidentally she also introduces Bridget to a young millionaire who at once becomes infatuated with her and in whose favor Bridget makes her choice of champion. Level-headed, shrewd, experienced as only the European can be experienced in playing her feelings instead of letting them play havoc with her, Bridget knows just the sort of help she needs and just how to secure it. The story closes with Percy prostrated in failure and with Millicent facing the tragic necessity of having to turn her life inward instead of—romantically—outward.

There have perhaps been other modern American novels—though at the moment I cannot name any—that have given one as vibrant a pictorial impression of New York as Miss Bolton's does. But *Do I Wake or Sleep* is surely unique for the cultural meanings it evokes in every stroke of its portrait of the city and for the way it demonstrates the human outcome of cultural fact, and the relation in both human and social terms of American and European culture. In a symbolic story like Miss Bolton's the temptation to either overstatement or oversimplification is enormous: Miss Bolton's ability to avoid both is the mark of a beautifully disciplined mind and heart. If one waits, for instance, for the character of Bridget to dissolve in satire or to merge into the usual picture of a glamorous European adventuress, one waits in vain: one's sympathies for Bridget increase as she comes more and more to reveal the cool springs of her conduct. Or if one looks for the young millionaire of the novel to become a caricature of stupid American openhandedness, one has the agreeable surprise of watching his author endow him with all the frank sweetness possible to his kind. Just as there is no hint of chauvinism or of any other easy value in Miss Bolton's comparison of the Old World and the New, so there is no touch of malice or of any other form of self-hatred in her approach to American character.

Then there are the myriad wonderful details with which Miss Bolton fills in the main outlines of her drama of American self-discovery. As striking as her descriptions of New York and her use of the World's Fair are Miss Bolton's descriptions of meals, of the protocol of restaurants, of a newsreel, her portrait of a cocktail party—the scene with the little doctor asserting his professional importance in the midst of so much alcoholic indulgence is a minor miracle—her asides on literary subjects, on Whitman, on Hart Crane, on why a modern cocktail party would be an unsuitable subject for a Restoration comedy. From time to time I have been accused of anti-intellectualism in my reviews because I have spoken so sharply against the modern "intellectual" novel. What I have been speaking against, of course, has been the use of the novel as a crude vehicle for argument or as an educational display-piece. The proper play of intellect in a novel is something quite different from this, both desirable and (now) rare, and I recommend *Do I Wake or Sleep* as a beautiful instance of its virtues and charm.

December 14, 1946

The jacket of Robert M. Coates's *The Bitter Season* (Harcourt, Brace, $2.50) is misleading when it tells us that this is a novel about how men who were a "little too old or a little too frail to be warriors" felt about their exclusion from war service.

199

Actually it is a novel about all of us in war time as we are seen by Mr. Coates's narrator and as this one person is representative of a broad segment of civilian life. The novel's protagonist, a painter-writer, is a typically decent product of his century, who came to maturity—or supposed he did—in the period following the First World War. Now, in the midst of another war, he finds himself little farther than where he was then in his own life and in the life of his country. The parallel between this narrator's personal history and the history of our times is Mr. Coates's means of tracing some of the antecedents and possible consequences of the present condition of the world: through the eyes of this sensitive observer of human behavior in a period of stress Mr. Coates attempts to assess the society that makes and is made by war. It is a large fictional undertaking, larger than the effort to analyze the state of mind of people unfit for military duty—though this too would of course be a good subject for a novel—and if Mr. Coates is not wholly successful in it, he at least deserves good marks for the attempt.

The failure of *The Bitter Season* to be equal to its intention is chiefly due, I think, to the confusion of its method which in turn would seem to reflect Mr. Coates's lack of confidence in the power of a fictional incident to communicate more than it may superficially appear to. Mr. Coates's narrative follows no time sequence. It is constantly interrupted for philosophical asides and rapid reports on war-time habits and manners, and even these contemporary social observations are so crowded and handled so fancily that their import is all but lost; it is only with a certain effort that one realizes that a single principal thread—the thread, and threat, of suppressed or only half-suppressed violence in our most ordinary human encounters—runs through all of them. There are few current novelists who see the small business of life, how bartenders and bar customers, waiters, taxi drivers and bus conductors act and talk, with Mr. Coates's accuracy and intelligence. This makes it the more regrettable that *The Bitter Season* doesn't do a better job of dramatic distillation.

Jerome Weidman's *Too Early to Tell* (Reynal and Hitch-cock, $3.00) is about the undisciplined goings-on in a bureau of psychological warfare which its author does not call the Office of War Information. It bears little relation to Mr. Weidman's earlier novels. Certainly one never thought to be able to accuse the author of *I Can Get It for You Wholesale* of dullness or lack of narrative flair, or of spreading himself transparently thin: in short, of sweating out a novel. It is true that because Mr. Weid-man's bureaucrats and other civil-service people are not particu-larly attractive, *Too Early to Tell* has been labeled another of his usual caustic efforts. But this is to look for trouble where for this reader any kind of trouble would have been preferable to tedium.

The literary case of Mr. Weidman interests me very much. Never a major talent or even the promise of one, Mr. Weidman has yet seemed to me to be one of the quirkily arresting writers of our time who has received a peculiarly bad deal from the critics. I have the impression, in fact, that he has been singled out as whipping boy for the bad conscience of a literary period sanctified to the doing of good works. Most notable has been the outraged response that has greeted his writing about Jews. Conspicuously ignoring the question whether the characters in his earlier novels were faithful representations of a section of the Jewish population, Mr. Weidman's critics have taken the attitude that in describing Jews who are not very nice people Mr. Weidman was himself as wicked as they, and that virtually singlehanded he was bringing Nazism to America. The unfor-tunate result of this kind of moral pressure was that in his novel called *The Lights Around the Shore* Mr. Weidman translated a group of obviously Jewish characters into Gentiles, thus robbing them of their ethnic reality, and that in his newest novel he touches no reality at all. Present-day liberalism, in all its astigmatism and self-righteousness, has many important cultural as well as political sins to account for at the Day of Judgment; I am not saying that its pressure upon one minor literary figure is among the largest of them. But I do feel that the unofficial censorship of Mr. Weidman cannot be overlooked if we are to understand the relation of politics and literature in our time.

The Liberators by Wesley Towner (A. A. Wyn, $2.75) is a pedestrian, earnest, decent study of the occupation of Germany. While I am unable to recommend it as a work of fiction, I can commend it as an unusually enlightened and honest report on our conduct in victory, something of a relief after such sentimental fantasies as *A Bell for Adano*.

If you have been puzzled by announcement of the publication of *The Memorial* by Christopher Isherwood (New Directions), you might want to know that this is an early novel published in England in 1932.

May 24, 1947

The publishers of Herman Wouk's novel about the radio business, *Aurora Dawn* (Simon and Schuster, $2.75), announce that they are going to put a new, more modest jacket on the book. I suppose we must acknowledge this achievement as all to the credit of the reviewers: they have been pretty unanimous in objecting to Simon and Schuster's claim that Mr. Wouk has rescued the beautiful English language from Hemingway and restored it to the tradition of Fielding. But while I join in rejoicing that an author is going to be allowed, however belatedly, to make his way without the embarrassment of excessive promotion, I am afraid I cannot become very excited about this token of the wholesome influence of the reviewers upon our literary life. The critics neglected several rather important opportunities in the case of *Aurora Dawn*. They did not point out, for instance, that Mr. Wouk's eighteenth-century affectations are pretentious and immature, that stylization is never style, and that there is something wrong with a society which thinks it is. Nor did they point out that the selection of *Aurora Dawn* by the

202

Book of the Month Club indicates that Mr. Wouk's mistakes have a considerable cultural backing.

Mr. Wouk should most certainly be spared the advertising genius of his publishers. But he should also be saved from the perversion of his own pleasant gifts. Behind the rosy anachronisms of *Aurora Dawn* there would seem to be a nice talent for light fiction. The reason we have no decent light fiction in this country is that we respect no literary work that is not heavy with portent or pretension. Mr. Wouk gives us plenty of evidence that he could write simple colloquial English if he thought it desirable. He is naturally witty. He is well educated. It is the sad mark of our times that he should find it necessary or favorable to roll in the full periods of a bygone prose, and display his book-learning like a college sophomore.

It is important to note that Mr. Wouk affects his eighteenth-century manner chiefly in his chapter titles and in his pages of straight narrative. He uses it, that is, to rid his story of intellection and moralization, to separate plot and commentary. He wants to take sides and to make moral and intellectual comment on his situations and characters, and he therefore turns to the manner of a century which expected the novelist to do just this. And because excursions of this sort are flamboyantly out of date, he is not only forgiven them but celebrated for his style. How different would have been the response if he had taken it for granted that he had the right to digress from his narrative, and had incorporated his comments directly and colloquially into his story! He would have been accused of the very faults of which he is now guilty but of which he would then have been innocent. He would have been told he was pretentious, over-intellectualized, old-fashioned.

Obviously what is involved here is a deep distrust, on the part not alone of Mr. Wouk but of our whole literary culture, of mind. We feel that mind has no rightful place in fiction. If it insists upon intruding itself, we demand that it not try to act as if it belonged but that it proclaim itself a rank outsider, a comic echo from a past age. It is this profound unease about our ideas and our relation to the people to whom we address our ideas that accounts for the extremes of barrenness and sonorousness in current writing and for our inability to create a clear, honest, flexible contemporary prose.

Similarly—and this is the connection between Mr. Wouk's anachronistic style and the self-consciousness with which he parades his learning, his endemic references to the Hundred Best Books—we are uncomfortable about education. Although we should like to think that knowledge is a private affair, we know it is also a form of authority and power. And if it is power, best to wear it like a badge.

The fact that Mr. Wouk has to go back to the eighteenth century to find a style which permits him to make moral comment on his story does not mean that ours is any the less a moral age. To the contrary, I doubt there has ever been a literary period that matched ours in fictional breast-beatings and threshings of conscience. But *Aurora Dawn* is not typical of contemporary fiction in this regard. That other novel about radio, *The Hucksters,* is far more so. Mr. Wakeman was much concerned with his own share in the sins of radio; Mr. Wouk, with commendable self-respect, does not believe himself to blame for this evil—except perhaps as every member of society shares all its responsibilities. Indeed, it is precisely because Mr. Wouk wished to keep a moral distance between himself and his subject that he had to borrow his style from so distant in time.

I have dealt only with the prose and pose of *Aurora Dawn,* to the neglect of its story. For the most part that is neat enough, a matter of a young radio executive who has to choose between his true love and the daughter of his chief sponsor. The book ends with Mr. Wouk's hero reunited with his sweetheart and saving his soul by departing from the radio business entirely. But I pause over the instrument of this salvation. Young Andrew Reale has come to fame by signing up for the Aurora Dawn programs a certain Reverend Stanfield, a Virginia preacher who captures the American radio audience by combining a short sermon with a public confessional: his followers come on the air to announce their misdoings and be forgiven. But this preacher and program, although they have their comic aspects, are not presented as part of the nonsense of radio. They are offered in salutary opposition to the other programs on the station. Mr. Wakeman's answer to radio was an apocalyptic dedication to art; Mr. Wouk's is evangelistic religion. Perhaps even more than his affectations of manner, this false vision of virtue makes one hesitant about Mr. Wouk's future of comic seriousness. The good comic-serious writer lives by common sense, not by big gestures of the spirit.

June 14, 1947

Vladimir Nabokov's new novel, *Bend Sinister* (Holt, $2.75), is about a professor of philosophy in an unnamed country who is destroyed by the tyrannical government that has come to power. By my count the book has four successful moments. Three are moments of amusement.

On page 50 Professor Krug, pressed by his university colleagues to present a petition to the Dictator with whom he had had a boyhood acquaintance, explains why the attempt would be ill-advised. When Krug and the Toad (the name by which the tyrant is privately called) were at school together, Krug had sat on the Toad's face, and not merely once or twice but regularly, as a habit. " 'I sat upon his face,' said Krug stolidly, 'every blessed day for about five school years—which makes, I suppose, about a thousand sittings.' "

On page 124 two organ-grinders arrive simultaneously in a backyard. The pair of musicians look very uncomfortable. Krug, watching them from a window, comments, "It is a very singular picture. An organ grinder is the very emblem of oneness. But here we have an absurd duality."

On page 142 Krug, on his way to an interview with the Toad, passes through a room equipped with a large radio-like machine attended by three doctors and two members of the secret police, from which there comes a steady beat like an African drum. It turns out that the machine amplifies the Dictator's heartbeats so that the strains on his health can be constantly controlled.

There is also in Mr. Nabokov's novel an instance of effective imagination. At the start of the story Krug's wife has died, leaving him with a small son to care for. There is a scarcity of servants, and Krug is forced to hire a very young girl as nurse-maid for the boy. This teen-aged domestic, at first only slatternly and incompetent, develops into a horror of lewdness, and Mr. Nabokov very tellingly suggests the root-connection between the nursemaid's degeneracy and the social-political degradation that surrounds her.

Such few moments of wit or enlightenment in a book of 242 pages would not ordinarily call for isolation and report. The reason I note them here is to indicate how little relief from tedium I was able to find in a novel presented by its publishers as an item of great literary prestige, its way prepared by the acclaim which its predecessor, Mr. Nabokov's *The Real Life of Sebastien Knight,* received in certain critical quarters. With such judgment I dare say there will be a certain amount of agreement. It will emanate from a public that has become so tired of the arid prose and method of contemporary naturalism that it welcomes any change. But in point of fact, what in Mr. Nabokov's style looks like a highly charged sensibility is only forced imagery and deafness to the music of the English language, and what looks like inventiveness is already its own sterile convention.

Here is a sample, a single sentence, of Mr. Nabokov's prose; the scene is on a staircase where Krug has to pass a young couple who have just come from a fancy-dress party, the boy dressed as a football player and the girl dressed as Carmen:

They separated and he caught a glimpse of her pale, dark-eyed, not very pretty face with its glistening lips as she slipped under his door-holding arm and after one backward glance from the first landing ran upstairs trailing her wrap with all its constellations—

Cepheus and Cassiopeia in their eternal bliss, and the dazzling tear of Capella, and Polaris the snowflake on the grizzly fur of the Cub, and the swooning galaxies—those mirrors of infinite space *qui m'effrayent, Blaise,* as they did you, and where Olga is not, but where mythology stretches strong circus nets, lest thought, in its ill-fitting tights, should break its old neck instead of rebouncing with a hep and a hop—hopping down again into this urine-soaked dust to take that short run with the half pirouette in the middle and display the extreme simplicity of heaven in the acrobat's amphiphorical gesture, the candidly open hands that start a brief shower of applause while he walks backwards and then, reverting to virile manners, catches the little blue handkerchief, which his muscular flying mate, after her own exertions, takes from her heaving hot bosom—heaving more than her smile suggests—and tosses to him, so that he may wipe the palms of his aching weakening hands.

I read this as elaborate chicanery. It is not daring, it is merely wilful. It is not original, it is anarchic in an already-established pattern. It bears the same relation to the prose of the contemporary leaders in innovation as the prose of, say, *Gentleman's Agreement* bears to the prose of the nineteenth-century masters.

But if Mr. Nabokov's novel is written in a claustrophobic style in which the reader's mind is allowed to do no work of its own and which leads us by meaningless associations into blind alleys where it traps us in boredom, Mr. Nabokov's story of the dehumanization of man under tyranny is, after all, a claustrophobic story. Whether or not it was the author's intention to model his prose system on the social system he is attacking, this is exactly what he has accomplished. When, then, Mr. Nabokov's book is praised as a new kind of literary force asserting itself against the weakness of the old naturalism, we perhaps need to be reminded of the way in which a people who have lost faith in liberal democracy welcome tyranny because it initially presents itself to them as a new strength.

The point is not to be pressed too far. I am obviously not suggesting that Mr. Nabokov is a literary precursor of dictatorship. But I do suggest that the passivity of mind and spirit demanded of the reader by *Bend Sinister* is not as far removed as may appear from the passivity of mind and spirit demanded by dictatorial governments, and that when we submit ourselves to it we are perhaps betraying a disenchantment with more than old literary methods.

July 5, 1947

It is not at all uncommon for light fiction to betray a deep hidden bitterness; the work of Angela Thirkell is a case in point. But it is rare to come across a light novel which, like Rupert Croft-Cooke's *Miss Allick* (Holt, $2.75), announces an open anger. The theme of *Miss Allick* is the bad condition of modern literature, particularly novels. It is a subject to which the author brings so much quiet passion that one must suspect him of having at some period in his career been that most unenviable of readers, a fiction reviewer.

Mr. Croft-Cooke believes—and I agree with him—that in novels as in love people by and large get only as good as they ask for. He believes too—and I agree with him—that literature is no mere decoration of life but an index of the health or sickness of a society, and that just as dictatorship, war, and all the other hideous phenomena of our political day undoubtedly answer a profound need in the modern mass-personality, so the debasement of our literary standards reflects a loss of standard throughout our lives. The Miss Allick of Mr. Croft-Cooke's title is a governess with a firm determination to become a best-selling novelist. She succeeds, and not only once but season after season. The secret of this grim lady's success is simple: she infallibly appeals to her times because she *is* her times. Her only values the easiest values of the moment, her opportunism indistinguishable from sincerity, Miss Allick is the perfect expression of a civilization diabolically contriving its own destruction.

There is a wonderful account of Miss Allick's dull fierce movement, as the cycles spin, from the romantic novel to bohemianism, to national pride, to social consciousness, to international politics, each step of the way hailed as a "classic" by the critics. Mr. Croft-Cooke's description of a modern writing career might have been funnier but it could not have been more accurate or better calculated to demonstrate the way in which literature marks our political path. Whatever liveliness is missing from *Miss Allick* is more than compensated for by its intelligence. And even the fact that Mr. Croft-Cooke's governess falls short of being humanly convincing, which we at first take to be a failure in character-depiction, assumes another significance as we grasp the full seriousness of his book. Miss Allick's inhumanity is her author's final argument that it is monstrosity rather than human enlargement that modern life and fiction celebrate.

Of the accumulated spring novels that I have been going through these last weeks I have so far found only one other, besides *Miss Allick,* that seems to me to be worth noting, Henry Morton Robinson's *The Great Snow* (Simon and Schuster, $2.75). The story of what happens to a family—husband, wife, two children, and some guests—marooned in a country house during a twenty-day snowstorm, Mr. Robinson's novel, although primarily concerned with states of mind, has a nice excitement about it: it stirs your Robinson Crusoe instincts. But it is less for this pleasant gratification than for its decency that Mr. Robinson's book must be noticed. *The Great Snow* is written out of an affection for people that is all but obsolete in current novels, especially if they claim psychoanalytical inspiration.

There is little question but that the chief motive in present-day psychiatric or psychoanalytical fiction is revenge against psychiatrists and analysts. It is as if we wanted to turn our dubious understanding of the workings of the mind against the very people who first invited us to self-knowledge, tell them that they are mad before they tell us that we are. This hostile attitude is of course new even in so-called Freudian fiction; up to a few years ago our chief impulse, as we tried to use the methods of analysis, was not so much the wish to make villains of the analysts as to make heroes of ourselves. And heroism was mostly a matter of sensitivity: the more a writer could reveal of his own delicate mechanisms, the greater his virtue and stature. There was undoubtedly too much loving self-reference in our past performance, but at least it was a step short of what seems to be the current need to hit out with blind passion against anyone who might question us.

In such a situation Mr. Robinson's novel, which regards the findings of psychoanalysis as an instrument of health, is something of a cultural anomaly. There is a great deal of muddle in Mr. Robinson's use of Freudian concepts but this is of less importance than the fact that Mr. Robinson uses the Freudian psychology to add to the size and well-being of his characters. In this purpose he is neither didactic nor mealy-mouthed. As best he can, he translates clinical information into novelistic terms and tries to avoid lifeless resolutions. The most interesting passage in his book deals with the ordeal of a markedly masculine father when he has to recognize the effeminacy of his young son. At first outraged, the father gradually begins to see not only his own responsibility for the boy's character but the kind of strength that resides beneath the son's seeming weakness. It is an insight which offers the father no absolute happiness but does help him to accept the good-and-bad of which life is compounded.

July 12, 1947

I don't suppose that three instances in six months of a new impulse to maturity on the part of our young writers can be taken as proof that we are witnessing a cultural change. But they do warm one's hope that fiction may at last be trying to free itself from the infantilism that has for so long now been considered a first signal of literary merit. Last winter, while I was on vacation from reviewing, I read two novels, Peggy

Bennett's *The Varmints* and Elizabeth Fenwick's *The Long Wing,* by young and gifted new writers. Both authors, writers of obvious sensibility, had unusually adult views of life. Now there is Daphne Athas's *The Weather of the Heart* (Appleton-Century, $2.75) which is also an effort to create life beyond the immediate world of the writer's own precious selfhood. *The Weather of the Heart,* written when Miss Athas was only twenty-two, her first published work, is strikingly talented. It is also an admirable attempt to put sensibility at the service of growth rather than of self-pitying retreat.

In fiction as in life one of the marks of growth is of course activity. In the novel activity shows itself as drama. Drama is the novelist's means of bringing inner conflict into the open and thus of advancing its resolution, and it seems to me that the static quality of so much present-day fiction must be understood as a refusal of growth, a willingness to rest in the conditions given at the start of the story. Especially in novels about childhood it is striking how little our authors desire maturity for their small protagonists; they all seem to end as they began, with their little heroes and heroines still troubled children. While this passivity often presents the face of revolt, the children never rebel in the direction of growing up. The first novel of an ambitious writer, which was once so likely to be a novel of development, in our present period is almost sure to be a novel of non-development.

This is not the case with Miss Athas's *The Weather of the Heart* any more than with Miss Bennett's book or Miss Fenwick's. These are novels of drama and of at least the attempt at resolution. Although the main characters of Miss Athas's book are children when we first meet them, by the time we leave them not so many years later their personalities have been deeply grooved by an expanded experience. They have acted and been acted upon, and we know the direction their adult lives must take. It is not a happy projection: Eliza Wall will be a dry, masochistic spinster; Hetty Wall will be a wan, semi-delinquent weakling—and how full of gracious possibility the two little sisters were on first appearance! Claw Moreau, the young precipitating agent of the girls' miseries, will always be edging criminality; Monty, the "nice" boy of the early years, will be a mild horror of concealed meanness. It is decidedly not a pretty picture but it *is* development, and inevitable development, from the conditions given at the start of the story. However much Miss Athas may deplore the fate that awaits her characters, she at least allows them to achieve it.

There is much fantasy in our literature of sensibility but it is predominantly narcissistic, unable to move beyond the range of the writer's self-love. The fantasy in Miss Athas's novel is almost frighteningly unhampered. On the one hand, Miss Athas can generate large dramatic conflict out of something as seemingly trivial as the murder of a pet canary. On the other hand, she can match Faulkner in the imagination of aberrant behavior. Her story is set in Maine and even her descriptions of landscape and weather are free and bold. It is only in her statement of the source of Eliza Wall's sexual fears that Miss Athas works by rote, looking to the textbook.

The circumstances surrounding the publication of *The Weather of the Heart* are unfortunate. The book has a singularly ugly jacket. More important, it is promoted by a blurb from Betty Smith of *A Tree Grows in Brooklyn* fame, which means that its publishers fail to make necessary discriminations. A writer with no literary reputation or connections, a writer, moreover, who fails to offer the usual reassuring signs of her literacy—Miss Athas makes no reference to Joyce or Kafka— has a hard enough time being taken seriously by the critics without being given this sorry send-off.

August 9, 1947

The Age of Reason by Jean-Paul Sartre (Knopf, $3.00) is the first novel in a projected trilogy, *Roads to Freedom,* by the leader of the French Existentialists; the second, already published in France, is promised in English translation later this year. What Sartre gives us, so far, is a canvas of the forlorn-ness—to use a term we frequently encounter in the writing of the Existentialists—of modern man. Huddled together in the Paris of 1938, on the eve of the war, is a group of middle-class bohemians committed to nothing and connected with nothing in life: Mathieu, a professor of philosophy; Marcelle, his self-invalided mistress; Daniel, a tortured homosexual; Boris and Ivitch, brother and sister, devotees of infantilism; Lola, an aging café singer and drug addict. This central circle of *The Age of Reason* is touched by another series of modern types: Jacques, Mathieu's fascist-minded bourgeois brother; Brunet, a Com-munist; Sarah, a maternal Jewess who takes too much pleasure in helping her troubled friends.

None of these people is heroic; each is the victim rather than the master of his fate. Only Brunet is firmly organized around a purpose, and only Mathieu suggests the possibility of a signifi-cant moral change in the future. In this first volume of his trilogy Sartre has done no more than lead his patients into the theater and described their symptoms. He has convinced us that his world is very sick but he has not yet prescribed a cure. For this we must await the succeeding volumes or refer to his other work.

We have been told that Sartre's fictional method has been influenced by Dos Passos. But even a summary listing of the characters in *The Age of Reason* should indicate the unsound-ness of pressing the connection. Dos Passos's social canvas is obviously much broader than Sartre's. Dos Passos also com-mands a much higher vantage in relation to his characters. Then, too, there is much more *event* in Dos Passos's novels than in this book of Sartre's, the whole of whose central action hinges on the fact that Mathieu's mistress has become pregnant and must either be allowed to bear her child or be provided with money for an abortion. *The Age of Reason* is indeed claustro-phobic in its limitation of movement and action: we recognize that this mood expresses Sartre's belief that only an understand-ing of the true meaning of freedom allows man to escape the increasing pressures of life. The characters in *The Age of Rea-*

son talk obsessively about freedom. They may mean anything from a refusal of the responsibility of marriage, to political quietism, to Gide's *acte gratuite*. But from Sartre's other work, not from anything he tells us in this book, we know that these are all false interpretations and that by "freedom" he means the taking of a full responsibility for our own lives, and that his notion of responsibility goes so far as to reach the categorical imperative of Kant: we must always act as if our choice were the rule for mankind.

Much closer than any resemblance of Sartre's method to that of Dos Passos is, I think, its resemblance to the microcosmic method of the early Aldous Huxley, where the miseries of a small, especially exacerbated segment of society—the society, roughly, of the author himself—is taken to stand for the whole modern dilemma.

But this is not the sole respect in which *The Age of Reason* brings Huxley to mind. Behind Huxley's present religious position there stretches a long search for an authority in life. Only in his last novels does Huxley openly personify this authority in a strong father-figure who is a sort of earthly liaison to God. But it has always been clear that his need of a some*thing* to which man might cling was actually the need for a some*one*. And what we have watched as his ideas have evolved is the process by which the actual-life parent-person has been transformed into an ideal parent-person, the alchemy by which parental flesh has been changed to parental spirit. Before Huxley could permit any authority to the father, he had to rid him of body. The sexual disgust and confusion from which his characters have always suffered is primarily a disgust with the sexual parent; it is only resultingly a disgust with themselves.

There is a striking similarity between the sexual atmosphere of *The Age of Reason* and that of Huxley's books. None of Sartre's bohemians is sexually at peace, each wars against his sexual impulses. It is in the sexual sphere that Sartre centers the conflict between good and evil. As in Huxley, *The Age of Reason* is heavy with unpleasant reminders—bad tastes in the mouth, self-inflicted bleedings, vomit, body odors—of the dominion the body can exercise over the spirit. And all the characters are concerned in some unsatisfactory child-parent relationship: Boris, Ivitch, Daniel all look to Mathieu as to a father; Mathieu's own crisis has to do with his fear of parenthood; Daniel "solves" his homosexual problem by assuming the incongruous role of father to Mathieu's child. We have the evidence of his book that Sartre believes that the deep alienation from which these people suffer has a sexual source.

Here the analogy to Huxley must sharply end. Where Huxley goes on to replace the authority of the physical father with the authority of God the Father, and His saintly representative on earth, Sartre remains rigorously atheistic and, as we know from his other writings, incorporates all authority in the individual himself. Where Huxley's philosophy ensues in passivity, the Existential philosophy insists upon man's involvement with his time.

And yet there seems to me to be a large suggestiveness in the common emotional ground from which the two take off—the fact that Sartre, like Huxley, is so concerned to destroy the parental figure of authority. Huxley has found another authority to substitute for it; might it not be possible that Sartre will need to do the same? While one hesitates to conjecture that the very fierceness of the Existentialist protest against authority may disguise a longing for it, we recall that Heidegger, the German Existentialist, became a Nazi. And we take note of the fact that the Communist Brunet in *The Age of Reason* is given, almost all unconsciously, a very different moral quality from the other characters. Huxley chose God; might not the Existentialist choose the State—the proletarian dictatorship, say, though not the fascist dictatorship? Might not the final act of freedom be the free choice to give up all purely personal freedom? In his little volume, *Existentialism,* Sartre acknowledges his "distress" that God does not exist to give man "essence," and thus his inescapable moral values. "Everything is permissible if God does not exist," he quotes Dostoievski. We need not be either

215

theists or lacking in moral principle to recognize that the overburdened individual is always tempted to seek an external organization, theological or political, which will lift the weight of an unguarded universe from his weak shoulders.

As an artistic performance, *The Age of Reason* is more than competent. I especially like its relaxed command of language, its easy movement between the colloquial and the educated idiom. Its chief interest is nevertheless that of a document in an extraordinarily interesting moral research.

August 23, 1947

The Steeper Cliff by David Davidson (Random House, $3.00) is not the distinguished literary performance it is being said to be. Nevertheless, the enthusiastic reception it has received can be read as one of the happier signs of the times. It must mean that we are at last ready to be told that all Germans need not be either anti-Nazi angels or Nazi devils, that a great many of them are ordinary people like us Americans, now capable of a shining moment of heroism, now weak and frightened, for the most part torn between their ideals of decency and their instinct to survive. *The Steeper Cliff* is about an American officer obsessed with the problem of personal bravery who, assigned to find Germans to staff the new democratic newspapers in the occupied zone, begins to identify himself with a missing journalist whose conduct under fascism seems to parallel what his own would have been in similar circumstances. The research into the career of this unknown German provides the dramatic suspense of Mr. Davidson's story and leads his hero to several important conclusions. He learns that courage is not an absolute, as he had always believed, but that it is nevertheless a good reality. He learns that even a brave person is not necessarily brave all the time. He eventually comes to understand that although it was far better to fight Nazism than to be passive under it, it is not always given to the individual to be as strong as he would wish to be; and that only to aid and approve Nazism was to be guilty of an absolute wickedness. He discovers, in short, that Germans are to be judged as human beings.

Nowadays, this is an unusually decent lesson for a novel to teach. *The Steeper Cliff* is also an unusually interesting report of Germany under American occupation; it has the ring of authenticity. Beyond this, except to say that the book sustains a pleasant narrative excitement, I cannot go. Aware as he is of the rich texturing of our lives, Mr. Davidson is not yet able to re-create it.

The Eagle on the Plain by Victor Wolfson (Simon and Schuster, $2.75) is a novel on two levels. First, it is a folk story of life in a poor backroads community in the Catskills; as such, it has much of the charm of tall-tale telling but also the senti-mentality that seems inevitably to accompany literary excur-sions into "simple" society. It is also a fable of freedom, at once affecting and uncomfortably inflated. As symbol of the unfet-tered spirit, Mr. Wolfson chooses a young Italian-American boy, son of a rural bootlegger, the fulfillment of whose dream of glory—to be a popular ballad singer—is interrupted by a brush with the law. Instead of submitting to imprisonment, this ap-pealing youngster organizes his old neighbors and friends, all of them as touched with the genius of individualism as himself, to make a large though hopeless gesture against the restricting authorities of modern life: they blow up roads and a dam, rocking the Catskills with their call to freedom. Treated realisti-cally, Mr. Wolfson's story might have had considerable dramatic power. Handled half realistically but half as fantasy, it loses weight both as psychological drama and as a parable of social protest.

The Other Room by Worth Tuttle Hedden (Crown, $2.75) is an odd, rather inept novel about the Negro problem by the author of the lively *Wives of High Pasture* of a few seasons ago. Straining probability, a young Virginia girl accepts a job teach-ing in a New Orleans college without knowing that it is a

217

colored school. Instead of running home she stays to learn some basic truths about the colored people, and to fall in love with one of the Negro instructors. The worthiness of its purpose and especially the courage with which it handles the theme of miscegenation makes one wish *The Other Room* were a better book, more committed to fictional construction, less to instruction. The subject of Negro-white relations has reached the point, so far as fiction is concerned, where goodwill without art is almost as dismaying as art without goodwill.

September 20, 1947

The only thing that makes Anna Kavan's *The House of Sleep* (Doubleday, $2.50) worth writing about—nothing makes it worth reading—is the point of view it shares with a considerable section of our literary culture, the most "advanced" section, that madness is a normal, even a better than normal, way of life. Although Miss Kavan's book is called a novel, it has no feature of fiction: no narrative, no characters, no insight into our common emotions. It carefully avoids reality except in so far as it uses words which, however arbitrarily arranged, manage to evoke fleeting glimpses of a momentarily recognizable universe. A kaleidoscope of the subjective states of an increasingly disordered mind, recorded half as if from within this sick psyche and half as if through the eye of an outsider much too closely identified with her subject, *The House of Sleep* seems to me to have been published out of our utter confusion as to what life and literature are all about. I haven't the slightest idea what it means to be told of such a pretentious piece of non-communication that it is a "penetrating insight into the subconscious world of dreams and shadows." To me, insight necessarily proceeds from some kind of organized sense of actuality. The world of dreams and shadows is interesting only if it adds to our information about the world of consciousness.

Miss Kavan has a principled disagreement with this point of view. She explains her own stand in an introduction sufficiently brief to be quoted entire:

The creative impulse is the result of tension; without tension life would not exist. If human life be accepted as the result of tension between the two polarities of night and day, the negative pole, night, must have at least equal importance with the positive day.

At night, under the negative influence, subjected to cosmic radiations of a different kind, human affairs are apt to come to a crisis; at night most human beings die and are born.

The House of Sleep describes in the night-time language certain critical stages in the development of one individual human being. No interpretation is needed of this dream tongue we all, as a matter of course, have spoken in sleep and childhood; but for the sake of absolute clearness a short paragraph at the head of each section indicates the corresponding day situation.

Every sentence of this statement invites examination but it is the second sentence that perhaps best reveals the serious mis-apprehension under which Miss Kavan conceived her book. For believing that human life is a tension between the two polarities of reason and non-reason and that non-rationality, instead of being an element in the human composition that normally is and should be under the dominion of reason, asserts an "at least equal" authority with reason, Miss Kavan refuses the usual atti-tude whereby the test of health lies in the delicate matter of degree. When a person's non-reason approaches a fifty per-cent dominion over his reason it means that the person is sick and of only questionable use to society. And it is by calculations such as these that even a threatened civilization preserves itself.

As to the sentences that follow, they too make rather singular assumptions. When Miss Kavan writes, "at night, under the negative influence," one might ask, why negative? What makes night negative? In support of Miss Kavan's affirmation that "at night most human beings die and are born," one asks for statis-tics. And in support of Miss Kavan's assertion that her text is written in the "dream tongue we all, as a matter of course, have

219

spoken in sleep and childhood" one wonders whom Miss Kavan means by "we all"—even as a matter very much *out* of course, this reviewer was certainly never capable of an infant speech or a sleep speech of such fineness as "the blessed genii who walk about in the light gazing with blissful eyes of still, eternal clearness. The perennially clear eye of the Heaven-Born opens to a stare of shockingly bright moonlight. The eye is located at presumptive Godheight so that the terrestrial globe is seen as if from an airplane cruising over it at about three thousand feet." I pick this passage at random. There are others even more rarefied.

But, as I say, none of this would be worth stopping over were Miss Kavan's book an isolated instance of its kind. The author of *The House of Sleep* not only has a distinguished reputation in her own England and here; she also speaks for an attitude that is now finding a frighteningly wide adherence along our advanced literary front. As our popular writing more and more undertakes to subserve our grosser realities and mold itself into a power instrument, the higher literary art increasingly claims for itself the realm of shadow and dreams. In substitute for an increasingly grim reality we are offered the poetry of nonrationality. In cure of a schizophrenic society we are offered the schizophrenic personality.

October 25, 1947

A reviewer who has persistently battled the popular notion that a novel is as good as its politics must do a bit of backtracking in the case of Humphrey Slater's *The Heretics* (Harcourt, Brace, $2.75). Perhaps, after all, a novel is as good as its politics in at least this one sense, that if it has a sound political core, the work as a whole will have some essential soundness. Certainly this would seem to be the case in Mr. Slater's instance where his disciplined political intelligence is consistently matched by a disciplined literary taste. But unfortunately Mr.

Slater's good sense and taste, while they save him from the common pitfalls of present-day political fiction, seem also to put a brake on his energies of imagination. *The Heretics* is lamentably underwritten in point of character development and drama. It is only a suggestion of the fine novel it might have been.

Mr. Slater divides his story into two sections, the first dealing with the Albigensian heretics of the early thirteenth century, the second with the Spanish civil war. The connection is only ideological; Mr. Slater is giving us a comparative study in fanaticism. But he also contrives a narrative link by carrying over the names of the chief characters in the first half of the book to the second. Four children are the main actors in the early section of *The Heretics*: a brother and sister, Paul and Elizabeth, their friend Simon, and Moro, the Moorish boy with whom they join forces after their parents are killed as heretics. Seven centuries later a Paul and an Elizabeth, brother and sister, and a friend Simon are again Mr. Slater's principal characters in the confusion of the Spanish war in which they become variously involved—Elizabeth as a correspondent for the English papers, Paul as a Trotskyite soldier, Simon as a Stalinist soldier and spy; and the old quartet is completed by Cordova, Elizabeth's Spanish lover. It is a stunty contrivance, without intellectual or emotional validity.

For the fact is that no more than Mr. Slater's modern characters are present-day counterparts of the Albigensian orphans is the Spanish civil war a modern equivalent of the heresy-hunting of the Middle Ages. *The Heretics* is not saying anything so mechanical as that history repeats itself. If I read it correctly, what it is saying is that the instinct to fanaticism has been fairly constant throughout history. Just as a dedication to the ideals of the church issued in the reign of terror against the Albigensians, so a dedication to the Soviet ideal produced the ruthlessness of the Spanish Communists. In either period the other side of the coin of principle is violence. Mr. Slater's parallels between the child victims of the church crusades and the Russian *bezprisoni,* between the Nominalist-Realist issue and the theoretical issues of radical dissidence, have a more than literal significance. They indicate the avenues of thought and feeling that connect man to man over the centuries.

The earlier portion of Mr. Slater's book is historically interesting. It was nevertheless a mistake for Mr. Slater to have included it in the same novel with his Spanish material, which, quite by itself, has such fine fictional potentialities. Probably no one who has written about the Spanish struggle is better qualified for the task than Mr. Slater, both in military knowledge—he fought in the Spanish war and he has published several books on military strategy—and in political insight. *The Heretics* has none of the sentimentality or political ambiguity that marred Hemingway's *For Whom the Bell Tolls*. Its author is not caught up in the myth of heroism nor is he afraid to move completely into the open with his indictment of the Stalinist command in Spain: the book's most brilliant passage is a short satiric chapter describing a meeting of the Operational Policy Commission, three Spaniards and three Russians. Nevertheless, as a work of imagination *The Heretics* is not to be compared with Hemingway's Spanish novel. Every human encounter in it, every occasion for drama is, if not thrown away, taken at its lowest possible pitch, quite as if the business of novel-writing were properly conducted on the scale of a well-bred drawing-room conversation.

And one's disappointment at Mr. Slater's undue reticence turns to bitterness if one happens, as I did, to read *The Heretics* hard upon Frederic Wakeman's *The Saxon Charm* (Rinehart, $2.75), which is one of the most inept books that has come my way, yet one of the most self-proclaiming. The new book by the author of *The Hucksters* has a novelist as its protagonist and a good deal to say about the profession of literature. Clearly Mr. Wakeman believes that the writing of novels is a superior pastime: he provides opportunity for everyone in his book to say so. Whenever Novelist Eric Busch, hero of *The Saxon Charm*, utters an inanity, which is whenever he opens his mouth, there is a bystander to murmur, "What wisdom!" And

I'm sure Novelist Busch would be no less admiring of Novelist Wakeman than Novelist Wakeman is of Novelist Busch.

Let other reviewers risk libel by naming the likely original of the villain of Mr. Wakeman's piece, the prodigious play-producer whose genius for the theater is so heavily encased in egotism that it finds no room for the genius of his playwrights. I am content to report that Mr. Wakeman calls him Matt Saxon, and that he comes nowhere near making him into a credible fictional character. We are intended to understand that Saxon's malign charm was the temporary undoing of a fine writer named Busch who had written a fine play about the life of Molière. (Happily Mr. Wakeman spells Molière correctly, which cannot be said of his repeated spelling of "Stendahl.") People who can believe in Busch and in the quality of his dramatic effort, or who can even remember with respect that there was such a person as Molière after Mr. Wakeman's manhandling of him, will no doubt also believe in the inordinate power for good and evil of Mr. Saxon. I am not one of them.

I should perhaps add that my untempered response to *The Saxon Charm,* however much it may result from the contrast between Mr. Wakeman's unwarranted confidence and Mr. Slater's unwarranted modesty, is also directed to a culture which encourages cheapness such as Mr. Wakeman's and pays such large sums of money for it. When the hero of *The Hucksters* left the advertising business and committed himself to the life of art, we had every reason to expect the kind of art we get in this novel which follows it. Mr. Wakeman's book about radio advertising didn't conceal the fact that the point of view of its author was identical with the point of view of its chief character, and that if, after he broke with his old world, Mr. Wakeman's hero went on to be a writer he would simply lay aside his "sincere" neckties for "sincere" ideas. But self-revelation was read as healthy self-criticism, Mr. Wakeman was credited with a conscious act of social good, and anyone who failed to appreciate his service to us was accused of refusing help when it was offered.

The same accusation will perhaps be leveled against the critic who fails to welcome Mr. Wakeman's newest seriousness. Here the ungenerosity may be found to lie in tracing so intimate a kinship between *The Hucksters* and *The Saxon Charm* and in failing to encourage Mr. Wakeman's journey from Mammon to literature. I risk the imputation in view of the substantial aid our society makes available for such travelers. The report is that the movies encouraged Mr. Wakeman with $250,000 for *The Saxon Charm* in advance of publication.

December 13, 1947

Ours being in all spheres such a "know-how" culture, a civilization so brilliantly skilled in turning out anything it sets its hand to and yet so appallingly ignorant of what is worth making or to what use the things it makes should be put, we cannot be surprised that our literature, too, shows a marked ascendancy of craft over conscience. Probably there has never been a time when so many people wrote so "well" as now but to such meager purpose; when, indeed, the emptier a novel's content, the surer its technical proficiency. It has reached the point where, remembering the great novels of the past—how dreary and inept they could be for long passages; how varied and nubbly were their textures—I think we can be forgiven the perversity of seeking out the *in*expert performance as promise that here at last there may be a book with something to say.

Certainly in the case of Josephine Herbst's new novel, *Somewhere the Tempest Fell* (Scribner's, $3.00), there is a significant connection between an author's perception of life and her faults of performance. I do not mean that Miss Herbst's technical mistakes are to be taken as the measure of her good achievement or, on the other hand, overlooked. Without question her novel would have been better for rigorous rewriting—if the dangling ends of narrative had been caught up, if there had been a sounder proportion between important incidents and trivialities, if the characters had been better projected, if—even—its mad punctuation had been corrected. But I do mean that Miss Herbst's gravest faults have an aspect of virtue because they proceed from a sense of urgency and a zest for experience which are all but gone from modern writing.

Partly because its bony structure is never fully articulated, partly because no large and ambitious narrative can ever be properly boiled down, *Somewhere the Tempest Fell* is difficult to synopsize. It is primarily about a mystery writer, Adam Snow, who under the pseudonym of George Wand has become a great popular success but who, in the middle of the war, suddenly wishes to re-establish himself in his own identity. Long resident in Italy, Snow had won the confidence of several members of the anti-fascist underground; he believes that he unwittingly betrayed one of them into Mussolini's hands. Now that he has returned to America, this guilt becomes the symbol of a general guiltiness about his life. His impulse to expiation finds its outlet in championing, against his wife's counter-claims, his seventeen-year-old daughter's budding love affair with a jazz musician.

But this is only the central theme of the novel against which numerous other themes are counterpointed: the story of the Brady household, connected with that of the Snows by Mrs. Snow's wealthy uncle who restores his sense of possibility by playing benefactor to one of the Brady daughters; the stories of various friends of Ada Brady; the stories of the swing musicians who meet for jam sessions in Ada's basement. It may be—it undoubtedly is—that these multiple threads of Miss Herbst's narrative are joined a bit carelessly but this very haphazardness is not the least of the signs of Miss Herbst's creative generosity. The right to be a victim of accident is, after all, one of the great freedoms with which a novelist can endow the people he creates and, by extension, his readers.

This freedom is rarely granted in present-day novels. The mood of most contemporary story-telling is suffocatingly static, almost claustrophobic; one has the impression that the current

225

novelist, like a neurotic parent, thinks he will lose prestige if he loses dominance over his fictional family and that once he permits his characters to take their chances in the world, he himself will cease to count for anything. The absence of this self-concerned author-figure from *Somewhere the Tempest Fell* is notable. Throughout her story Miss Herbst is present only in such light as is reflected from her characters. This is very unfashionable. Equally unfashionable is Miss Herbst's prose, and the quality of her imagination. Whereas in most current writing the imagination is like nothing so much as a series of dye-pots in which the author successively dips his or her own image, each time bringing it up with fresh surprise at how pretty it looks in its new tint, in Miss Herbst's novel it colors the objective world.

Somewhere the Tempest Fell proceeds, that is, from an attitude toward novel-writing which I so much favor that I could passionately wish that in refusing the false restraints of what passes for artistic taste Miss Herbst had not also refused the necessary discipline of all good art; that in accepting the happy mess of life she had not herself produced something of a mess; and that in giving her characters the license to be free she had also given them the gift of being more compelling. Especially I regret that in padding the flesh of her book to the weakening of its basic anatomy Miss Herbst obscured the portions of her story which concern the jazz musicians. Jazz enters often into present-day fiction but its acute relevance to present-day culture is usually not well understood. *Somewhere the Tempest Fell* is the first novel I have come across which seems to comprehend some of the complicated values which meet in the jazz world: its decent and its disturbing political overtones, the marijuana route it travels toward criminality, the personal and artistic idealism it both satisfies and frustrates. It would have been a fine accomplishment if Miss Herbst had expressed this understanding more fully and boldly.

It is a special pleasure for a reviewer who did not admire Saul Bellow's first novel, *Dangling Man,* to report of his second, *The Victim* (Vanguard, $2.75), that it is not only in every way a striking advance over its predecessor but also hard to match in recent fiction for brilliance, skill, and originality. There are of course certain clear connections between the two performances: Mr. Bellow still writes of a world where the sunlight penetrates only with difficulty and of people whose nerves are rubbed too raw. But however cheerless the universe of *The Victim,* the new novel is not open to the charge, as the earlier volume was, of reducing the world to the mean stature of some of its least expansive inhabitants or of neglecting to suggest the reprieve from misery which is always the promise of art. Mr. Bellow has remarkably transcended, in his second book, the self-pitying literalness which robbed his first of scale. He is still puritanically fearful of charming us but he is at least willing to excite our emotional participation.

So much of the virtue of *The Victim* lies in its wonderful physical evocations—the domestic detail, for example, of its hero's existence: the dreadful decency of his apartment, the ghastliness of his quick solitary meals, the suffocating routine of his habits of personal cleanliness—that not to linger over them is to do Mr. Bellow's talents much injustice. But it is also impossible to deal adequately with the philosophical content of Mr. Bellow's book in a short review: like all good novels, it can be read on so many levels that to stay with any of them is to put false limitations on a large experience.

Mr. Bellow tells the story of a young man, a Jew named Asa Leventhal, who is suddenly accused of having ruined another man's life in revenge for some anti-Semitic remarks. Several years before, when Leventhal had been out of a job, a Gentile acquaintance, Kirby Allbee, had given him an introduction to his employer, the editor of a chain of publications. The editor had received Leventhal so coldly that Leventhal had turned the interview into a violent quarrel. Now Allbee reappears in Leventhal's life and announces that the reason Leventhal had attacked his boss was that Allbee had once spoken offensively about Jews; he insists that as a consequence of Leventhal's misconduct he, who had introduced Leventhal to the editor, had himself been fired; out of work, he had taken to drinking heavily, lost his wife, and become a complete down-and-outer. He places the responsibility for this débâcle squarely upon Leventhal, attaches himself to him, and demands that his persecutor make restitution for the ruin he has caused.

The exciting problem of Mr. Bellow's novel is to figure out who in this complex of circumstances is the "victim" of the book's title. There is certainly no doubt that Leventhal is being madly persecuted by Allbee who has suddenly appeared out of nowhere to drop the full burden of his disintegrated life upon the other man. Leventhal remembers all the incidents of his former association with Allbee but there is no reason for him to feel that when he lost his temper with Allbee's boss he was acting to affect the fate of a third person. And even supposing that Allbee had been fired as a result of Leventhal's behavior, is it Leventhal's responsibility that Allbee then went to pieces? On the other hand, not only is Allbee himself convinced that *he* was victimized by Leventhal; there are mutual friends whom Leventhal respects who—it turns out—agree that he had an important share in precipitating Allbee's downfall. The accusations and defenses move back and forth between the two men: each is forced farther and farther into examination of his motives both conscious and unconscious while Mr. Bellow brilliantly explores the whole problem of guilt. What emerges from the investigation is a beautiful balance of forces: no man is without responsibility for his neighbor but neither is any man really responsible for his neighbor or free of responsibility for himself. In addition, there is accident or, if you will, the biological determination which it would be hopeless to suppose one can entirely master.

Not the least impressive aspect of Mr. Bellow's novel is that he dares to place this study of the difficult problem of responsibility in that most charged of spheres, the sphere of inter-racial relationships. More and more these days, under the guise of increasing our "realism" about minority situations, progressive thought has actually been lending itself to myth-making. Instructing us to defend the rights of minorities, it also teaches us that members of minorities are not adult human beings like other citizens, with similar responsibility for their own destinies, but born victims—the innocent sufferers of the will of the dominant groups. Probably there is no less fashionable idea in current liberalism than that Jews exist in reciprocal relationship with Gentiles or Negroes with white people. But Mr. Bellow cuts across this pleasant fantasy to confront us with the disturbing idea that the social "victim" may himself assist in the creation of his unhappy condition. It would be a mistake to read *The Victim* as only a novel about anti-Semitism: its implications are far wider and its insights are as relevant to members of majority groups—that is, to any human being—as to members of oppressed minorities. Yet even read solely as a novel about the Jewish situation, it is morally one of the farthest-reaching books our contemporary culture has produced.

A good deal of nonsense is written by the book reviewers about the novel of ideas. Our professional readers like to assume that there is an unbridgeable separation between the novel of thought and the novel of feeling whereas the simple truth is that ideas not only necessarily adhere in emotions and emotions in ideas but there is no such thing as a novel *without* ideas: a good novel has good ideas, a bad novel has bad ideas. Actually when reviewers protest the novel of thought, what is really bothering them is confrontation with new, serious, or provocative thinking. A book has only to be sufficiently soft or shoddy in its ideas for the reviewer to announce himself deeply stirred by its message. *The Victim* is solidly built of fine important ideas; it also generates fine and important, if uncomfortable, emotions. One need only compare it to Mr. Bellow's earlier *Dangling Man* to have a striking lesson in the way in which intellect has the power to alter the quality of a novelist's feeling and enhance his art.

January 31, 1948

It is seldom I have so double a response to a book as I have to Truman Capote's *Other Voices, Other Rooms* (Random House, $2.75). This is a first novel—or, more accurately, long novelette—by the twenty-three-year-old writer whose shorter fiction has already brought him much notice from the advance talent scouts. I can well understand what the shouting has been about: not since the early work of Eudora Welty has there been an example of such striking literary virtuosity. Even if Mr. Capote were ten or twenty years older than he is, his powers of description and evocation, his ability to bend language to his poetic moods, his ear for dialect and for the varied rhythms of speech would be remarkable. In one so young this much skill represents a kind of genius. On the other hand, I find myself deeply antipathetic to the whole artistic-moral purpose of Mr. Capote's novel. In Mr. Capote's case, as with so many of our gifted contemporary artists, I would freely trade eighty percent of his technical skill for twenty percent more value in the uses to which it is put.

In some respects *Other Voices, Other Rooms* can be read as a realistic story. Set in the rural South, it is about the miseries, fears, and loneliness of a thirteen-year-old boy who, on the death of a beloved mother, comes to live with his unknown father, only to discover that the father is a helpless paralytic, the father's newest wife an imbecile, and Randolph, the remaining member of the household, a middle-aged degenerate aesthete. We can even include in the generally realistic pattern

230

certain of the other characters that surround the young Joel in his new environment: the tomboy Idabel who is incapable of the tender girlishness that Joel needs in a friend; the century-old Jesus Fever, the Negro mule-driver; Zoo, the colored housemaid whose native warm-heartedness we watch disappear in a developing religious hysteria. But this realism, which from the start is sufficiently faced in the direction of nightmare, is eventually overlaid with so many trappings of horror that the book has predominantly the air of a work of surrealist fantasy. Thus, as if it were not bad enough that Joel's father is a paralytic, he is a paralytic whose only means of calling for help is to drop red, not even white, tennis balls from his bed, which bounce slowly down the stairs to the lower floor of the house—though there is no reason why he should not simply ring a bell—and Miss Amy, the father's wife, in addition to being feeble-minded, must have a wooden hand on which she always wears a glove. And Cousin Randolph, in addition to his other pleasant habits, must collect the wings of bluebirds which Miss Amy has killed for him with a poker! This claptrap, however skilfully written, paradoxically enough changes what might be a valid symbolic statement of the loneliness and decay of modern life into our latest chic example of Southern Gothic. In large part it transforms a sincere if ambiguous psychological study into a self-conscious titillation of the reader's nerves.

But happily for Mr. Capote's future as a novelist, the transformation is not complete. Despite its fantastic paraphernalia, *Other Voices, Other Rooms* does manage to convey a serious content. At the end of the book the young Joel turns to the homosexual love offered him by Randolph and we realize that in his slow piling up of nightmare detail Mr. Capote has been attempting to re-create the emotional background to sexual inversion. What his book is saying is that a boy becomes a homosexual when the circumstances of his life deny him other more normal gratifications of his need for affection.

Well, I am not equipped to argue whether or not this is a sound explanation of the source of homosexuality. Nor does the question interest me here. Much more arresting is the implication of Mr. Capote's book that, having been given an explanation of the *cause* of Joel's homosexuality, we have been given all the ground we need for a proper attitude *toward* it and toward Joel as a member of society. For what other meaning can we possibly draw from this portrait of a passive victim of his early circumstances than that we must always think of him in this light, that even when Joel will be thirty or forty we shall still have to judge him only as the passive victim of his early circumstances? But in exactly the same sense in which Joel is formed by the accidents of his youthful experience, we have all of us, heterosexuals no less than homosexuals, been formed by our early experience. Is no member of society, then, to be held accountable for himself, not even a Hitler?

Let me make myself unmistakably clear. I do not oppose the attitude set forth in Mr. Capote's novel simply as it refers to homosexuals, but as it refers to all people. For it seems to me to create an adult world of passive acceptance in which we are rendered incapable of thinking anybody responsible for anything.

The point asks to be paused over because this blanket indorsement of the deterministic principle is extraordinarily current in contemporary fiction. With startling regularity our most talented young novelists present us with child heroes who are never permitted to grow up into an adulthood which will submit them to the test of *conduct*. Or in novels where there are grown characters, there is seldom any action in which moral attitudes are seriously assessed. Fiction leads us, that is, into opting for a world of irresponsibility.

The problem is of course a very complex one. Obviously, in standing against an absolute of determinism, I do not mean to close out all social or personal causality. I do ask, however, for some degree of mediation between the extremes of causality and freedom. Is this not, after all, what fiction is peculiarly suited to do, to mediate between extremes? Surely the novel, compounded as it is or should be of both psychological insight and dramatic choice, is par excellence the medium for bringing both sympathy and moral-social judgment to bear upon the individual fate.

But I am afraid that this is not the function of the novel as Mr. Capote sees it nor as a large percentage of present-day readers see it, for were we to ask of fiction, as we once did, that it base its claim to accomplishment on its moral stature, most of the writing we celebrate today would fall into its proper place as no more than a feat of literary athletics.

February 21, 1948

Before the reviews of Merle Miller's *That Winter* (William Sloane Associates, $3.00) appeared, I had set the book aside as one of those young efforts which might just as well be allowed to live out its short life undisturbed by critical comment. For one thing, it works a literary vein which is too nearly exhausted to merit further consideration. For another, even within its established genre, it seemed to me to be too dull a performance to fuss about. But there is apparently no limit to our capacity for mistaking a battered old hat for a shining new helmet. Himself convinced that he speaks fresh and strong for his generation, Mr. Miller has put over the idea on a good proportion of his reviewers.

It is true, of course, that Mr. Miller's three leading characters—Ted, an alcoholic millionaire; Lew, a Jew all but corrupted by his response to the status of his people; and Peter, who wants to write novels—are veterans and very conscious of the drama of their particular situation in history. And such action as there is in the story takes place in the first season of their re-entrance into civilian life. Mr. Miller's novel, that is, is all set to be a significant statement of post-war attitudes. But an author's awareness that his materials *ought* to yield fresh interest is little assurance that they will: I, for one, am only embarrassed by Mr. Miller's insistence that his people drink in a meaningful new way when all they do is drink a lot, or that they earn their livings in a meaningful new way when they still hold their same old radio and *Time* jobs, or that they love in a meaningful new way when their emotions are as stereotyped as their vocabularies. The sophisticated modernity of *That Winter* was corn long before Lew and Ted and Peter ever saw a uniform, and if Mr. Miller does not recognize this fact, it is the duty of his critics to recognize it for him instead of encouraging a young writer in the unfounded belief that he is breaking new literary ground.

It no doubt puts an undue weight on John Cobb's *The Gesture* (Harper, $2.75) to counter it to *That Winter*. A first novel, Mr. Cobb's story of an American airfield in England is modest in intention and technically just adequate to its purpose. But if any post-war novel can be said to express or even work toward a new point of view, it is Mr. Cobb's, for *The Gesture* is concerned with the absolutism that can reside in idealism and this is a theme peculiarly pertinent to these post-war times but one which most of our writers are not up to grasping.

The rigid idealist of *The Gesture* is the new officer who has come to command the airfield, a man incapable either of compromise with principle or any adjustment to the human needs of the men with whom he must deal. Major Harris's standards are of the highest: he believes in order, duty, responsibility, he has a gentleman's notions of decency and a gentlemanly regard for the more delicate fruits of education, he feels an obligation to be as courageous as his subordinates, and he believes that a position of leadership requires one to put one's best social theories into practice. When he first arrives, the men at the field are merely conventionally prejudiced against Harris. The better they know him the more they loathe him. Soon even the novel's first-person narrator, a character who is most remarkably not an autobiographical projection of his author, finds it necessary to dissociate himself from someone who, although closer to him in class and principles than anyone else at the field, is so far removed from him in common humanity.

It will be interesting to compare the critical response to Mr. Cobb's book with that to Mr. Miller's. I can scarcely be optimistic that a manner as unfashionable as Mr. Cobb's, and a literary tone that is pitched so low, will be attractive to the contemporary taste. Nevertheless *The Gesture* indicates a fresh and rewarding literary direction. Mr. Cobb's is still only a wee bud of a talent but it promises what is much worth nurturing.

March 6, 1948

The Patchwork Time by Robert Gibbons (Knopf, $3.00) is about a young man, Johnny Somers, aged twenty-one, a high-school teacher of history in a small Southern town, who is taking his first steps away from the parental home and suffering his first adult sexual experience. The title of the book refers to the desperately troubled months which follow from the fact that the young man's long-awaited sexual consummation happens to coincide with the death of his father. To no better than a sterile mechanical purpose, Mr. Gibbons uses a variety of experimental prose techniques derived from Joyce and Dos Passos and Cummings to explore the psychic confusion which threatens to overwhelm Somers in his traumatic progress from adolescence to young manhood. There are nevertheless two things that make his novel worth mention: one, an appealing innocence in Mr. Gibbons's approach to people; the other, its refusal of the sexual conventions of contemporary fiction.

The Patchwork Time is concerned with the problem of virginity. But according to our fiction, no such problem any longer exists. On the contrary, it is assumed that in all sexual situations our heroes and heroines are perfectly equipped to live out their authors' fantasies of ease and power. The changing sexual conventions of literature are of course a fascinating subject. Compared to even two decades ago our fiction would seem to have attained to a complete sexual freedom, what with the boldness with which the marital, pre-marital, non-marital or adulterous bed is bared to the public eye. Yet in actual fact the current novel is as much bound by sexual convention as ever it was; we have merely substituted a set of conventions of revelation for the older conventions of reticence. Thus our present-day romantic hero moves with a sexual directness and assurance as rigidly prescribed for him as was ever the effort for gentlemanly self-control ordained for his grandfather; and it is as necessary for our present-day heroine to be lively, ready, and withal sweet in bed ("good" is the word used, *ad nauseam*) as for her ancestress to blush and tremble at the bedroom door. In much the way that a decade of anti-Nazi adventure fiction was built on the pleasant assumption that no man would be in trouble with the Gestapo who was capable of reading a compass, tracking down fresh water, or binding his own wounds, our present fictional generation proposes the pleasant illusion that sexual competence is within the reach of anyone with an arm long enough to embrace the first available partner. One comes to wonder whether the strange conclusion drawn by Dr. Kinsey after his hour and a half interviews—it is much at variance with the observation of psychoanalysis—that the American male is not at all worried by his sexual problems, is not perhaps an instance of life imitating art; if, that is, it is not possible that Dr. Kinsey's respondents had simply read so many novels in which successful sexuality was taken for granted that only after long hours of self-investigation would they themselves become aware of the fears and miseries which belie their premise of command.

In our period Mr. Gibbons's willingness to devote almost a whole novel to a young man's anxiety in approaching his first adult sexuality is so unfashionable, then, as to constitute a small act of cultural revolution.

I suppose if Alan Paton had written about the American Negro or Indian in the idyllic vein in which he writes about the Zulus in *Cry, the Beloved Country* (Scribner's, $3.00), I would be the first to dismiss him as a sentimentalist. But distance from a novelist's materials helps to give us critical latitude, and despite its sweet elegiac manner I found myself much absorbed

236

by Mr. Paton's account of South African life. I had no idea that the Zulus led such an embattled minority existence, torn between the white culture of the cities, where the pressures of poverty and discrimination are a constant invitation to criminality, and an indigenous life which they pursue only at the cost of conscious removal from the main stream of civilization. Indeed, as Mr. Paton states it, and one is sure he states it honestly, the problem of the South African peoples, in all its racial, economic, and social complexity, is a paradigm of the modern political dilemma throughout the world. That is undoubtedly why so valid a note of tragedy makes itself heard even through his excessive lyricism.

October 30, 1948

If anyone has illusions about the happy life of a book reviewer, I suggest he read the three novels I comment on this week: *The Running of the Tide* by Esther Forbes (Houghton Mifflin, $4.00), *Remembrance Rock* by Carl Sandburg (Harcourt, Brace, $5.00), and *Guard of Honor* by James Gould Cozzens (Harcourt, Brace, $3.50). The total mileage of the three volumes is 2,330 pages—big pages too—of which I suppose I covered about half. But even slacking on the job, I feel as if I had completed some wonderful enterprise of fortitude and folly, like crossing the Rockies backward.

The Running of the Tide is so clearly a pot-boiler—and this despite Miss Forbes's reputation as a historian—that it should not be reviewed at all in a serious periodical. In fact, I had set it aside when I saw it described on the front page of the *New York Times Book Review* as a major artistic achievement. While it may not be entirely fair to submit an author to harsh judgment in one journal because she has been unwisely praised in another, it would be crueller to allow the readers of this magazine to discover the disappointment of Miss Forbes's book for themselves. Miss Forbes's story of the seafarers of Salem has but a single thing to recommend it, its presumable historical accuracy. For the rest it is a tedious romance aimed at the movies, remote indeed from the important experience it was called by the newspaper which is the chief molder of literary opinion in this country.

On the other hand, I can be grateful to another front-page *Times* review—Perry Miller's review of Carl Sandburg's *Remembrance Rock*—for minimizing the constraint I naturally feel at having to report that a first novel by so long-established and valued a member of the literary community is such an unhappy performance. In a poem about Lincoln in Mr. Sandburg's *The People, Yes* there are the lines:

> Death was in the air.
> So was birth.
> What was dying few could say.
> What was being born none could know.

They are not very good lines but they are at least concise. They also announce a modesty before the historical process of which Mr. Sandburg's verbose novel about three centuries of American life gives no evidence.

Remembrance Rock is about the American Dream, whatever that may now turn out to be or to have been: I gather from a couple of dozen novels on the subject that it is the idealism which guided the growth of our country. In order for America to be as it is, so the argument runs, all the jobs that Americans have done have had to have a special motive and quality, the democratic motive and quality. Every ordinary emotion and drive has been subordinated to the purpose of producing a country which, sometime in the twentieth century, would be worth dying for. The logic of this kind of historical thought has always eluded me. After Mr. Sandburg's novel it escapes me even further. Even the dull scalpel of dialectical materialism is more useful in laying bare the tissues of our national growth than such mystic sentimentalism. What country in the world, fascist or democratic, could not make an equally persuasive and accurate case for its having been built not of simple human materials, good and bad mixed, but of the energy of such a dream?

Anyone acquainted with Mr. Sandburg's poetry will find its familiar elements in his novel: the same soft affirmation and optimism, the same excessiveness about social unity, the same love of the rhythms of balladry and religion, the same massing together of the people and objects which compose our national strength. But for some curious reason this paraphernalia is much more troubling when we come on it in *Remembrance Rock* than in Mr. Sandburg's verse. For like all patriots who are more ardent than thoughtful, Mr. Sandburg reminds us in his novel of how thin is the line between too fervent democratic nationalism and other kinds of nationalism, including the kind against which democracy recently went to war. Instead of fortifying our democratic emotions, *Remembrance Rock* transcendentalizes them. Transcendental political emotions are dangerous things.

The only previous novel of Mr. Cozzens's I have read is *The Last Adam*. I remember it as far too good a book to have been written by the author of *Guard of Honor*. A report on three days in the life of an army airfield in Florida, *Guard of Honor* is a thoroughly tedious document of the war effort, as frazzling and unilluminating as a minute-by-minute account of any three days in any big-business bureaucracy.

November 13, 1948

It is inevitable that Theodor Plievier's *Stalingrad* (Appleton-Century-Crofts, $3.00) should be compared to Erich Remarque's *All Quiet on the Western Front,* since it stands in much the same relation to the fiction of this war that Remarque's novel did to the fiction of World War I. So far as I know, it is the first novel of this war to appear in this country that is written from the point of view not of the winning but the losing side. It is also the first to portray German soldiers as capable of a full range of human suffering instead of as puppets of their political fate. Like *All Quiet,* Plievier's *Stalingrad* is published here after an enormous success in its original German publication, and like Remarque's book it chiefly owes its impact —and a very considerable impact it is—to its passion of protest against the hideousness of war.

To be most effective I suppose this protest must always come from the side of defeat. Triumph in war can look like a justification of its miseries: one's soldiers bled and died to achieve the victory of one's principles, and everyone knows that only right can be victorious. It is the lost battle that is stripped of illusion, without meaning or purpose.

By concentrating upon the German débâcle before Stalingrad, Mr. Plievier has chosen the quintessential moment of meaningless suffering for the Germans in the recent conflict. When the story opens—if it can be called a story: actually, it is more a panorama than a narrative—the defeat of the German forces has already been guaranteed. What follows is the slow turning of the pages of a book of foretold doom. Every level of the military hierarchy is caught in the giant process of annihilation, from the lowliest gravedigger trying to bury the ever-mounting pile of frozen corpses to the frenzied generals compelled to hold out long after the loss of hope. To the usual paraphernalia of tortures—the starvation and pain, the madness and fears of war—the scene before Stalingrad added the special nightmare of cold. One would have thought oneself inured, through the fiction and movies of the last decade, to even the grisliest details of human degradation and hardship but it is Mr. Plievier's sad distinction to have recorded a history of horrors to which no sane mind can come with sufficient preparation not to sicken and refuse to believe. Alongside the war of *Stalingrad,* or perhaps what I must say is, after the lessons taught us in the last twenty-five years, the war of *All Quiet on the Western Front* is a children's story.

In view of Mr. Plievier's background, his novel is singularly unpolitical both in its approach and conclusions. There is no attempt to place its many characters where they resided within the Nazi system, no impulse to correlate their personal and political behavior—this is one of the commendable aspects of the book. Less impressive is the political irresolution in which the book ends, its belief that the therapy for a desperately ill society is love, the unnamed and unasking love of man for man which is exemplified in Mr. Plievier's book by the devotion of the humble Sergeant Gnotke to his stricken comrade, or by the socially-undifferentiated association in affection which is represented by the understanding between Gnotke and his colonel. Any decent person would agree with Mr. Plievier that we should all love one another. Very likely even the least decent members of society live by the same principle, according to their own lights. There remains the crucial job not only of definition but of investigation into the private and social sources of this most desirable human condition. As in the matter of the love of God—and Mr. Plievier would seem to be moving toward a religious position—so in love of man: it is not produced merely by asking for it, nor maintained without governance.

Before the question of the literary quality of Mr. Plievier's novel, the reviewer must lay down arms. If the communication of profound terror and suffering is a valid measure of literary merit—and I believe it must be, else one would respond to *Stalingrad* with revulsion—the book is an achievement. Yet how good can a novel actually be the whole of whose content is its message of horror, the whole of whose accomplishment is its communication of a not-to-be-imagined insanity? This can scarcely constitute a conventional critical recommendation.

It is much easier to deal, in the usual ways of the reviewer, with Joel Sayre's *The House Without a Roof* (Farrar, Straus, $2.75) or Samuel Spewack's *The Busy Busy People* (Houghton Mifflin, $3.00), each of which provides a pleasant and literate evening's entertainment. Mr. Sayre's book is less a novel than fictionalized reporting, an educated American's quick smooth view of what it could have been like to be a nice person in Nazi

Germany. Mr. Spewack's book has the pace and gloss of standard good light fiction but underneath its gay exterior takes itself, one suspects, too seriously as teacher of an important lesson about the Soviet Union. Not that I disagree with anything Mr. Spewack says about dictatorships in general and Russia in particular. It just strikes me as being a bit late in the day for giving people that pill in so much sugar-coating. There was a time when one had to bore from within the ranks of blind adherence to the great experiment; then I think it would have been useful to combine, as *The Busy Busy People* does, so much entertainment with so much sound counter-propaganda. But now those ranks are thinned, and the care with which Mr. Spewack balances fun and education is anachronistic, even embarrassing.

November 27, 1948

Hubert Creekmore's *The Welcome* (Appleton-Century-Crofts, $3.00) is described on its jacket as a novel of modern marriage but it is difficult to sum up precisely what it is saying about that unsteady institution. With no wish to parody its content, it would seem to add up to something like this: if women were truly feminine and feeling, they would forgive men for loving other men; they would marry them, respond to them sexually despite the fact that for these men women represented only second best in the sphere of love, and thus help them be happy in a society based on matrimony.

It sounds like an odd thesis for a novel. It also sounds rather hard on women. But perhaps neither humor nor feminine bias should make us dismiss *The Welcome* too easily. If Mr. Creekmore is muddled about the problem of homosexuals in our society, so is our society muddled about most sexual things. The Kinsey report has startled us with its statistics on the incidence of homosexual activity among married men. While it doesn't attempt to investigate the relation between this fact and the success or failure of American marriage, we must guess that a connection exists and, pending scientific information on the subject, learn what we can from our novelists. The very dimness of Mr. Creekmore's resolution of the conflict in which his two main characters find themselves is instructive: certainly it is worth knowing that in the opinion of at least some small section of society it is woman's function to serve as a therapy for male homosexuality. But *The Welcome* has an even more useful purpose. Of the novels about homosexuality which have appeared in the last few years, it makes the most ingenuous and therefore the most disturbing statement of the damage done to and by society by our refusal to recognize how widespread is the homosexual preference and by pushing people to the conformity of marriage who are emotionally unfit for it.

This pressure is of course not nearly as intense in the big cities as in smaller places, and Mr. Creekmore sensibly sets his novel in a small Southern town which he describes with a patient and gentle accuracy; indeed, his novel owes such literary virtue as it has to its honesty as a study in small-town manners. Undoubtedly in Mr. Creekmore's Ashton it would be harder to identify the sexual element in a male friendship than it would in New York, and the intellectual isolation in which Mr. Creekmore's Don and Jim live would be more acute, therefore a larger contributing factor in the growth of their attachment. In order to qualify for membership in the community life of Ashton one must be married, and despite the incomparably richer feeling which Don and Jim have for each other than either has for any woman, they make the conventional choice. The trouble is that Mr. Creekmore traces this sad course without seeming to be aware that a marriage contracted under such cruel circumstances is inevitably fated to bring misery to both partners.

The ingenuousness of his story lies in its curious assumption that homosexuality is something one can leave behind one simply by the wish to outgrow it, much as a man might discipline himself to give up his youthful idealism in favor of a life of

243

commerce or finance. The influence that our society exerts upon a man to make money is acknowledgedly blind and powerful; but neither in its force nor in its ignorance nor yet again in its effect upon the individual's emotions is this to be regarded as similar in kind to the pressure society exerts upon a man to be sexually "normal." The novel which will give us real insight into this aspect of our social-sexual morality will itself have to transcend not only the conventions but also the confusions by which we now live. In the meanwhile the best to be said of *The Welcome* is that by its very muddledness it indicates how much enlightenment we need.

January 8, 1949

Perhaps the first thing to be remarked of Ira Wolfert's *An Act of Love* (Simon and Schuster, $3.95) is that its hero is not, like his author, a newspaper correspondent. This is unusual, since to most newspapermen or advertising men or radio men with an ambition to write fiction, the world seems to offer but a single type of hero—a newspaperman or an advertising man or a radio man with an ambition to write fiction. It confirms the impression retained from Mr. Wolfert's earlier novel, *Tucker's People,* that Mr. Wolfert has a larger notion of the range of fiction than is general among practitioners of the fringe profession of literature.

However, once it has been reported what *An Act of Love* is not about, the question arises what it *is* about—and then the reviewer's difficulties begin. It is common to good novels, and proper, that they defy easy summary of their contents. I think it can even be said that one of the things most obviously wrong with the present-day novel is that we can so baldly report its subject matter: it deals with intermarriage, or alcoholism, or incipient fascism in a Southern town with a population of fifty thousand, or tobacco-growing in Connecticut. Mr. Wolfert's novel has no such limitation of content. The story of some white people thrown together on a Pacific island in wartime and having to battle out their feelings about themselves and each other, about love and death and destiny, its purview is intended to be as wide as man's possibilities of glory or despair. It is designed, that is, to be what D. H. Lawrence called the novel, a book of life. But unfortunately instead of capturing the strange and wonderful swarm of life, it is a book of artifacts; it is not itself truthful so much as it is a book of poses in relation to truth.

Some time ago I wrote of the fact that so many of our most conscientious writers, or writers with pretension to talent and conscience, use language to call notice to themselves rather than to the object they are presumably examining. Less guilty of stylistic posturing than most, Mr. Wolfert is far from free of it. He can write the following internal monologue:

> Harry the fixer, he sneered at himself, the square-it boy. . . . Take a square look at the jerk. He's a guy who needs a vote. He's a champ when there's somebody in the corner for him, but leave his corner empty and he can't lift his hands to pick his nose. . . .

which wholly sacrifices the logic of one of his characters, a sensitive and literate young man, in order to strike on the author's own behalf the fashionable pose of tough-boy virility. But worse, he postures with ideas, in particular with ideas as they touch on the emotions. *An Act of Love* has all the paraphernalia of an intense psychological investigation. It operates in the realm of our most deeply hidden motives, and of the fierce tensions of love and hate which bind or separate people. It commands a sophisticated psychoanalytical vocabulary. Yet not a single perception in Mr. Wolfert's long research into human motivation has the ring of validity. To undertake to exemplify the way in which Mr. Wolfert substitutes the simulacrum of emotional insight for the real thing is like trying to describe mist by bringing a handful of it into the living room. Indeed, *An Act of Love* is like nothing so much as an obscurity through which one glimpses dim familiar lights. But perhaps a passage in which Mr. Wolfert analyzes the dark forces involved in his hero's rejection of the sexual overture of Julia, his sweetheart, can adequately suggest the vaporous method by which the novel proceeds. Naturally enough, Julia has been shocked by Harry's refusal, tries to understand it. Mr. Wolfert writes:

> He had spurned her. He had fought himself free of her grasp. . . . But he hadn't spurned her, she thought. He had spurned being led. He had spurned her taking of him. He had spurned her wanting to yield himself up when it was she who must yield to him. But she had not wanted him to yield. No, she had wanted her mother to yield.
>
> Julia's face had been red with rage. It turned pale as she realized what had been behind her desire for Harry. She resented her mother, and because she resented her mother she had set herself deliberately to do the opposite of what her mother wanted. . . . He had not spurned Julia. He had spurned her taking him in hate of her mother.

False as such a passage is in itself, for surely no woman would think like this in the moment of a sexual rejection, it is doubly false in the context of what precedes and follows it because the whole of the novel, including the background of Julia's relation with her mother, is compounded of a myriad of such fabrications. What Mr. Wolfert gives us isn't insight into human behavior but a construct of all the psychological bits and pieces which float around so freely in our advanced culture— that big boys would wish to regress to the condition of little boys, that little boys are passionately committed to their mothers, that little boys cannot mate with big girls until they grow up themselves, that mothers have private reasons for not wishing their daughters to mate at all.

But surely the world is too demanding to give place to such prides of misleading knowledge. It screams to be truthfully revealed to us so that it may live for a better day. Yet here is the sickness of contemporary fiction, that so sharp is our writers' sense of alienation from their society that the only way they

246

seem to have of asserting their existence in it is by alerting us to their own very special presence in it and special awareness of it. To be is to be perceived in the act of perceiving.

To anyone who came of literary age in the period between wars the appearance of a new novel by John Dos Passos is bound to be an occasion for sentiment. It is therefore pleasant to be able to report that, however sharp one's divergence from Mr. Dos Passos's present political opinions, one can still read his new and very political novel, *The Grand Design* (Houghton Mifflin, $3.50), as one might spend an evening with an old friend from whom one has been long removed: animated by common recollections, warmed by the energy of his responses to the world, pleased that in disagreement he at least remains a sizable adversary.

Yet despite this old loyalty, or perhaps because of it, there is also the aching realization of how sad it is that a novelist who was once so boldly radical in his social opinions should now have let himself be pushed to such an extreme of reaction. Mr. Dos Passos's disillusionment with the organized political left is certainly understandable: who that has lived through the last decade and a half and retained a jot of his wits and integrity could feel otherwise? But what is there, one wants to know, in the emotion of radicalism—is it the taste for absolutes?—which makes for this swing of the pendulum when the revolutionary ideal has been shattered? Why could not the acute vision of the world which Mr. Dos Passos had as a radical novelist have widened with the years to the compass of tragedy rather than narrowed, as it has, to the compass of bitterness?

For one need not be a passionate Roosevelt partisan to be dismayed by the bitter tone and unfairness of Mr. Dos Passos's estimate of the Roosevelt Administration. *The Grand Design* is a panorama of the years from 1932 to 1942, a Washington story of the way in which the idealism of the New Deal disappeared under the pressure of political opportunism and the urge to personal power. The devil in the machine, we must understand, is Roosevelt himself who never actually appears in the book but whose presence is kept in our minds by repeated reference to the famous smile, the famous radio voice, the familiar long cigarette holder: "that man in the White House" is the chief character in a book from which he is absent. Only secondary in importance and malignity is Walker Watson, a not very successful composite of Harry Hopkins and Henry Wallace. To the blind, wilful, demagogic course pursued by Roosevelt, and the spurious, undisciplined, self-deceiving course pursued by Watson, Mr. Dos Passos bends the fate of all the subsidiary people in his novel—the fate, that is, of American democracy in our time. It is his belief that although there were some true idealists in government in this decade of our national degeneration—like his Millard Carroll and Paul Graves who sacrifice their decent quiet private lives in order to devote themselves to the public good—they were doomed to defeat by their leadership. And down to defeat with them went the radiant hopes of the American people.

Even the briefest outline of Mr. Dos Passos's case against the New Deal indicates his use of the attitudes of reaction as a stick with which to beat the liberals. But the bias of his case against the New Deal is broad indeed: he fails to point out that a Millard Carroll or Paul Graves would never have considered working in government, let alone been given important posts, had it not been for the Roosevelt dispensation; he neglects to take into account the alternatives the country faced in 1932: from the perspective of a recovered prosperity the pump-priming of the Thirties has a different look from what it would have had if this country had continued in the hands-off private-enterprise spirit which led us into the depression; he dwells on Roosevelt's manifest errors in the sphere of agrarian policy but fails to give the credit which even the most disillusioned radical

248

should be willing to grant the New Deal for the permanent gains it won for industrial labor. And even more dismal than this unjust weighting of his argument is Mr. Dos Passos's apparent commitment, if only in reverse, to that most unworthy of notions of the complex historical process: the great-man notion of history. Mr. Dos Passos holds one man, Roosevelt, liable for the whole course of our national development since the days of Hoover. He ignores the degree to which, for better or worse, the President represented the general will of the country. This is a peculiarly unthoughtful attitude for a man as sophisticated in politics as Mr. Dos Passos. It is also dangerous since it implies that the democratic method has finally no validity in practice and that such a phenomenon as, say, the re-election of Truman represents only the persistence of the Roosevelt image, and not the desire of the American people that the basic direction of the Roosevelt Administration be maintained.

In short, what Mr. Dos Passos has done is to launch an essentially irresponsible attack upon an historical situation which requires great judiciousness; and we must suspect that its excess stems from the frustration of his old impulse to perfection. In all his novels we recognize Mr. Dos Passos's profound impatience with people because they are less than ideal. Now it is politics itself which falls so lamentably short of the ideal because it is the creation of fallible people.

As I have said, the chief and most erring character in *The Grand Design* never actually appears in it. But even the people who do enter its pages are no more than insignificant figures in the wide landscape of corruption. It is with his Communist caricatures, brief as they are, that Mr. Dos Passos does best: evidently a novelist can hate well only where he has once loved well. But surely no one who is not already convinced will be persuaded that Mr. Dos Passos is not falsifying his picture of the Washington comrades—especially among liberals where persuasion is most needed, the price Mr. Dos Passos pays for exposing himself as such a prejudiced observer is that he seriously weakens the force of his accurate and knowledgeable report on Communist infiltration into the higher echelons of government.

In fact, all along the line Mr. Dos Passos has compromised his power to speak to that part of the reading public which should be his proper audience. There has always been among liberals a cloud of piety around the Roosevelt years, an effective conspiracy of silence on the many opportunistic or ill-advised or stupid policies whose results we still suffer. It is about time this self-imposed censorship were broken, the clouds dispersed, but by writers who remain basically sympathetic with the liberal aims of the New Deal, not by opponents from the right. Because Mr. Dos Passos no longer thinks in terms of the reactionary "enemy," he no longer fears giving comfort to it. This freedom might well be borrowed from him, but for the purpose of investigating actual political decisions and their consequences, not to obscure them still further.

February 5, 1949

Because Edward Newhouse's *The Hollow of the Wave* (Sloane, $3.50) wears no air of importance, is entirely understandable and even lively, it must be singled out from the run of current fiction: these are rare, if relative, virtues. It is some time since I have read a novel whose author comes through his book so attractively. Even where Mr. Newhouse's manner is less than striking and his characters less dimensional than is their human privilege, we see the former fault as a defect of modesty, the latter as a defect of kindliness.

The Hollow of the Wave is about some men and women in and around a Communist-dominated reprint house in New York. The group includes a millionaire angel with whose portrait Mr. Newhouse is most successful; a typography man who tells the story in the first person and thereby borrows from his author a certain credibility to which he is not wholly entitled

250

in his own fictional right; a pair of party stooges, convincing only as shadows of the authority they serve; some believable wives; some assorted minor figures of various political view. Involved with one another and their jobs, these people turn out to be essentially involved with the problem of personal salvation; and personal salvation turns out to be a problem of power. For the comrades the solution is simple: subservience to the strength of the Party. For the wealthy connections of Larry Holland, Mr. Newhouse's troubled young millionaire, salvation is also available; theirs is the haven of entrenched class. But for Holland himself and for Mr. Newhouse's narrator there is no such easy way out or up. They are the men of the humanist tradition for whom present-day society provides no clearly defined line of feeling and action. Unable to command even their women, they are themselves commanded, and therefore happy, in a war whose principles engage them. The war ends and they drift back into the army to wait out the quiet days before being picked up in the next conflict. As for the women of *The Hollow of the Wave,* they suffer the usual minority fate. As dependents of an ascendant power they find an at least temporary satisfaction. As dependents of a dispossessed caste they are themselves unpossessed and miserable.

Read this way, Mr. Newhouse's novel is of course a parable of the contemporary personal-political dilemma, but a bit too neat in the opinion of this reviewer who doesn't believe that people are so directly the product of their political condition and who thinks that fiction is suicidal as well as murderous when it so patly delivers human beings over to their political destinies. But the book need not be read as parable; it can be read as the play of its author's pleasant personality, and this is its own sweet small victory. For despite Mr. Newhouse's estimate of the power that the political situation can exercise over the human spirit, the triumph of his own spirit over this assumption is a telling argument against him, suggesting as it does how far people can move beyond the boundaries into which we try to fence them. I suspect, though, that the author of *The Hollow of the Wave* is too modest a man to generalize himself into a counter-principle.

There is a certain kinship between Mr. Newhouse's book and David Davidson's *The Hour of Truth* (Random House, $3.00). The new novel by the author of *The Steeper Cliff* is also a sweet-intentioned performance and uncommonly readable: swift, lively, dramatic. Its political content is more overt than that of *The Hollow of the Wave;* indeed, in a sense it is a pedagogic book though without the didactic tone we have come to associate with novels that have a lesson to teach. Mr. Davidson writes of a backward South American country—he calls it Alba—and the nature of our neighborly relations with it. Perhaps he tells us no more than most liberals might have guessed of the behind-the-scenes story of our recent benevolent policy, but he tells it pungently and usefully, documenting his case with excellent reporting of what life is like in Alba, both natively and by importation. Early in the war America sends a mission to Alba with a million-dollar budget and a fine program of benefits. The Albanese are for the most part cynical and respectful. They have reason to be cynical—by the end of *The Hour of Truth,* the redemption of Alba has been made the bounty of a group of men who are themselves in sore need of redemption.

Mr. Davidson's account of the personal evolution of the men who make up the American mission is beautifully relevant to his political intention: with the exception of William Harmon, the young lawyer who is the book's central character, each member of the group, far from staying the selfless savior he originally appears to be, betrays himself as a corrupt or corruptible weakling who naturally gravitates to a section of the globe which is so depressed that, in contrast, he seems strong. The picture of the mission is thus an effective dramatization of the unsound motives which animate even the nobler gestures of imperialism; one could wish Mr. Davidson had not diverted so much of his energy to a secondary story of Harmon's search for his lost manhood. Long subdued by the apparently predatory females of his family, Harmon has become impotent; he regains his sexual powers in an affair with a South American beauty

252

bred in the Latin tradition of female docility, and then, from the vantage of his renewed sexual confidence, is able to make a fresh assessment of North American women.

I have no doubt that in a person like Harmon there exists a connection between sexual and other expressions of character, but it would have been well if Mr. Davidson had not yielded to the temptation of romancing with the sexual psyche and, too, if he had not yielded to another even more insidious influence of literary fashion. I like books in which men learn to be heroes. The quest for greatness is an eminently proper subject for fiction. But the novelist who now attempts it must beware a peculiar pitfall prepared for him by our culture, the sentimental danger of supposing that someone can come to moral stature merely by identifying himself with the righteous cause of an oppressed people. A person is not necessarily as big as his cause is right. In a novel as in life, it is not enough that a Harmon ally himself with the corruption-ridden against the corrupters in order to achieve personal grandeur, or even enough that at the end of his story he at some risk take a dramatic stand for justice. He must have the *style* of greatness: even his weaknesses, and they can be major, must be told us in a language which implies his capacity for moral distinction. Mr. Davidson is unable to confer this gift on either Harmon or Hidalgo, the Albanese drunkard-martyr to whose size Harmon tries to grow, and the result is that even at their best final moments the two men seem to have attained only to the pose of heroism and not to a grand consummation.

March 19, 1949

With her second novel, *The Christmas Tree* (Scribner's, $2.75), Isabel Bolton establishes herself as the best woman writer of fiction in this country today. If I link her with the novelists of only her own sex, it is because Miss Bolton's work is essentially so feminine in the modesty of the face it turns to the world. It nevertheless avoids the self-imposed limitations of most contemporary female writing. I have often spoken in this column of the fact that external reality seems to exist for our most talented and conscientious women authors chiefly as a means of reflecting their own highly developed consciousness. Miss Bolton has no such over-arching self-reference. Her sensibility is as keen as that of Katherine Anne Porter or Eudora Welty, Carson McCullers or Jean Stafford—to name the women writers who have come to most renown in this country—but unlike them she has what we must call a masculine readiness, now rare enough even in our male novelists, to place her gifts of feeling and observation at the service of an objective universe.

In her first novel, *Do I Wake or Sleep,* Miss Bolton undertook to contrast the moral climates of modern Europe and America. It was a short, concentrated, technically brilliant performance, and if, to my taste, its tone was a little too precious, I could easily forgive this fault because the content of the book was so bold. With her new novel, Miss Bolton advances the position she won with its predecessor. *The Christmas Tree* is less "written" than *Do I Wake or Sleep*. Its emotions are more open, warmer, wider. A wonder these days, it is a novel whose sympathies enlarge rather than simply confirm our own. Dealing with that most hazardous of themes, the sources of homosexuality, it adds a new dimension of feeling to anything our fiction has yet given us on the subject.

The Christmas Tree is as little clinical as it is fashionable in other ways. Miss Bolton asks herself the question so many people are now asking: what is there in our society that accounts for the alarming increase in male homosexuality? And her answer—whether it is correct or not is irrelevant; we have no reason to believe there is a single correct answer—is that the disruption of our sexual patterns is another inevitable manifestation of the disruption throughout our culture. Her line of reasoning runs something like this: the rigors of Victorian society were a last-ditch protection against the encroachments of science and of a rising industrialism upon a world previously ordered by faith in God. Victorian morality was a firm façade for a crumbling house whose inhabitants were left with no place to lodge their emotions. When the women, so paralyzingly trained to be ladies, suddenly found themselves without the security of the drawing-room life for which they had been prepared, they were incapable of making a rough public way for themselves. Their charms, their human drives, their intellects had but a single respectable outlet—their sons. So they seduced their sons with all the strength for life and love that was dammed up within them and then turned the sons, their nerves aquiver, into a world which by now had lost even its façade of order, to make their own fates and find their own loves.

Such a summary of Miss Bolton's novel makes it sound didactic. It is anything but that. Miss Bolton works like a mosaic-maker, piecing together bits of scenes and persons—but it is a full panorama and a full cast, though given us in such tiny fragments—until finally, in unbelievably small compass, the whole pattern and intention are laid out before us. By what miracle of selection and organization she catches in 212 pages all we need to know of four generations of her Danforths, a story which in the hands of any other writer would have been a giant tome, is a not-to-be-fathomed secret of her craft. She could not have done it, one is sure, had she used a different narrative manner. The reader may be too conscious of, even irritated by, her long Proustian sentences but they admirably connect past and present, and permit Miss Bolton to recollect, create, and comment upon, all at the same time and with greatest economy. Only occasionally does she indulge the temptation to be "fine." For the most part her language is quiet and forthright, her lengthy sentences firm.

We learn that when she wrote *Do I Wake or Sleep,* Miss Bolton was past sixty. Her talent is not a youthful one though it has the energy and promise of growth. On the contrary, it redefines and celebrates maturity, teaching us what it means to grow older in wisdom: it is something we are likely to forget in a culture like ours in which the beginnings are always so dramatic and so often all; for Miss Bolton has not only the social perspective of her years but also a beautifully ripened understanding of the relation between pain and perversity, love and destruction, art and death. Reading *The Christmas Tree*, I kept thinking of Truman Capote's *Other Voices, Other Rooms*, with its effort to assign blame for its young hero's homosexuality, and thereby excuse him of responsibility. Miss Bolton blames no one, neither Larry Danforth nor his mother nor his mother's mother, for Larry's homosexuality. She and we suffer for him and with him, as we suffer with his mother, his lover, his wife, his child. She has, however, the impulse to take such responsibility as belongs to all of us as grown persons. In her universe as in the theology of St. Paul we are all part of one another, and if the world goes down, we all go down with it, together. But together not in torments of accusation but in affection and knowledge.

May 7, 1949

After a poor start, whose shallow and mechanical humor seems designed to capture an easy audience, Howard Nemerov's *The Melodramatists* (Random House, $3.00) develops into a considerable first novel, literate, entertaining, with a nice satiric barb. The chief objects of its attack are the church and psychiatry, those two therapies most generally prescribed for the ailing modern soul. Claire and Susan Boyne of Boston are the suffering heroines of Mr. Nemerov's book, and ailing souls indeed; the former's attachment to Rome and the latter's to Vienna win stability and security for neither of them. When the novel ends with Susan dead and Claire working out a classical fugue on the harpsichord amid the debris of a sexual brawl which is the result of a religious effort to transform the Boyne home into a refuge for prostitutes, we gather that Mr. Nemerov means us to understand that his own happy principle of harmonious living is an acceptance of reality in all its confusion, the will to find order without authority.

The Melodramatists makes no pretension to major literary stature. Nevertheless everything it includes and excludes makes it a most precise post-war document, and this despite its being set in the period of 1940–41 so that it takes no cognizance of America at war. Thus, where a Boston novel of even a decade ago would have been centrally concerned with the class structure of Boston society, *The Melodramatists* scarcely recognizes even the heritage of class feeling in its well-placed Boyne family. Or where a novel of twenty years ago would have strung the dilemma of two such youthful heroines on the strong line connecting children and parents, and a novel of ten years ago would have wanted its parental figures in the forefront of the story if only as persons of affectionately outrageous fancy, Mr. Nemerov's novel casts its mother and father into a quick and almost entire outer darkness—the Boyne offspring have the slimmest of fiduciary ties with their mad father and vaporous mother, both incarcerated in an expensive Virginia rest home. Or where a novel of the Thirties would have offered its troubled young people the choice, not between the individualistic principle of psychiatry and the selflessness of the church, but between capitalistic individualism and the selflessness of communism, there is not as much as a mention of political salvation in Mr. Nemerov's book. Or where a novel of five years ago must have resolved its personal conflicts in terms of the new world war, Mr. Nemerov deliberately dates his story before Pearl Harbor and introduces even the European war as merely a convenient shadow into which the inconsequential brother of Susan and Claire can escape from full participation in the narrative.

These are all, I think, important evidences of cultural change. But perhaps they are of less intellectual moment than Mr. Nemerov's strictly contemporary attitude toward psychiatry. The practitioner of the dark science of the mind in *The Melodramatists* is a Dr. Einman; his unsavory counterpart appears in

257

every third novel one picks up these days. Dr. Einman is the villain-father, the figure of presumed strength who turns out to be the very symbol of weakness and disintegration, the guardian of the sexual secret who is himself disclosed as a dirty little boy. The medicine he dispenses, though presumably derived from Freud, is of course pure charlatanry, with no relation whatsoever to Freudianism or to any other school of legitimate psychiatric thought. In "serious" fiction it is now always a Dr. Einman who pushes precarious sanity beyond the point of balance; in more frankly commercial fiction a Dr. Einman is likely to compound his lecheries with murder—the psychiatrist is the devil of modern literature. The frequency with which he is raised makes one wonder if, in some dim way, we are this much interested in Satan because we are this much interested in God.

May 28, 1949

Although Joyce Cary's *To Be a Pilgrim* (Harper, $3.00) may not be as odd an experience for an English reader as for an American, for at least one American reader it is odd indeed. I do not mean that it is esoteric in the sense of being abstract or surrealist, like the fiction of Nabokov or Sansom. For all its strangeness it wears the unmistakable signs of what we carelessly call "popular" writing. But it has so queer a way of going about its popular business that it has left me wholly confused as to what, if anything, it is supposed to be saying.

It is one of those novels which hinge on the ability to separate the sanity from the insanity in a certifiable character, always a confusing issue. The narrative is the journal of a seventy-one-year-old man in which he recalls his own long life and the lives of his family; between its various entries old Tom Wilcher is locked up in his room by his doctor-niece lest he commit still more of the public nuisances to which he has been addicted in his later years. But we learn this salient truth of Mr. Wilcher's condition—that he has been given to pinching the bottoms of pretty young women on dark streets—only as the book reaches its close. Through most of *To Be a Pilgrim* Mr. Cary's narrator has appeared a prig and a meddlesome old person, yes, but also someone meant to be taken into account. He has been the mouthpiece for opinions about morals and politics and especially religion which we are given no solid reason to suppose his author offers in irony. If, having finished the story, we are then intended to understand that throughout it Tom Wilcher spoke the views of a hypocrite and lunatic—that, for instance, his ardent pleas for religious faith are to be a priori discredited—I am afraid Mr. Cary's is the kind of playful mind which bumps into itself skipping around corners.

But it is not alone the opinions that Mr. Cary entrusts to his unbalanced narrator that we find hard to assess. *To Be a Pilgrim* is a detailed family portrait, and the American reader is bound to be confounded by certain aspects of the Wilcher family situation. In the domestic life of the English gentry as it is described in modern fiction, there is of course always an atmosphere of fortuitousness to which American home life provides no parallel. County sons have a way of disappearing for years on end with no one so much as remarking their absence; county daughters contract marriages on the basis of relationships no more intimate than that of being partners at tennis; babies are born who might just as well have come from cabbages; whole households are not merely sustained but presumably well nourished on meals so vaporous as to require neither marketing nor preparation; her personal correspondence and family bookkeeping are capable of undermining the health of a woman who can produce and rear ten children without a nervous tremor. And finally there is the matter of drains. All this may be bewildering enough, but it is when we are asked to believe the career of a Lucy Wilcher, sister of old Tom, that the foreign imagination balks. Lucy is the brilliant spirited daughter of the Wilcher ménage; every good family in English fiction has one such. Usually they marry Army and get properly tamed, but not Lucy—Lucy for no determinable reason suddenly turns religious and joins, indeed marries the leader of, a sect called the Benjaminites. This sect is as dreary and dirty an evangelical fancy as has ever found its way to paper but no one in the Wilcher family is given anything approaching a normal response to Lucy's membership in it—they are not shocked, they do not consider their daughter and sister demented. Lucy's maniacal choice of vocation causes as little stir as her brother's choice of the law. The American who is moved to ponder what would go on in a similarly placed American family whose most gifted offspring suddenly decided to become a Holy Roller must conclude either that English county life is beyond the comprehension of an outlander or that Mr. Cary swings a bit free. Myself, I tend to the latter opinion.

In fact—and I suppose this is the only reason to take Mr. Cary's novel with anything of the seriousness with which it has been taken by many reviewers—there is more than a suggestion of anarchy in Mr. Cary's whole conception, and of a kind which is now sufficiently prevalent in fiction to have worn out such attractiveness as it may once have had. When Mr. Cary entrusts his views on religion and politics to a senile bottom-pincher this is not very different, after all, from Mr. Steinbeck or Mr. Saroyan entrusting their views on life to ne'er-do-wells and vagrants—we keep it in mind, too, that one of our most successful current plays, *The Madwoman of Chaillot,* assigns the best of its wisdom to the insane. There may have been a time when such a juggling with the established social values served some useful purpose: the outrage of convention could force us to a fresh appraisal of accepted attitudes. But now it is no longer an outrage of convention, it has itself become a convention. Anarchy no longer has the power to jolt us—which means that we should perhaps take heed of our condition.

Because Philip Wylie describes his new volume, *Opus 21* (Rinehart, $3.00), as a novel, it has come to this department for comment. There would seem to be little fiction about it. The author speaks in the first person and in his own name and describes a few days in his recent life: a trip to New York to consult his physician about a possible throat cancer, an involved encounter with a girl he picks up in a bar, a trying experience with a young nephew who has got himself engaged to a prostitute. Upon this slight narrative skeleton he hangs discussions of politics, art, science, love, psychiatry, sexual morality, and so on which are, of course, the reason he wrote the book. Not having read any of Mr. Wylie's previous work, I do not know if this is his usual method but I admit myself drawn to the unorthodox form he has contrived for himself.

I also admit a rather disarmed affection for the author of *Opus 21:* when one deals with so personal a performance—Mr. Wylie tells us not only what he thinks on all the topics of our times but also what he likes to eat and drink, what he enjoys and what he fears, how he feels about his wife and daughter, how much money he earns and how much insurance he has accumulated—it is impossible not to be personal oneself. But eventually his egocentricity is embarrassing and his lapses of taste too numerous to specify. He is nevertheless so aware of his own error that one has the impulse to overlook his excesses and to protect him as one protects a small boy who cannot help misbehaving.

Still, Mr. Wylie's is the role of an educator in morality. He boasts a large public influence, and he is probably reaching a wide and susceptible audience with his opinions. He must therefore be held to some intellectual and moral account, especially for his sexual ideas which are the ones that will be most in-

teresting to most readers. Mr. Wylie claims the authority of
Freud and Jung: Jung is still alive and can refuse his spokesman
but the reviewer has a responsibility to make the disclaimer for
Freud. Enough nonsense is already ascribed to Freud without
Mr. Wylie's notions being laid at his door.

I refer particularly to Mr. Wylie's mad prescription for the
sexual health of the young woman he picks up in a bar. The girl
is reading Kinsey: she has recently discovered her husband in a
homosexual partnership and is trying to find enlightenment on
this woeful marital problem. Mr. Wylie talks to the girl at great
length, learns that she has herself been frigid in her marriage
and promptly diagnoses her trouble: it is her own sexual repres-
sion that sent her husband to a male companion and that accounts for her dismay at his present behavior. And Mr. Wylie
not only diagnoses, he cures: he introduces the girl to a prosti-
tute with whom he encourages her in a Lesbian relationship.
The girl experiences her first sexual fulfilment; she becomes
transformed. Accepting her own bi-sexuality, she is now able to
accept her husband's as well. She returns home with the author's
happy assurances that her matrimonial difficulties have been
solved; she and her husband will now achieve a fine sexual
union.

This reconstruction of a marriage is only half the "plot" of
Mr. Wylie's novel but obviously it will be the whole lesson most
casual readers will draw from the book. It is not only foolish
talk and a total perversion of Freudian theory and practice
but very dangerous stuff to bandy about. Yet among all the
reviews of Mr. Wylie's book I have so far seen, not one has
questioned this "therapy" to which the author of *Opus 21* devotes so much unlicensed zeal.

And it is a particular shame that it is in the sexual sphere that
Mr. Wylie goes so wrong because he has a basic perception
about the sexual source of our ills which one might be glad to
help him propagandize. Mr. Wylie understands what few better-
disciplined moralists are willing to acknowledge, the extent to
which a faulty attitude toward man's biological nature creates

the horrors of modern society. He knows that politics begins in the cradle, that the distortions we force upon our emotions, especially our sexual emotions, in infancy are of a kind which are hardly amenable to correction at peace tables or in atomic commissions. But the general public will need more discrimination than it is yet equipped with to be able to take Mr. Wylie's sexual premise without the faulty construction he builds upon it. Either the one will be thrown out with the other, or the one accepted as an inevitable development of the other—and it is hard to say which outcome is the less desirable.

June 25, 1949

George Orwell's *Nineteen Eighty-Four* (Harcourt, Brace, $3.00) is a brilliant and fascinating novel but the nature of its fantasy is so final and relentless that I can recommend it only with a certain reservation. This is Mr. Orwell's picture of the way the world ends; actually it does not end at all—one might welcome some well-placed atom bombs—but continues in a perpetual living death. Thirty-five years from now, by Mr. Orwell's grim calculation, there will be three great powers on this planet, any two of which will be constantly at war with the third not for ascendancy but in order to maintain the political and economic status quo—"War is peace," as the party slogan has it. For the rulers of the future state it is enough that people will be allowed to exist; their welfare, in any sense in which we understand the word, doesn't have to be taken into account. The dehumanization of man reaches its ultimate development. Love, art, pleasure, comfort, the sexual emotions: all are recognized as the consumer products of a society based upon the freedom of the individual and have been liquidated. Life, so-called, continues in order that power may continue.

Mr. Orwell's description of how this dictatorship operates is ingenious in the extreme. The population is divided into Inner

263

Party, Outer Party, and "proles." The economy of the state is always a war economy. The head of the government is Big Brother, he of the ubiquitous face, whose all-seeing eye follows one wherever there is light. The strong arm of power is the Thought Police; the greatest sin against the state, Crime-think. To help the police detect subversion every public or private room is equipped with a telescreen which records each move and utterance of the individual citizen. There is a Ministry of Truth whose function is to eradicate whatever may have been said yesterday which is no longer policy today, and a Ministry of Love where dissidence is educated into orthodoxy before it is exterminated. There is a state language, Newspeak, consisting only of such words as make freedom of thought impossible.

The fact that the scene of *Nineteen Eighty-Four* is London and that the political theory on which Mr. Orwell's dictatorship is based is called Ingsoc, which is Newspeak for English socialism, indicates that Mr. Orwell is fantasying the fate not only of an already established dictatorship like that of Russia but also of Labor England; and indeed he clearly states that "by the fourth decade of the twentieth century all the main currents of political thought were authoritarian. . . . Every new political theory, by whatever name it called itself, led back to hierarchy and regimentation." From any immediate political point of view this assimilation of the English Labor government to Soviet communism is dismaying. On the other hand, whatever our partisanship for the present English revolution as against the present situation in Russia, we recognize that the generalization in the lesson Mr. Orwell is teaching is a proper one. Even where, as in his last novel, *Animal Farm,* Mr. Orwell seemed to be concerned only with unmasking the Soviet Union for its dreamy admirers, he was urged on by more than sectarianism; what he was telling us is that along the path that the Russian revolution has followed to the destruction of all the decent human values there have stood the highest ideals of modern social enlightenment. This idealism he has wished to jolt into self-awareness. In the name of a higher loyalty, treacheries beyond imagination have been committed; in the name of socialist equality, privilege has ruled unbridled; in the name of democracy and freedom, the individual has lived without public voice or private peace—if this is true of the Soviet Union, why should it not eventually be true of the English experiment as well? Mr. Orwell is warning us against the extremes to which the contemporary totalitarian spirit can carry us so that we will be warned against Russia but also so that we will understand the danger we confront wherever unimpeded power moves under the guise of order and rationality.

With this refusal to limit his attack to Soviet totalitarianism, Mr. Orwell reasserts the ability, so rare among intellectuals of the left, to place his own brand of idealism above political partisanship. It is difficult to pin a political label on the author of *Nineteen Eighty-Four:* if one has heard that Mr. Orwell is now an anarchist, one can read his new novel as the work of an anarchist. But one can just as easily read it as the work of an unfashionable democrat or libertarian. Yet one cannot help being thrown off, I think, by something in the book's temper, a fierceness of intention, which seems to violate the very principles Mr. Orwell would wish to preserve in the world. Whereas *Animal Farm* was too primitive a parable to capture the emotions it wished to persuade, the new book exacerbates the emotions almost beyond endurance. Even apart from the cruelty of its imagination—and Mr. Orwell has conceived the inconceivable—one is disturbed by the book's implacable tone and the extreme of pressure it exerts upon the reader, in contrast to the relaxed tone of Mr. Orwell's literary and sociological essays. To make this criticism is not to ask for quietism as a means of combating the passions which are destroying modern life. But it is to wish that there were more of what E. M. Forster calls the "relaxed will" in at least those of us who, like Mr. Orwell, are so acutely aware of the threats of power.

Index of Authors
and Titles Reviewed

271